17 July 2019

Dear Michael,

Thank you, for everything.
Words can't express my
gratitude

yours

Noam

THE CHILD'S RIGHT TO DEVELOPMENT

This book provides a comprehensive account of how child development and the right to development of children have been understood in international children's rights law.

It argues that any conceptions of childhood focussed either on children's future as adults or on children's lives in the present, overlook the hybridity of children's lived experiences. The book therefore suggests a new conception of childhood – namely, 'hybrid childhood' – which accommodates respect for children's agency and human dignity in the present, in the process of growth and in the outcomes of this process when the child becomes an adult. Consequently, and building on the capability approach's idea of human development, the book presents a radical new interpretation of the child's right to development under the UN Convention on the Rights of the Child.

NOAM PELEG is a lecturer at the Faculty of Law, University of New South Wales, Australia, where he researches and teaches international children's rights law and family law. He is a member of the editorial board of the *International Journal of Children's Rights*.

THE CHILD'S RIGHT TO DEVELOPMENT

NOAM PELEG

University of New South Wales, Faculty of Law

CAMBRIDGE UNIVERSITY PRESS

CAMBRIDGE
UNIVERSITY PRESS

University Printing House, Cambridge CB2 8BS, United Kingdom

One Liberty Plaza, 20th Floor, New York, NY 10006, USA

477 Williamstown Road, Port Melbourne, VIC 3207, Australia

314–321, 3rd Floor, Plot 3, Splendor Forum, Jasola District Centre, New Delhi – 110025, India

79 Anson Road, #06-04/06, Singapore 079906

Cambridge University Press is part of the University of Cambridge.

It furthers the University's mission by disseminating knowledge in the pursuit of education, learning, and research at the highest international levels of excellence.

www.cambridge.org
Information on this title: www.cambridge.org/9781107094529
DOI: 10.1017/9781316146804

First published 2019

Printed and bound in Great Britain by Clays Ltd, Elcograf S.p.A.

A catalogue record for this publication is available from the British Library.

Library of Congress Cataloging-in-Publication Data
Names: Peleg, Noam, 1978– author.
Title: The child's right to development / Noam Peleg, University of New South Wales.
Description: Cambridge, United Kingdom ; New York, NY, USA : Cambridge University Press, 2019. | Based on author's thesis (doctoral – University College London, 2012), | Includes bibliographical references and index.
Identifiers: LCCN 2019001102| ISBN 9781107094529 (hardback : alk. paper) | ISBN 9781107476509 (pbk. : alk. paper)
Subjects: LCSH: Children (International law) | Child development–Law and legislation.
Classification: LCC K639 .P45 2019 | DDC 342.08/772–dc23
LC record available at https://lccn.loc.gov/2019001102

ISBN 978-1-107-09452-9 Hardback

CONTENTS

v

ACKNOWLEDGEMENTS

I'm not sure how long it took me to write this book. One possible starting point is when I created the folder 'Book' on my cloud drive some six years ago. But a more plausible moment happened nearly 10 years earlier, when I represented two siblings, a brother and a sister, aged 9 and 6, in a challenging family law case. The children had been sexually, emotionally and physically abused by their father. When I met them, they were living with their mother, who suffered from a number of mental health illnesses. The father had not had any contact with them for months, the children refused to see him, and he insisted on bringing a case to court. At one of the many hearings, I asked the judge to consider the effect of a decision to force the children to meet their father on their right to development. That suggestion was met with silence. It was then when I decided to look for some answers.

The book is based on my PhD thesis, which I wrote at University College London (UCL), and it was in the making for a long time. During those years, I was fortunate to receive the help and support of numerous people and institutions. I cannot do justice to all of them. Colm O'Cinneide was a wonderful supervisor, and his insights, as a 'children's rights fan in the closet', as he once described himself, were invaluable. Michael Freeman was the reason why I wanted to study at UCL to begin with, and his ongoing support, curiosity and intellectual leadership encouraged me at every step of the way. Alison Diduck was a wonderful colleague, mentor and friend. I would also like to thank UCL Laws for its generous research scholarship, which enabled me to be a full-time student and for letting me stay for additional two years as a postdoctoral fellow. The UCL Chaim Herzog Alumni Award enabled me to leave practice and study for my LLM at UCL, and for that opportunity I will always be grateful.

The Faculty of Law at the University of New South Wales has been my home since 2015. I truly appreciate the amazing collegiality, the intellectual environment and the institutional patience with the time that it took me to bring this project to completion. Cambridge University Press, especially Finola O'Sullivan and Tom Randall, deserves recognition too, not least because they gave me the opportunity not to rush things.

The manuscript benefitted from the comments and feedback of many colleagues who were very generous with their time, which is probably the most important commodity in academia these days. I would especially like to thank Ros Dixon, Fleur Johns, Kathryn Hollingsworth, Laura Lundy, and Helen Stalford. Aoife Nolan's encouragement and advice over the years were invaluable too. Many thanks to Angela Kintomanis for her excellent research assistance, and to Michelle Nichols for her wonderful editing skills.

A special thank you goes to my parents, Hava and Uri. Their unconditional love is the parenting model for which every child can hope.

Lastly, I wish to thank the two people without whom I would not be the person I am today: my partner, Lana, and our son, Neal. Life with Lana is a fascinating, challenging, thoroughly enjoyable and ever-rewarding journey. You mean everything to me. The arrival of Neal completely changed my life. He has been my inspiration, and I hope that I am worthy of the title 'Aba'.

〜

Introduction

'I want to be big,' says 12-year-old Josh Baskin to Zoltar Speaks, an arcade machine, in Penny Marshall's 1988 film *Big*. The next morning, Josh wakes up inside the body of a 30-year-old man. Overnight, Josh has skipped the process of growing up and is transformed from a child into an adult. For international children's rights scholars and advocates, the process of transformation is far more fraught. In fact, international children's rights law dedicates much attention to this process by establishing the right of children to develop. This book shows how the process might be rethought, and why that might be worth doing for the intended agents and beneficiaries of international children's rights law: children.

Ever since the League of Nations adopted the Declaration of the Rights of the Child in 1924, one of the main objectives – if not the most important one – of international children's rights law has been to enhance children's development. This objective is derived from a certain conception of children as developing human beings that dominated studies of childhood throughout the twentieth century.[1] For these reasons, Article 6(2) of the 1989 UN Convention on the Rights of the Child (the Convention), the most ratified of all international human rights treaties, protects the child's right to development. In addition, five other Articles of the Convention – Articles 18(1), 23(3), 27(1), 29(1)(a) and 32(1) – mention eight specific aspects of child development that are worthy of attention and protection: physical development, mental development, moral development, social development, cultural development, spiritual development, development of the personality, and development

---

[1] Martin Woodhead, 'Child Development and the Development of Childhood' in Jens Qvortrup *et al.* (eds.), *The Palgrave Handbook of Childhood Studies* (Palgrave, Basingstoke 2009, 2011) 46–61.

1

of talent. No other binding international human rights treaty contains a protection of the right to development that is similar, either in its breadth or in its language.[2]

The right to development of children is not often discussed in human rights scholarship, or in children's rights practice. When the right to development is mentioned or debated, it is usually as a derivative of other rights of the child,[3] while its articulation in human rights terms is overlooked.[4] As an independent right of children, and as one of the four guiding principles of the Convention,[5] the right to development deserves much more attention. This book analyses the context in which this right was created and developed. It asks how the right has been understood and how it can be better substantiated. Arguing that the current interpretation of the child's right to development is insufficient, too abstract, and falls short on respecting children's agency, the book suggests a new way to look at children, childhood, and the process of transformation into adulthood. This book is premised on the suggestion that the child's right to development should be critically analysed within the context of the Convention, while considering the impact that different images of 'the child' and different conceptions of 'childhood' (namely 'a hybrid childhood') have on the interpretation of children's rights. It therefore considers the subsequent space that this new interpretation can open for the right to development.

---

[2] At the regional level, Article 5(2) of the African Charter on the Rights and Welfare of the Child protects the child's right to 'survival, protection and development'. The 1986 Declaration on the Right to Development recognises such a right, but it is not a binding treaty.

[3] Manfred Nowak, *Article 6: The Right to Life, Survival and Development* (Martinus Nijhoff Publishers, Leiden 2005) 43–49; James R. Himes, 'Children's Rights: Moralists, Lawyers and the Right to Development' (1993) 1 *International Journal of Children's Rights* 81; Douglas Hodgson, 'The Child's Right to Life, Survival and Development' (1994) 2 *International Journal of Children's Rights* 369; Geraldine Van Bueren, *The International Law on the Rights of the Child* (Martinus Nijhoff Publishers, The Hague 1998) 318–320.

[4] Martin Woodhead, 'Early Childhood Development: A Question of Rights' (2005) 37 *International Journal of Early Childhood* 80.

[5] UNCRC, 'General Comment No. 5 (2003): General Measures of Implementation of the Convention on the Rights of the Child' (27 November 2003) UN Doc. CRC/GC/2003/5. But see Karl Hanson and Laura Lundy, 'Does Exactly What It Says on the Tin? A Critical Analysis and Alternative Conceptualisation of the So-Called "General Principles" of the Convention on the Rights of the Child' (2017) 25 *International Journal of Children's Rights* 285.

Childhood Studies and the Image of the Developing Child

Childhood is neither a natural nor a neutral concept.[6] It is a socially constructed conception[7] that changes over time[8] and among societies,[9] in accordance with shifting views about family, gender roles, the labour market, crime and punishment, and religion, to name just a few factors.[10] An illustration of the fluid content of the term is the perception of childhood as a time of innocence and purity, or conversely as a period of depravity.[11] Children have been seen as both 'little angels' and 'little devils'. Thomas Hobbes, for example, characterised the children of the seventeenth century as being as malicious as adults, thus eliminating any difference in that regard, while John Locke thought that it was parents' economic pressure that shaped children's behaviour.[12] At the turn of the twentieth century, with the growing influence of capitalism and consumerism in the West, childhood was seen as a time of happiness and cheerfulness, and therefore children became worthy of investment of

---

[6] Allison James et al., Theorizing Childhood (Polity Press, Cambridge 1998) 126–128.

[7] Allison James and Adrian James, Constructing Childhood: Theory, Policy and Social Practice (Palgrave Macmillan, Basingstoke 2004) 10–26.

[8] Colin Heywood, 'Centuries of Childhood: An Anniversary – and an Epitaph?' (2010) 3 Journal of the History of Childhood and Youth 343, 357–358; Richard T. Vann, 'The Youth of Centuries of Childhood' (1982) 21 History and Theory 279. Though he was at the early stages of writing the history of childhood a half-century ago, Philippe Ariès argued in Centuries of Childhood that childhood, as a social conception, was invented only in the seventeenth century: Philippe Ariès, Centuries of Childhood: A Social History of Family Life (trans. Robert Baldick; Jonathan Cape, London 1962). For a contesting argument, see Rex Stainton Rogers and Wendy Stainton Rogers, Stories of Childhood: Shifting Agendas of Child Concern (University of Toronto Press, Toronto 1992) 65–66. Ariès's method and sources were grounds for harsh critique: see Adrian Wilson, 'The Infancy of the History of Childhood: An Appraisal of Philippe Ariès' (1980) 19 History and Theory 132.

[9] Suzanne Shanahan, 'Lost and Found: The Sociological Ambivalence towards Childhood' (2007) 33 Annual Review of Sociology 407.

[10] James and James, supra n. 7, 70–74. On childhood and 'time', see Judith Ennew, 'Time for Children or Time for Adults?' in Jens Qvortrup et al. (eds.), Childhood Matters (Ashgate, Farnham 1994) 125–134.

[11] Colin Heywood, A History of Childhood (Polity Press, Cambridge 2001).

[12] Cynthia Price Cohen, 'The Relevance of Theories of Natural Law and Legal Positivism' in Michael Freeman and Philip Veerman (eds.), The Ideologies of Children's Rights (Martinus Nijhoff Publishers, Dordrecht 1992) 53–70; Peter O. King, 'Thomas Hobbes's Children' in Susan M. Turner and Gareth B. Matthews (eds.), The Philosopher's Child: Critical Perspectives in the Western Tradition (University of Rochester Press, Rochester, NY 1998) 65–84. For a claim that no conclusions can be drawn from Locke's writing about children, see David Archard, 'John Locke's Children' in Susan M. Turner and Gareth B. Matthew (eds.), The Philosopher's Child: Critical Perspectives in the Western Tradition (University of Rochester Press, Rochester, NY 1998) 85–104.

time and energy.[13] The declining mortality rates for infants and children also meant that middle-class mothers had fewer pregnancies and fewer children to bury, thus transforming children into a symbol of joy.

These social attitudes towards children and childhood shape the legal treatment of children. But law, as a powerful social instrument, also plays a pivotal role in the institutionalisation[14] and conceptualisation of childhood.[15] It is thus simultaneously a reactive and a constructive force. Law shapes, develops, and reconfigures childhood,[16] thus affecting children and adults alike[17] – for example, in setting the minimum ages for criminal responsibility and for marriage, and in determining the duties of care that parents owe their children. Despite changes in the image of childhood and in the jurisprudence concerning children, which are discussed in more detail in the next chapter, the 'human becomings' approach to children[18] has prevailed in the twentieth century. That conception sees children as passive actors, lacking in agency, weak, vulnerable, and in need of protection.[19] It positions children against adults, describing childhood as 'the absence of adult qualities'.[20] Positioning children against adults has ultimately enabled adults to define 'the child' as the negative other.[21] And, as Erica Burman argues, this separation of people on the basis of their age has also enabled adults to assume control over children, to colonise them, and, eventually, to 'civilise' them.[22]

---

[13] Peter N. Stearns, 'Defining Happy Childhoods: Assessing a Recent Change' (2010) 3 *Journal of the History of Childhood and Youth* 165; Paula Fass, *The Damned and the Beautiful: American Youth in the 1920s* (Oxford University Press, Oxford 1977) 15.

[14] James and James, *supra* n. 7; Emily Buss, 'What the Law Should (and Should Not) Learn from Child Development Research' (2009–2010) 38 *Hofstra Law Review* 13.

[15] Michael King and Christine Piper, *How the Law Thinks about Children* (Gower, Vermont 1990) 36–37.

[16] James and James, *supra* n. 7, 64–70.   [17] *Ibid.*, 214.

[18] Nick Lee, *Childhood and Society: Growing Up in an Age of Uncertainty* (Open University Press, Buckingham 2001) 8.

[19] For non-Western perspectives, see, for example, Charles Stafford, *The Roads of Chinese Childhood* (Cambridge University Press, Cambridge 1995); Toshiko Ito, 'New Education for Underprivileged Children: The Condition of Children's Rights in Japanese Law' (2012) 48 *Paedagogica Historica* 153. See also Robert A. LeVine and Rebecca S. New, *Anthropology and Child Development* (Blackwell Publishing, Malden, Mass., and Oxford 2008).

[20] David Archard, *Children: Rights and Childhood* (Routledge, London 2004) 38.

[21] David Archard, 'Philosophical Perspectives on Childhood' in Julia Fionda (ed.), *Legal Concepts of Childhood* (Hart Publishing, Oxford 2001) 43–56, 46.

[22] Erica Burman, *Deconstructing Development Psychology* (3rd edition, Palgrave, London, 2017), 123.

The child is seen as an 'unfinished product',[23] a human being in the making. Therefore, childhood is a 'journey toward a destination'.[24] As James and Prout argue, under this conception, childhood is 'a highly complex and engineered trajectory towards adulthood'.[25] The virtue of fostering this developmental trajectory is, according to Richard Kraut, good not only for the individual but also for society.[26] As Chapters 1 and 2 argue, this 'desire'[27] to enable children to 'grow up'[28] led to the creation of their right to development in international law, and to a large extent has dictated the interpretation of this right.

A good example of the prominence of the human becomings approach to childhood in Western culture is Émile Durkheim's article on education, published in 1911:

> The essential function of this age, the role and purpose assigned to it by nature, may be summed in a single word: it is the period of *growth*, that is to say, the period in which the individual, in both the physical and moral sense, does not yet exist, the period in which he is made, develops and is formed.... In everything the child is characterized by the very instability of his nature, which is the law of growth.[29]

Durkheim's vision of childhood is very clear: the child does not yet exist as an individual with agency, and the 'law of growth' should therefore govern childhood and dictate the treatment of children. The field of anthropology, as another example, was also dominated by the 'law of growth' approach. The first major research into the lives of children was Margaret Mead's seminal book *Coming of Age in Samoa*, published in 1928.[30] In her study,

---

[23] Carol Smart *et al.*, *The Changing Experience of Childhood* (Polity Press, Cambridge 2001) 1.

[24] Lee, *supra* n. 18, 8.

[25] Allison James and Alan Prout, 'Re-Presenting Childhood: Time and Transition in the Study of Childhood' in Allison James and Alan Prout (eds.), *Constructing and Reconstructing Childhood: Contemporary Issues in the Sociological Study of Childhood* (2nd edition, Falmer Press, London 1997) 230–250, 235.

[26] Richard Kraut, *What Is Good and Why: The Ethics of Well-Being* (Harvard University Press, Cambridge, Massachusetts 2007) 165.

[27] Erica Burman, 'Desiring Development? Psychoanalytic Contribution to Antidevelopmental Psychology' (2011) 24 *International Journal of Qualitative Studies in Education* 1, 9.

[28] James *et al.*, *Theorizing Childhood*, *supra* n. 6, 196. See also Onora O'Neill, 'Children's Rights and Children's Lives' (1988) 98 *Ethics* 445.

[29] Émile Durkheim, 'Childhood' in W. S. F. Pickering (ed.), *Essays on Morals and Education* (trans. H. L. Sutcliffe; Routledge, London 1979; first published 1911) 150.

[30] Margaret Mead, *Coming of Age in Samoa: A Psychological Study of Primitive Youth for Western Civilisation* (Penguin Books, Harmondsworth 1943; first published 1928).

Mead observed the maturation process of girls from childhood to adult-hood, focusing her attention on what the future held for these children.[31] *Growing up in Samoa* led to the establishment of the 'Culture and Person-ality' school of anthropology,[32] in which anthropologists and developmen-tal psychologists teamed up to study the ways that 'children became adults'.[33] Another important anthropological study that was published around the same time was Katharine Bridges's *The Social and Emotional Development of the Pre-School Child.*[34] This research, which was described by the *Lancet* at the time as one of the most influential studies on children's lives and behaviour,[35] observed the daily lives of children in the classroom and the playground, in order to create a 'development scale' of the child.[36]

Since the late nineteenth century, developmental psychology has heav-ily influenced social and legal attitudes towards children.[37] It has replayed and legitimised evolutionary ideas about growth and domin-ation,[38] dividing childhood into sequential stages with the child moving from one developmental phase to the next. Over time, the child trans-forms from being incompetent to being competent, gradually learning the necessary skills to 'achieve the fully social state of adulthood'.[39] There is a range of developmental psychology theories, some more influential than others. Sigmund Freud, for example, focused on sexual develop-ment, while Erik Erikson emphasised psychosocial development. Jean Piaget's theory of cognitive development and Lev Vygotsky's theory of proximal development, which concerned the child's process of trans-forming into a healthy adult, probably had the most influence on law and on legal discourse on children's capacities.[40] The prominence of these

[31] For a critique on Mead's work, see Derek Freeman, *Margaret Mead and Samoa: The Making and Unmaking of an Anthropological Myth* (Harvard University Press, Cam-bridge and London 1983).

[32] Heather Montgomery, *An Introduction to Childhood* (Wiley Blackwell, Chichester 2009) 22–23.

[33] *Ibid.*, 23.

[34] Katharine M. Banham Bridges, *The Social and Emotional Development of the Pre-school Child* (Kegan Paul, Trench, Trubner & Co., London 1931).

[35] Anonymous note, 'The Development of Young Children' (1931) 218 (5638) *The Lancet* 668.

[36] See also LeVine and New, *supra* n. 19.

[37] Lloyd deMause, 'The Evolution of Childhood' in Lloyd deMause (ed.), *The History of Childhood* (Souvenir Press, London 1976) 1–74.

[38] Burman, *Deconstructing Development Psychology*, *supra* n. 22.

[39] Smart *et al.*, *supra* n. 23, 4.

[40] Buss, *supra* n. 14, 48–50; Woodhead, 'Early Childhood Development', *supra* .

Euro-American psychological theories has been widely challenged,[41] and their cultural, gender,[42] and class biases[43] have been highlighted. According to Michael Wyness, the combination of the child's biological growth and psychology makes it 'difficult for us to view childhood any differently'.[44] And, as John Modell rightly notes, the history of childhood is written from a developmental perspective.[45] Childhood, therefore, seems to be important only in terms of the child's future.[46] 'Development', then, is not only a hypothesis, but also the prognosis of childhood. Thus, it is clear why, according to this paradigm of childhood, 'children didn't have rights'.[47] As persons in the making, children were subject to the 'law of growth' and not to human rights law. But, despite its theoretical and conceptual shortcomings,[48] developmental psychology still has significant influence on law – including international children's rights law.

After the First World War, one of the main projects of childhood studies was to define the 'normal' and 'abnormal' child,[49] and to understand how children's lives, bodies, and minds should be treated.[50] Dozens of manuals were published in the United Kingdom targeting parents. These guides used medical and psychological jargon to explain how to educate and discipline children, essentially seeking to enlighten parents about how to raise a 'healthy child'.[51]

---

[41] Erica Burman, 'Deconstructing Neoliberal Childhood: Towards a Feminist Antipsychological Approach' (2012) 19 *Childhood* 423, 425. See also Alison Diduck, *Law's Families* (LexisNexis, London 2003) 74–77.

[42] Carol Gilligan, *In a Different Voice* (Harvard University Press, Cambridge, 1982).

[43] Burman, *Deconstructing Development Psychology*, *supra* n. 22, 18–19.

[44] Michael Wyness, *Childhood and Society: An Introduction to the Sociology of Childhood* (Palgrave, Basingstoke 2006) 18.

[45] John Modell, 'How May Children's Development Be Seen Historically?' (2000) 7 *Childhood* 81.

[46] James and Prout, 'Re-Presenting Childhood', *supra* n. 25, 239.

[47] Michael Freeman, 'The Human Rights of Children' (2010) 63 *Current Legal Problems* 1, 9.

[48] Lindsay O'Dell *et al.*, 'Introducing Normative and Different Childhoods, Developmental Trajectory and Transgression' in Lindsay O'Dell *et al.* (eds.), *Different Childhoods: Non/Normative Development and Transgressive Trajectories* (Routledge, Abingdon 2018) 1–6.

[49] André Turmel, *A Historical Sociology of Childhood: Developmental Thinking, Categorization and Graphic Visualisation* (Cambridge University Press, Cambridge 2008). See also Helga Kelle, '"Age-Appropriate Development" as Measure and Norm' (2010) 17 *Childhood* 9.

[50] For a good review on this point, see Annemieke van Drenth and Kevin Myers, 'Normalising Childhood: Politics and Interventions Concerning Special Children in the United States and Europe (1900–1960)' (2011) 47 *Paedagogica Historica* 719.

[51] John Stewart, '"The Dangerous Age of Childhood": Child Guidance and the "Normal" Child in Great Britain, 1920–1950' (2011) 47 *Paedagogica Historica* 785.

How children grow up and what constitutes a normal process of maturation are themes explored in anthropology, sociology, medicine, history, psychology, social work, political science, the built environment, and educational pedagogy. Child development is the subject of numerous other studies – including, for example, research into children's play and development, language and development, social bonding and development, brain development, bodily development, sexual development, cognitive development, and biosocial development.[52] These studies attempt to 'reveal' how children develop, what factors have positive or negative influences on their development, what qualifies as 'good' development and what is considered a disability. But such studies should be treated with caution, according to Brian Hopkins. He writes in *The Cambridge Encyclopedia of Child Development* that 'development is one of those terms that we freely use in everyday language and yet when we try to pin it down with a precise definition it assumes an almost evanescent-like quality'.[53]

The findings and conclusions of these studies are of less significance in our context. What concerns me is the volume of diverse meanings of 'child development' that they create. The colossal corpus of literature is evidence of the dominance of a conception of children as human becomings.

An alternative conception of childhood, the 'human beings' approach, emerged in the 1970s,[54] embracing more diverse and complex notions of childhood.[55] The human beings approach perceives children as persons rather than as 'projects',[56] suggesting that the study of childhood and children should be accomplished without comparing children to adults.[57]

---

[52] See Brian Hopkins (ed.), *The Cambridge Encyclopedia of Child Development* (Cambridge University Press, Cambridge 2005); Kathleen Stassen Berger, *The Developing Person* (7th edition, Worth Publishers, New York 2006).

[53] Brian Hopkins, 'What Is Ontogenetic Development?' in Brian Hopkins (ed.), *The Cambridge Encyclopedia of Child Development* (Cambridge University Press, Cambridge 2005) 18–24, 18.

[54] Karen Wells, *Childhood in a Global Perspective* (Polity Press, Cambridge 2009) 1–24.

[55] Alan Prout, *The Future of Childhood: Towards the Interdisciplinary Study of Children* (Routledge, London 2005) 7–34; Alan Prout and Allison James, 'A New Paradigm for the Sociology of Childhood? Provenance, Promise and Problems' in Allison James and Alan Prout (eds.), *Constructing and Reconstructing Childhood: Contemporary Issues in the Sociological Study of Childhood* (3rd edition, Routledge, Oxon 2015) 7–33.

[56] Smart *et al.*, *supra* n. 23, 13.

[57] Prout and James, 'A New Paradigm', *supra* n. 55, 8. See also Berry Mayall, *Towards a Sociology for Childhood: Thinking from Children's Lives* (Open University Press, Buckingham 2002) 33.

According to this approach, children are active human beings who can and should participate in shaping their own lives and play an active role in their communities.[58] An essential component is respecting children's agency, which is probably 'one of the most important theoretical developments in the recent history of childhood studies'.[59] As human 'beings', children are defined in their own right[60] and not by comparison to adults. This also means that children are considered to be human-rights holders.[61] As Michael Freeman notes, rights and agency are interdependent and indivisible, as those who have human rights 'can exercise agency . . . as agents, rights bearers can participate. They can make their own lives, rather than having their lives made for them'.[62]

An important implication of respecting children's agency is giving children a voice in their own lives. This is reflected in Article 12 of the Convention, which protects the child's right to participation.[63] Children can surprise you, as Baroness Hale of the United Kingdom Supreme Court has said,[64] by how much they know about their lives and about their world. Children, for example, can make sense of their experiences of poverty (and what qualifies as well-being)[65] and of living on the street.[66] They contemplate their health and their fear of dying,[67] enabling them to

---

[58] James and James, *supra* n. 7, 38–39.

[59] Allison James, 'Agency' in Jens Qvortrup *et al.* (eds.), *The Palgrave Handbook of Childhood Studies* (Palgrave, Basingstoke 2011) 34–45, 34.

[60] Lee, *supra* n. 18, 54.

[61] Michael Freeman, *The Moral Status of Children* (Martinus Nijhoff Publishers, The Hague 1997).

[62] Michael Freeman, 'Why It Remains Important to Take Children's Rights Seriously' (2007) 15 *International Journal of Children's Rights* 5, 8.

[63] For an analysis of Article 12, see Laura Lundy, '"Voice" Is Not Enough: Conceptualising Article 12 of the UN Convention on the Rights of the Child' (2007) 33 *British Educational Research Journal* 927.

[64] *ZH (Tanzania) (FC) v. Secretary of State for the Home Department* [2011] UKSC 4 at [37].

[65] Laura Camfield *et al.*, 'What's the Use of "Well-Being" in Contexts of Child Poverty? Approaches to Research, Monitoring and Children's Participation' (2009) 17 *International Journal of Children's Rights* 65; Haridhan Goswami, 'Social Relationships and Children's Subjective Well-Being' (2011) 107 *Social Indicator Research* 575; Zoran Pavlovic and Tina Rutar Leban, 'Children's Rights International Study Project (CRISP) – A Shift from the Focus on Children's Rights to a Quality of Life Assessment Instrument' (2009) 2 *Child Indicators Research* 265.

[66] Udi Mandel Butler, 'Freedom, Revolt and "Citizenship"'(2009) 16 *Childhood* 11. See also Marcela Raffaelli, 'How Do Brazilian Street Youth Experience "the Street"?: Analysis of a Sentence Completion Task' (2001) 8 *Childhood* 396.

[67] Myra Bluebond-Langner, *The Private Worlds of Dying Children* (Princeton University Press, Princeton 1978) 5.

participate in the design of paediatric wards.[68] They think about how their relationships with friends and family members affect their happiness and well-being.[69] If given the opportunity, they can also contemplate what human rights mean,[70] how they would like to see the Convention interpreted,[71] and how they would have drafted it. They have views about what rights they should have,[72] how they would change government spending,[73] and how to exercise their civil and political rights.[74] Children can also provide accounts of their well-being and development.[75] For example, one participatory study found that children distinguish between the evolution of their development and the aims that this process should achieve. Children understand 'development' as something that gives their lives a sense of direction, seeing it as their natural process of maturation.[76]

The capacity of children to make sense of the world around them does not have any age limits.[77] As Priscilla Alderson *et al.* (2005) have shown,

---

[68] Katherine Bishop, 'Challenging Research: Completing Participatory Social Research with Children and Adolescents in a Hospital Setting' (2014) 7 *Health Environments Research & Design Journal* 76.

[69] Goswami, *supra* n. 65.

[70] Martin D. Ruck *et al.*, 'Children's and Adolescents' Understanding of Rights: Balancing Nurturance and Self-Determination' (1988) 64 *Child Development* 404; Martin D. Ruck *et al.*, 'Adolescents' and Children's Knowledge about Their Rights: Some Evidence for How Young People View Rights in Their Own Lives' (1998) 21 *Journal of Adolescence* 275.

[71] Wiebina Heesterman, 'An Assessment of the Impact of Youth Submissions to the United Nations Committee on the Rights of the Child' (2005) 13 *International Journal of Children's Rights* 351.

[72] Laura Lundy *et al.*, 'What If Children Had Been Involved in Drafting the United Nations Convention on the Rights of the Child?' in Alison Diduck *et al.* (eds.), *Law in Society: Reflections on Children, Family, Culture and Philosophy – Essays in Honour of Michael Freeman* (Brill, Leiden 2015) 223–242.

[73] Laura Lundy *et al.*, *Towards Better Investment in the Rights of the Child: The Views of Children* (Belfast, Queens University Belfast, 2015).

[74] Karen Orr *et al.*, *Enabling the Exercise of Civil and Political Rights: The Views of Children* (Save the Children, London 2016).

[75] Hanita Kosher and Asher Ben-Arieh, 'What Children Think about Their Rights and Their Well-Being: A Cross-National Comparison' (2017) 87 *American Journal of Orthopsychiatry* 256.

[76] Helga Kelle, 'The Discourse of "Development": How 9- to 12-Year-Old Children Construct "Childish" and "Further Developed" Identities within Their Peer Culture' (2001) 8 *Childhood* 95, 109. In a different context, see Richard Maclure, 'The Dynamics of Youth Participation: Insights from Research Fieldwork with Female Youth in Senegal' in Myriam Denov *et al.* (eds.), *Children's Rights and International Development* (Palgrave, New York 2011) 155–174.

[77] Jérôme Ballet *et al.*, 'Children's Agency and the Capability Approach: A Conceptual Framework' in M. Biggeri *et al.* (eds.), *Children and the Capability Approach* (Palgrave, Basingstoke 2011) 22.

premature babies can also actively participate in their own life, and they have the capability and the capacity to express their preferences and needs. These young children do so by using body language and the only mode of vocal communication that is available to them: crying.[78] Adults and children with limited or no verbal skills can also communicate in nonverbal ways – for example, through drawing.[79] But these modes of communication require the willingness of listeners, usually adults. Therefore, respecting children's agency and right to participation should not be limited to children of a particular age.[80] The realisation of this right depends on the space that children have in which to exercise it, and the willingness of adults to listen to them. Even when some forms of participation are seen by adults as tokenistic, children – as Laura Lundy eloquently writes – claim them as spaces for exercising their agency.[81] Needless to say, it is not always easy to facilitate children's participation, and there are numerous methodological and structural challenges in doing so.[82] But problems in implementation should not undermine the foundations of the principle and its pursuit. The importance and implications of respecting children's agency and voice in the context of the right to development will be further explored, especially in Chapters 4 and 5.

Traditionally, the concept of childhood embraced a universal image of childhood and children's development.[83] Childhood and child development were constructed in light of a premise of Euro-American developmental psychology that all children should develop similarly[84] and

---

[78] Priscilla Alderson *et al.*, 'The Participation Rights of Premature Babies' (2005) 13 *International Journal of Children's Rights* 31.

[79] Amanda Ajodhia-Andrews and Rachel Berman, 'Exploring School Life from the Lens of a Child Who Does Not Use Speech to Communicate' (2009) 15 *Qualitative Inquiry* 931. See also Amanda Ajodhia-Andrews, *Voices and Visions from Ethnoculturally Diverse Young People with Disabilities* (Sense Publishers, Rotterdam 2016).

[80] See Articles 5 and 12 of the Convention, which take age as a factor in deciding how much weight children's views should be given in a decision-making process, and not as a precondition for enabling them to participate in this process to begin with.

[81] Laura Lundy, 'In Defence of Tokenism? Implementing Children's Right to Participate in Collective Decision-Making' (2018) 25 *Childhood* 340.

[82] Sally Holland *et al.*, 'Power, Agency and Participatory Agenda: A Critical Exploration of Young People's Engagement in Participative Qualitative Research' (2010) 17 *Childhood* 360.

[83] Martin Woodhead, 'Reconstructing Developmental Psychology – Some First Steps' (1999) 13 *Children & Society* 3, 5–6.

[84] *Ibid.*, 8–9.

linearly[85] – thus ignoring intersections of identity, ethnicity, race, culture, gender, sexuality, dis(ability), and socioeconomic conditions.[86] Childhood was framed in coherent and homogeneous terms, and therefore the universal child was a standardised child too. In that sense, the universal child represents an ahistorical child – a concept that, according to Allison James, is mostly vested in the notion of bodily development.[87] The new sociology of childhood and newer approaches to developmental psychology (such as cultural psychology)[88] have challenged this perception, making it 'possible to think beyond the developmental/socialization framework for understanding children'.[89] But the moral–political assumptions that underpin developmental psychology have yet to be substantially undermined,[90] and still dominate the field of childhood studies.[91] One reason for this, according to Erica Burman, is that even contemporary childhood discourses represent and consolidate traditional gendered, racialised, and psychologised views.[92]

The Convention accommodates both the human becomings and the human beings conceptions of childhood.[93] Nonetheless, as far as the right to development is concerned, the Convention supports the view that there is one appropriate way for a child to develop.[94] The child is also represented as being in need of protection.[95] Another implication of this approach is that the right to development provides generic protection for the same 'development' to all children, without setting any 'milestones or qualitative shifts in the child's understanding or behavior across the years from birth to 18'.[96] This book seeks to challenge these premises and to offer an alternative and context-sensitive framework that respects

[85] Nancy E. Dowd, 'Black Boys Matter: Developmental Equality' (2016) 45 *Hofstra Law Review* 47, 55.
[86] *Ibid.*, 57–62.
[87] Allison James, 'The Standardized Child: Issues of Openness, Objectivity and Agency in Promoting Childhood Health' (2004) 13 *Anthropological Journal on European Culture* 93.
[88] Woodhead, 'Reconstructing Developmental Psychology', *supra* n. 83, 9–12.
[89] Smart *et al.*, *supra* n. 21, 12.
[90] Burman, *Deconstructing Development Psychology*, *supra* n. 22, 298.
[91] Barrie Thorne, 'Crafting the Interdisciplinary Field of Childhood Studies' (2007) 24 *Childhood* 147.
[92] Burman, 'Deconstructing Neoliberal Childhood', *supra* n. 41, 1.
[93] Freeman, 'The Human Rights of Children,' *supra* n. 47, 11–12.
[94] Ashleigh Barnes, 'CRC's Performance of the Child as Developing' in Michael Freeman (ed.), *Law and Childhood Studies* (Oxford University Press, Oxford 2012) 392–418.
[95] Colette Daiute, 'The Rights of Children, the Rights of Nations: Developmental Theory and the Politics of Children's Rights' (2008) 64 *Journal of Social Issues* 701, 710.
[96] Ibid.

children's agency and embraces a broad definition of 'child development' and the heterogeneity of childhood in order to create a coherent and meaningful interpretation of the right to development.

Is There a Right to Development?

Children's rights scholarship tends to focus on three main themes: Article 12 and the right to participation; the parent–child relationship; and the implementation of the Convention in various contexts.[97] In that sense, greater attention has been given to the realities of the Convention as a legal and advocacy tool while less – and arguably insufficient – attention has been dedicated to analysing the Convention itself. Ann Quennerstedt partly attributes this trend to the concern of children's rights scholars and advocates that investigating some of the weaker or problematic elements of the Convention could undermine the image of children as rights holders.[98] But putting your head in the sand, as John Tobin rightly argues, is the wrong approach; validating and reaffirming the importance of the human rights of children requires critically engaging with argumentative challenges, rather than ignoring them.[99] Similarly, the lack of scholarly engagement with the right to development is partly because of the ambiguity surrounding the term 'child development' and the hesitation to suggest either that Article 6 is not very clear, or that it does not provide any distinct protection for children's development. This book therefore takes up the challenge of confronting these arguments. It does so by suggesting that Article 6 protects a distinct right of children – namely, the right to development – which in turn offers comprehensive and unique protection for children's developmental trajectories.

While the language of Article 6(2) does not use the phrase 'right to development', but rather refers to states' obligation to ensure 'to the maximum extent possible' the survival and development of children, I argue that the Convention recognises the right to development as an independent right of children, for at least four reasons:

---

[97] Reynart, D. et al., 'A Review of Children's Rights Literature since the Adoption of the United Nations Convention on the Rights of the Child' (2009) 16 *Childhood* 518.

[98] Ann Quennerstedt, 'Children's Rights Research Moving into the Future – Challenges on the Way Forward' (2013) 21 *International Journal of Children's Rights* 233.

[99] John Tobin, 'Justifying Children's Rights' (2013) 21 *International Journal of Children's Rights* 395.

- First, other Articles in the Convention do not use the term 'right to' or 'right of,' but nonetheless have been interpreted – including by the UN Committee on the Rights of the Child – as protecting a right of the child. The most prominent example of this is Article 3 and the principle of the best interests of the child. While Article 3 names the best interests principle as a 'consideration', the Committee suggests in General Comment No. 14 (2013) that the principle is a 'substantive right' of children.[100] Therefore, the Convention language, as important as it is, does not preclude an interpretation that a right to development is protected under Article 6.
- Second, the drafting history of the Convention – which is reviewed and analysed in detail in Chapter 2 of this book – shows that the drafters intended to create a broad protection for child development. Introducing a right to development was not ruled out, nor was it strongly pursued.
- Third, the lived reality of the Convention, as interpreted by the UN Committee on the Rights of the Child, suggests that Article 6 protects three distinct rights: the right to life, the right to survival, and the right to development.
- Fourth, a similar recognition in this interpretation of the Convention – namely an interpretation that reads 'the right to development' in the Convention – can be traced in the relevant scholarly literature about children's rights in general, and about the Convention in particular. As such, this interpretation allies with the views of the relevant scholarly community, a factor deemed important by the Vienna Convention on the Law of Treaties (1969).

The Structure of the Book

The book consists of five chapters preceded by this introductory chapter. Chapter 1 reviews various ways and justifications for the protection of child development in international children's rights law, focusing on key children's rights theorists and their paradigms (at least, those in the English-speaking world). The chapter connects the ways in which childhood is conceived in law and the nature and content of the legal protection ascribed to 'child development'. It begins by reviewing late nineteenth-century attitudes towards childhood, focusing on the writings

---

[100] UNCRC, 'General Comment No. 14 (2013) on the Right of the Child to Have His or Her Best Interests Taken as a Primary Consideration (art. 3, para. 1)' (29 May 2013) UN Doc. CRC/C/GC/14, para. 6.

of three key theorists who pushed the boundaries of this field in the early twentieth century: Ellen Key, Janusz Korczak, and Eglantyne Jebb. It then analyses the first two key instruments of international children's rights law: the 1924 League of Nations Declaration of the Rights of the Child and the 1959 UN Declaration of the Rights of the Child. The images of children in these documents are compared with the image of the child under the Universal Declaration of Human Rights and the two 1966 Covenants (the International Covenant on Civil and Political Rights and the International Covenant on Economic, Social and Cultural Rights). Finally, Chapter 1 studies the texts of the 1970s child liberation movement – which was active mainly in the United States and essentially called for the elimination of the different legal treatment of children and adults – and the movement's approaches toward children's development and human rights. In Chapter 1, I argue that despite shifts in the ways in which questions of vulnerability, agency, parental role, states' duties, child protection, and children's rights have been addressed, one constant theme in nearly 100 years of children's rights law and scholarship is the protection of child development. However, the question of what child development means – beyond the general notion of care for the future – has rarely been explicitly addressed.

Chapter 2 explores the drafting history of the Convention. Based on original archival research, it unveils and analyses the discussions, ethical considerations, and conceptions of childhood, rights and child development that led to the creation of the child's right to development. I argue that while the drafters paid much attention to the various ways in which child development is protected by the Convention, the question of what child development means was rarely raised. Furthermore, no significant discussions about the implications of formulating the care for child development as a matter of legal right can be found, but the option for recognizing such right was not ruled out.

The drafting process resulted in the creation of a complex structure wherein the Convention relates to eight domains of child development, including a general clause that protects the right to development. Considering the history of international children's rights law, the drafting process, and the prevailing conception of childhood at the time of its drafting, I suggest that the right to development can be understood as a right of the child to have her needs for healthy growth met in order for her to become an adult.

Chapter 3 analyses the interpretation of the right to development by the UN Committee on the Rights of the Child. By reviewing all the

Committee's Concluding Observations issued between 1993, when their publication began, and 2016, and its General Comments Nos. 1 through 23, published between 2001 and 2017, the chapter analyses the Committee's interpretation of the right to development and its relationship with other rights in the Convention. The main argument in this chapter is that the Committee subjugates most of the Convention's rights to support the child's maturation process. But, at the same time – like the Convention's drafters – the Committee overlooks the right to development. I further argue that although the Committee repeatedly emphasises the importance of protecting the child's right to development – which it defines as one of the Convention's four guiding principles – its jurisprudence falls short of providing a workable definition of the right. This abstract engagement with the right to development is influenced by the human becomings conception of childhood, which inherently limits the Committee's outlook and leads it to overlook the articulation of children's development as a matter of human rights.

Chapter 4 looks at three identified impediments to the process of interpreting the child's right to development: the meanings of 'child development', the utility of articulating the protection of child development in human rights terms, and the prospects for concretising this objective. The chapter therefore analyses the meaning of 'development' in two other contexts: the general right to development in international law (that is, international human rights law that is not group specific) and the capability approach (also known as 'the human development paradigm'), which in general is 'under-theorized in relation to children'.[101] According to both frameworks, 'human development' refers to collective mobilisation, emancipation, and the democratic values of participation. I argue that since both the general right to development and the child's right to development share the same yardstick of growth – either economic development or personal maturation – a comparison between the two can enable us to expand the interpretation of the child's right to development. I further argue that using the capability approach's concept of human development can broaden the scope of the right to development so that it means more than ensuring an optimum result for the child's process of growth and provides concrete measures for implementation. The chapter also analyses the various methods utilised by the child indicator movement – a title used to describe scholarly work that

---

[101] Kaushik Basu, 'Prologue' in Mario Biggeri et al. (eds.), Children and the Capability Approach (Palgrave Macmillan, Basingstoke 2011) x.

seeks to measure children's development and well-being – to conceptualise child development. I argue that these indices have the potential to concretise the analysis of the child's right to development.

Finally, Chapter 5 brings together the past and present treatment of the right to development and rethinks the operationalisation of this right. In this chapter, I offer a new framework for the interpretation of the child's right to development. This framework upholds three key principles: a new conception of hybrid childhood, which synthesises the human beings and human becomings approaches; an increased respect for the child's agency in the context of her development; and a distinction between the right to development as a guiding principle of the Convention and as a separate human right of children. I argue that this framework can be meaningful and can be implemented if used in conjunction with a cross-disciplinary understanding of child development. Without a common language and shared knowledge about the various meanings of child development, the interpretation of this right is destined to continue to suffer from a lack of coherence and an inability to concretise it in human rights terms.

The book argues that conceptualising children as human becomings and seeing childhood only as a journey towards adulthood[102] have led international children's rights law to create a web of rights that provide wide protection for children's development. Consequently, the right to development has been created and interpreted against what seems to be the natural cycle of life: the transformation of a child into a competent adult. The fixation with caring for children's future did not end with the paradigm shift in childhood studies during the 1970s. According to the human beings approach to childhood, children are seen as active agents in their life, their families, and their communities, and as human rights bearers.[103] While the Convention includes some provisions that reflect this new paradigm – for example, the recognition of children's right to participate in decisions concerning their life (Article 12), the right to freedom of expression (Article 13), and the right to freedom of thought, conscience, and religion (Article 14) – the human beings conception has thus far not been utilised in the interpretation of the right to development. This is not least because, this book suggests, the human beings approach is in tension with the normative grounds that underpin the Convention and the right to development and the Convention's endorsement of a human becomings approach.

---

[102] Lee, *supra* n. 18, 5–19. [103] Prout and James, 'A New Paradigm', *supra* n. 55.

The focus on the child's future as an adult – while paying little attention to the child's life in the present, to the process of growth, or to the importance of childhood independently of adulthood – is where the main difficulty in the interpretation of the right to development lies. The concern with the child's future is not without significance, but it is not sufficiently respectful of children's agency and dignity. Recognising children's right to be active agents in shaping their own destiny, while respecting their right to grow up and become whatever they want to be and can be, requires conceptual shifts. First, it requires recognising that child development is a matter of protecting the child's human rights, and not merely a matter of welfare or kindness. Second, it requires reconstructing the conceptions of childhood and child development in the context of the right to development, so that the term 'child development' incorporates broad cross-disciplinary meanings, rather than being bound by the discourse of developmental psychology. Third, it requires abandoning the polarised views of childhood, which position adulthood against childhood, in favour of a hybrid conception that simultaneously respects children's present, their future, and their voice. These three changes can enable us to redefine the meaning of the child's right to development and to understand it as the child's right to fulfil her human potential to the maximum.

Children's rights scholarship, as Quennerstedt has shown,[104] is often limited by the conceptual and positivist boundaries of the Convention. This book, in many senses, is no different. It traces and analyses the origins of the right to development and the treatment of child development in international children's rights law, and dedicates much attention to the Convention itself, as a constitutive instrument, and to its monitoring body, the UN Committee on the Rights of the Child. I take this approach for two reasons: first, to understand why and to what extent the care for child development is embedded in international children's rights law, and second, to argue that this stands in sharp contrast to the inadequate treatment of this right so far. I argue that we should realise just how limited and biased the Convention is, and that, in order to improve our understanding of the right to development of children, we should think beyond the Convention and beyond the conceptual confinements of international human rights law. The book will therefore speak to children's rights scholars and practitioners, and I hope to

---

[104] Quennerstedt, *supra* n. 98.

anyone who makes decisions and creates policies that affect children. Unlike other legal scholarly work, it should also speak to, and I hope open the door to a conversation with, scholars and practitioners from other disciplines – not least because, as the book argues, child development is an issue of investigation, concern, and practice to many other professions, but also because lawyers must engage in these sorts of conversations in order to advance the utility of law itself.

*

After living as a middle-class white man for a few weeks, during which he has dated a woman, spent money on luxuries, climbed up the corporate ladder, and neglected his best friend, Josh Baskin realises that he is not ready to be an adult. He wants to return to his home, to his parents and to his childhood. The movie *Big* ends with Josh walking down the all-American suburban road, once again in his 12-year-old body, while wearing an adult suit, leaving the viewer to wonder about the nature of child development, and of childhood and adulthood. This book suggests that the right to development of children should be considered as an independent right of the child, and as a guiding principle of the UN Convention on the Rights of the Child, and that in the process of interpreting and protecting it, equal attention should be given to the process of development and to its potential outcomes. As Josh's journey demonstrates, the two dimensions of childhood are intertwined, but time, nonetheless, is linear and only moves forward. Legal adulthood is the inevitable ending point for the journey that legal childhood takes. The book suggests that this journey deserves a closer attention from a children's rights perspective.

1

Embedding the Protection of 'Child Development' into International Children's Rights Law

> Children are not the people of tomorrow, but are people of today. They have a right to be taken seriously, and to be treated with tenderness and respect. They should be allowed to grow into whoever they were meant to be – the unknown person inside each of them is our hope for the future.
>
> Janusz Korczak, *The Child's Right to Respect* (1927)

> The child is given rights so that he may become a complete and perfect human being.
>
> Cuevas Cancino, Speech to UN General Assembly (1959)

This chapter analyses the different ways in which child development and related concepts – such as autonomy, capacity, and agency – have been understood and interpreted in child law scholarship during the last century. The chapter begins in the nineteenth century, at a time when the legal conception of 'the child' in the Western world was changing, and the law, as a social agent, began to embrace new positionalities of children in society. The view that children are the property of their fathers was replaced by romantic middle-class ideas of children as a source of pleasure and joy for their parents. Legal measures that reflected political interests in children's lives and futures were introduced, particularly in the realm of welfare, education and health.[1] International law underwent a similar change with the adoption of the 1924 League of Nations Declaration of the Rights of the Child.[2] This was the first

---

[1] Priscilla Robertson, 'Home as a Nest: Middle Class Childhood in Nineteenth-Century Europe' in Lloyd deMause (ed.), *The History of Childhood* (Souvenir Press, London 1976) 407–431, 407.

[2] The term 'law' refers also to what is known as 'soft law' in international law. Although the 1924 Declaration of the Rights of the Child is not a binding international treaty, it nevertheless has a normative significance in international law. Christine Chinkin, 'The Challenges of Soft Law: Development and Change in International Law' (1989) 28 *International and Comparative Law Quarterly* 850.

international legal instrument dedicated solely to the human rights of children, and it continues to inspire international children's rights today.[3] The Declaration, analysed in detail below, pinned down 'child development' as a key concept and object of concern. The chapter also examines the work of three influential thinkers – Ellen Key, Janusz Korczak, and Eglantyne Jebb – who advocated for recognising the rights of children at the beginning of the twentieth century. Despite some differences in their views, all three emphasised the need to facilitate the process of growth (the 'human becoming' paradigm). They planted the seeds for thinking about children, their future as adults, and the law, while also accounting for children's lives in the present.

The chapter then moves on to analyse the second international legal instrument to acknowledge children's rights, the 1959 UN Declaration of the Rights of the Child. This Declaration is much broader in scope than the 1924 Declaration and includes many additional rights of children. Similar to the 1924 Declaration, the 1959 Declaration embraces protection of child development. The chapter continues by briefly analysing some key changes in child law during the 1960s, and the rise of the child liberation movement in the 1970s, as a means to contextualise the historical evolution of the legal treatment of child development and the background against which the UN Convention on the Rights of the Child was drafted. The liberation movement's key argument was that children should be seen as equal to adults and therefore should be recognised as human rights holders in the same way that adults are. The liberationists challenged the developmental model and its assumptions concerning children's capacities, arguing that society's attitude towards children must change, and that relationships between children and their parents, teachers, and governments should be redefined.

The Nineteenth-Century Children's Welfare Laws

The last quarter of the nineteenth century marked a period of significant economic, social, political, and legal changes in the Anglo-American world, all of which changed the conception of childhood. The perception of children as their father's property began to fade away, and children's

---

[3] Dominique Marshall, 'The Construction of Children as an Object of International Relations: The Declaration of Children's Rights and the Child Welfare Committee of League of Nations, 1990–1924' (1999) 7 *International Journal of Children's Rights* 103, 104.

humanity gained recognition.[4] Childhood began to be seen as a period of 'purity', rather than of 'sin',[5] and, subsequently, children were no longer seen as 'little devils' that ought to be disciplined, but as in need of protection. Declining infant mortality rates disentangled pregnancy from grief, and the rise of capitalism, consumerism, and new advertising techniques contributed to the association of happiness with childhood and parenthood – especially motherhood.[6] Mothers internalised this new paradigm and strived to turn their children into 'happy and productive citizens',[7] rather than a domestic workforce that could provide for the family.

The dawn of the Victorian era also saw the rise of a new social responsibility towards children.[8] Along with parents, the public began to show interest in promoting children's welfare and health[9] and in protecting children from the hardships caused by poverty.[10] One of the legal implications of this change was the introduction of welfare and protection laws in the Anglo-American world. On the one hand, these laws followed and perpetuated the new image of the humanised children by establishing a range of means to aid children whose living standard fell below a newly established minimum (in terms of nutrition, health, and the parenting skills and practices of their parents). But, on the other hand, the laws victimised children by conceptualising them as subjects in eternal need of protection.[11] The duality of images – of the child as a happy human being and as a victim – and the ongoing need to balance the two competing narratives of childhood have been at the heart of children's law ever since.

---

[4] For a review of the evolution in attitudes to children, see Michael Freeman, *The Rights and Wrongs of Children* (Frances Pinter, London 1983) 13–19.

[5] Karen Sanchez Eppler, *Dependent States: The Child's Part in Nineteenth-Century American Culture* (University of Chicago Press, Chicago 2005) xv; David Archard, *Children: Rights and Childhood* (2nd edition, Routledge, London 2004).

[6] Peter N. Stearns, 'Defining Happy Childhoods: Assessing a Recent Change' (2010) 3 *Journal of the History of Childhood and Youth* 165.

[7] Paula S. Fass, 'A Historical Context for the United Nations Convention on the Rights of the Child' (2011) 633 *Annals of the American Academy of Political and Social Sciences* 17, 21.

[8] Hugh Cunningham, *The Invention of Childhood* (BBC Books, London 2006) 145–175.

[9] Mary Ann Mason, *From Father's Property to Children's Rights: The History of Child Custody in the United States* (Columbia University Press, New York 1994) 87–92.

[10] Robert L. Geiser, 'The Rights of Children' (1976–1977) 28 *Hastings Law Journal* 1027, 1028–1034.

[11] Fass, 'A Historical Context for the United Nations Convention on the Rights of the Child', *supra* n. 7, 22.

One significant implication of society's assuming responsibility for children was the introduction of compulsory education. This not only provided educational opportunities for children from all classes,[12] who could later become healthy and skilled workers,[13] but also provided a physical space where children could come together and receive care from health professionals (for example, meals, vaccinations, and routine health checks). A parallel effort focused on reducing the number of working children and incentivising parents to send their children to school. Some legislative reforms along these lines were introduced – for example, in the United Kingdom, the 1847 Larceny Act and the 1854 Reformatory School Act[14] established a minimum age for employment, limited working hours for children under age 16, and made primary school education compulsory.[15]

The newly assumed state responsibility for ensuring children's future also featured in tackling domestic child abuse.[16] New laws regulated child-rearing practices, enabling and mandating state intervention – including by giving authorities the power to remove children from parental custody in cases of failure to properly care for children's welfare. These social ideas of what childhood should look like, and how it should be experienced, also enabled the implementation of racist programs of cultural genocide – for example, indigenous children in Australia and First Nations children in Canada were taken away from their parents via the legal pathways that welfare laws created.[17] In the United States, the creation of the first juvenile court in Illinois in 1899 is another example of the ways in which the new conception of childhood changed the legal treatment of children. The court was established on the premise that the state is under a duty to provide the child with 'aid and protection and to

---

[12] Mary Jo Maynes, *Schooling in Western Europe* (State University of New York Press, Albany 1985).

[13] Fass, 'A Historical Context for the United Nations Convention on the Rights of the Child' *supra* n. 7, 17.

[14] Freeman, *The Rights and Wrongs of Children*, *supra* n. 4, 66–67.

[15] C.R. Margolin, 'Salvation versus Liberation: The Movement for Children's Rights in a Historical Context' (1977–1978) 25 *Social Problems* 441, 443–445.

[16] Geiser, *supra* n. 10, 1030; Rex Stainton Rogers and Wendy Stainton Rogers, *Stories of Childhood* (University of Toronto Press, Toronto 1992) 22–24.

[17] Australian Human Rights Commission, *Bringing Them Home: The 'Stolen Children' Report* (1997). See also Heather Douglas and Tamara Walsh, 'Continuing the Stolen Generation: Child Protection Interventions and Indigenous People' (2013) 21 *International Journal of Children's Rights* 59–87.

direct it into a path that leads to good citizenship',[18] thus facilitating children's process of 'growing up and transforming into citizens'.[19]

However, from a child's perspective, all these changes can be rather confusing. As Steven Mintz claims:

> The young are told to work hard and value school, but also to enjoy themselves. They are to be innocent but also sexually alluring. They are to be respectful and obedient, but also independent consumers beholden to no one. They are to be youthful but not childish. The basic contradiction is that the young are told to grow up fast, but also that they needn't grow up at all.[20]

It was the concern for children's welfare, rather than their human rights, that stood at the heart of the law. This was similar to the treatment of women, people of colour, and other minorities in their struggles for rights. Despite the recognition of their humanity,[21] children were not perceived as human rights holders. Instead, the law catered for their welfare, continuing to conceptualise them as human beings in the making.[22]

The domination of the welfare approach to childhood at the dawn of the nineteenth century cast a shadow over other models. Three children's rights pioneers, to use Philip Veerman's description[23] – Ellen Key (1848–1926), Janusz Korczak (1878–1942), and Eglantyne Jebb (1876–1928) – advocated for different and radical approaches towards childhood, children and their rights. The core of their approaches was that children should be treated by considering not only the adults they could become, but also the children they are. For different reasons, they therefore called for respect of children as human rights holders. Their illuminating approaches deserve to be discussed in detail.

---

[18] Flexner, as quoted in Margolin, *supra* n. 15, 443. See also Anthony M. Platt, *The Child Savers: The Innovation of Delinquency* (2nd edition, University of Chicago Press, Chicago 1977) 101–136.

[19] Mason, *supra* n. 9, 85–120.

[20] Steven Mintz, *Huck's Raft: A History of American Childhood* (Harvard University Press, Cambridge 2004) 381.

[21] Paula S. Fass, *The Damned and the Beautiful: American Youth in the 1920s* (Oxford University Press, New York 1977) 23.

[22] Nonetheless, it should be noted that the welfare legislation concerning children is part of the process of recognising children's citizenship: Bryan Turner, 'Personhood and Citizenship' (1986) 3 *Theory Culture Society* 1, 8–10.

[23] Philip E. Veerman, *The Rights of the Child and the Changing Image of Childhood* (Martinus Nijhoff, Leiden 1992) 73.

Ellen Key and the Relationship between Children's Education, Development, and Public Policy

In 1900, Ellen Key, a Swedish teacher, published the book *The Century of the Child*.[24] This manifesto calls upon society to adopt a new approach towards children and to put them at the centre of attention in matters concerning their lives – including marriage, family life and education.[25] In contemporary terms, Key suggested recognising children as agents on their own terms and protecting their human rights accordingly. She offered a list of specific rights that she deems to be fundamental for children, with the right to choose one's parents at the top of the list. This is followed by the right to education, the right to participation in the context of education, the right to have a home, the right to be free from religious instruction, and the right to be free from labour. Most of these rights can now be found in the Convention on the Rights of the Child (Articles 28–29, 12, 14–15, and 32, respectively) but, in comparison to Key's suggestions, the Convention seems to be a rather protectionist document. The Convention, for example, recognises the child's right to be brought up by her parents (Article 9), but does not recognise children's right to 'divorce' their parents and does not respect their right to emancipation.

Writing against the background of the welfare approach, Key presents a less paternalistic and protectionist attitude towards children. She is not afraid to point the finger at parents, as well as society, for failing to protect children, and she does not think that one (the state) is better than the other (the parents, in case they fail to deliver on their responsibilities). Her book touches upon the issue of child abuse in a bold way, suggesting that the veil of privacy that covers the family should be lifted so that children can be protected from all forms of abuse, including corporal punishment, and other cases of abuse that do not meet the

---

[24] Ellen Key, *The Century of the Child* (G. P. Putnam's Sons, New York and London 1909). On the influence of this book, see Kriste Lindenmeyer and Bengt Sandin, 'National Citizenship and Early Policies Shaping "The Century of the Child" in Sweden and the United States' (2008) 1 *Journal of the History of Childhood and Youth* 50. For an overall appreciation of Key's influence on the twentieth century, see Jeroen J. J. Dekker, 'The Century of the Child Revisited' (2000) 8 *International Journal of Children's Rights* 133.

[25] The book was translated into English in 1909. In the same year, US President Theodore Roosevelt called the first White House conference on children, which dealt with the 'care of dependent children': Rochelle Beck, 'White House Conferences on Children: An Historical Perspective' (1973) 43 *Harvard Educational Review* 653.

threshold of serious harm.[26] Considering the contemporary global land-scape of legislation concerning parental abuse, where the majority of countries still accept the usage of physical force, it is evident that Key's propositions are far from being the accepted norm. She also advocates in favour of abolishing the social stigma and legal label of 'illegitimate' child, arguing that defining the legal status of a child based on the nature of her parents' relationship inherently harms the child and can undermine her future possibilities when she has in fact not done anything wrong.[27] In other words, this stigma limits the child's future development and narrows down the opportunities that she will have as an adult due to a situation that is beyond her control and a result of patriarchal order that asks to control and regulate women's sexuality.

Schools and education are also subjects of concern for Key. She claims that young children should be homeschooled by their mothers, in order to avoid the risk that their souls will be 'murdered' by teachers.[28] Compulsory education should therefore start only at the primary school level. While in school, children should not be subject to curricula that focus on producing future citizens. Instead, the program should 'give to each separate individual as much development and happiness as possible'.[29] In that sense, Key's concern with both the child's future and the child's present ('being' and 'becoming' simultaneously), and her rejection of the capitalist-informed objectives of education that had gained traction at that time, resonate with the romantic views of Jean-Jacques Rousseau, who asked to nurture the soul of the young child[30] and help her in 'setting [her] feet on a narrow path'.[31]

A significant part of Key's book is dedicated to questions of child-rearing, the process of growing up, and the appropriate public policies to nurture this process. She calls for the establishment of a 'pedagogical culinary science' that will determine what children should learn.[32] More specifically, this science, according to Key, would support the belief that 'harmonious development is the finest result of man's training, but it is only to be attained by his own choice. It implies a harmony between the real capacities of the individual, not a harmony worked up from a

---

[26] Key, *supra* n. 24, 128–138.   [27] *Ibid.*, 44–45.   [28] *Ibid.*, 203–232.   [29] *Ibid.*, 207.
[30] Julia Simon, 'Jean-Jacques Rousseau's Children' in Susan M. Turner and Gareth B. Matthews (eds.), *The Philosopher's Child* (University of Rochester Press, New York 1998) 105–120, 111; Kevin William Ryan, 'The New Wave of Childhood Studies: Break-ing the Grip of Bio-Social Dualism?' (2011) 19 *Childhood* 439, 444–446.
[31] Simon, *supra* n. 30, 114.   [32] Key, *supra* n. 24, 256. [

pedagogical formula'[33] (emphasis added). Variations of this statement, which sets an optimum stage of development that the child should achieve, can be found in every subsequent discussion about international children's rights law. One notable difference between Key's work and the other discussions that will be described in this chapter and in the rest of the book is the respect for children's agency and voice as key factors in developing the child's own capacities, which Key emphasises but which later receives little or no attention.

Janusz Korczak and Children's Present and Future Lives

Janusz Korczak, a paediatrician, was the director of Dom Sierot, an orphanage in Warsaw, for 30 years, from 1912 until his murder in Treblinka on 7 August 1942.[34] In a series of short books – some written in essay form, some as advice books for parents, and others as children's fiction – Korczak explains his unique approach towards childhood and children's lives and rights. Essentially, he argues that children are fully competent human beings, and not merely persons engaged in a process of becoming adults. As such, children's personhood should be acknowledged, and their dignity and rights should be respected. 'Our indolence keeps us from discovering beauty in the present', Korczak writes. 'When I approach a child, I have two feelings: affection for what he is today and respect for what he can become.'[35] Korczak is reluctant to use the jargon of psychoanalysis to characterise childhood, arguing that Freud was a 'dangerous maniac' who 'reduced childhood to a psychosexual stage'.[36] He also rejects the developmental approach that sees childhood as a sequence of stages that ought to be accomplished in order for a child to be successfully transformed into an adult, arguing instead that childhood is an important stage in itself. 'Is there a life that exists as some joke?',

---

[33] *Ibid.*.

[34] Veerman, *supra* n. 23, 93. See also Irena Sendlerowa, 'I Saw Korczak and the Children Walking from the Ghetto to Their Death' in Janusz Korczak, *The Child's Right to Respect: Janusz Korczak's Lectures on Today's Challenges for Children* (Council of Europe, Brussels, 2009),, 43–45, 43.

[35] Janusz Korczak, *Loving Every Child* (Algonquin Books of Chapel Hill, North Carolina 2007; originally published in 1919) 17.

[36] As quoted in Betty Jean Lifton, *The King of Children: A Biography of Janusz Korczak* (Chatto & Windus, London 1988) 125.

he rhetorically asks. 'No, childhood years are long and important ones in the life of a man.'[37]

Therefore, like Key, Korczak sees education not as a mean of transferring knowledge and skills aimed at creating a contributing citizen, but rather as a process that respects the child's dignity in a participatory way. Children, he claims, should take part in the educational process and should be given the space necessary to influence the content of education, as well as its administration. Korczak implemented these views, and the orphanage he directed was self-governed by children. The children ran their own parliament, where they debated and decided different issues concerning the operation of the institution. They published their own newspaper, as well as governing a court of peers where children and staff alike – including Korczak himself – could face trial if they broke the house's code, a code that was written and adopted by the children.

In his seminal essay 'The Child's Right to Respect', published in 1927, Korczak defines 'the child' and the time of 'childhood' in the following terms:

> The basic idea that the child is not now but will become later, does not know anything but will do so, is not capable of doing anything but will learn, makes us live in a perpetual state of expectation.
>
> For the sake of tomorrow we fail to respect what amuses, saddens, amazes, angers, and interests him today. For the sake of tomorrow, we steal many years of his life.[38]

Korczak argues that society should pay attention to children's experiences and expectations of the world, and should respect and appreciate the importance of the time of childhood, rather than seeing the child through the lens of her future. The child should be seen not only as a future citizen, he argues, but rather as a person in the present, and the process of growth should be acknowledged and celebrated, rather than being a justification for imposing more suppression on the child. 'We should have more respect for the mysteries and fluctuations of the hard business of growing up!', he says.[39] 'We search for signs of the future; we'd like to be able to foretell, to be certain; this anxious anticipation about what the future holds increases our indifference towards what it is.'[40] In other

---

[37] Korczak, The Child's Right to Respect: Janusz Korczak's Lectures on Today's Challenges for Children (Council of Europe, Brussels, 2009), 33.

[38] Ibid., 18–19.   [39] Korczak, Loving Every Child, supra n. 35, 63.

[40] Korczak, The Child's Right to Respect, supra n. 37, 24–25.

words, there is no reason to prioritise the care for an optimal or normal development, not least because it results in failing to value the time of childhood in itself and because the future is not more important than the present. In that sense, Korczak may have been the first to conceptualise the child as a human 'being' rather than merely as a human 'becoming'. But this is not his only contribution to childhood studies. In his work, Korczak also rejects any binary definitions of childhood, arguing in favour of an inclusive definition that respects children for both who they are and who they will become. In Chapter 5, I use this idea to develop further the 'hybrid conception' of childhood.

Korczak also writes about children's rights and the law. He suggests the adoption of a bill of rights for children, which he titles 'Magna Carta Libertatis concerning the Rights of the Child'.[41] This version of the Magna Carta includes the following rights:[42] the right to respect, the right to autonomy, the right to make mistakes, the right to fail, the right to participate, the right to human dignity, the right to information, the right to privacy, the right to own property, the right to education, the right to belief and the right to resist any educational influence, the right to due process and 'to a children's court', the right to freedom of religion, the right to love, and the right to respect for the child's grief. This is a much more comprehensive and progressive list of rights compared to most human rights instruments that existed at the time, including the 1924 Declaration of the Rights of the Child (which will be discussed later in this chapter), and some later human rights instruments such as the 1959 UN Declaration on the Rights of the Child. The list captures many nuances of children's lives and is attuned to children's needs, thus departing from liberal models of rights that are based on respecting the privacy and autonomy of an allegedly competent rights holder. For example, recognising the right of the child to fail runs in sharp contrast to any paternalistic approaches to education, which encourage success and disincentivise – and sometimes even punish – children who fail, irrespective of the reasons for their failure. The list does not focus on the protection of children's future or their

---

[41] As quoted in Gabriel Eichsteller, 'Janusz Korczak – His Legacy and Its Relevance for Children's Rights Today' (2009) 17 *International Journal of Children's Rights* 377, 385.

[42] Janusz Korczak, 'How to Love a Child' in M. Wolins (ed.), *Selected Works of Janusz Korczak* (National Science Foundation, Washington DC 1967) 355–356. *C.f.* Lifton, *supra* n. 36.

welfare, nor does it seek to prevent any harm to the child's ability to bloom as an adult.

The list is also an example of Korczak's groundbreaking approach towards children and childhood. It establishes a broad legal framework for caring for the child's future, positioning the right to grow up and the right to live in the present not as mutually exclusive rights, but rather as complementary to each other. The list essentially, even if not explicitly, acknowledges the right to development of children, and it defines 'development' in complicated terms. This approach to children, childhood, human rights, and child development – as this chapter and the next one show – has been lost over time.

Eglantyne Jebb and the Salvation of Children

Eglantyne Jebb, an English teacher, made an important contribution to the creation of international children's rights law by drafting and advocating for the adoption of the 1924 League of Nations Declaration of the Rights of the Child. She also founded the influential charity Save the Children, which was launched in London in 1919.[43]

At the end of the First World War, Jebb was concerned with the disproportionate effects that the famine spreading through Europe was having on children. She believed that because children are innocent people who have no culpability in the wars generated by adults, some mechanism should be established to ensure that they are protected from wars and their aftermath – including mass killings, the loss of family members, and other major traumas. Taking a somewhat naïve approach – surely one that had no basis in history – Jebb based her advocacy on the somewhat naïve proposition that 'common people could not bear to see children die without at least trying to help'.[44] She therefore decided to establish Save the Children as a service organisation, providing relief – especially food and toys – to children in need.[45] As its name suggests, the organisation reflects the Christian spirit of salvation and the desire to physically 'save' children – especially, similarly to Key's aspiration, their mental and spiritual well-being.

Jebb thought that, along with her charity work, the newly established League of Nations could be an avenue for advocacy, as this body

---

[43] See Clare Mulley, *The Women Who Saved the Children* (Oneworld, Oxford 2009).
[44] Veerman, *supra* n. 23, 89.   [45] *Ibid.*, 88.

could help create an international legal framework for the protection of children:

> The world's children stand in urgent need of better protection, because it is they who pay the heaviest price for our short-sighted economic policies, our political blunders, our wars. Adults can pass through a period of stress and strain and perhaps be none the worse for it, once it is over, but if we fail to give children their physical requirements and we restrict their educational advantages, they may well be handicapped in consequences for the rest of their lives.[46]

It seems that Jebb's main concern is with the effect of adults' 'short-sighted' views on children's 'physical requirements' and education, which in turn compromise children's future. Worrying that children could become 'handicapped' in the future, and thus denied the opportunity to fulfil their potential, Jebb suggests that their needs should be satisfied in the present. But unlike Key or Korczak, Jebb utilises the paternalistic welfare approach when arguing in favour of protecting children's future as adults. This rhetoric, and the approach to children's needs and development, would later be used by the League of Nations in the Declaration of the Rights of the Child.

Despite the differences among them, what unites Key, Korczak, and Jebb is their respect for children's agency and their sensitivity to the hardship and inferior treatment that children might experience due to their young age. They also share the view that children should be provided with the opportunity to grow up and, to different extents, develop into the adults whom they would like to be. Korczak and Key spoke about this process in human rights terms, but it was Jebb who translated the aspiration into concrete legal terms in the form of an international legal instrument.

1924 Declaration of the Rights of the Child

The League of Nations was established in 1919 in the aftermath of the First World War. One of its main objectives was the rehabilitation of war victims, including children,[47] and the main manifestation of this commitment was the establishment of the Child Welfare Committee, which was tasked with the unprecedented challenge of adopting a children's rights charter.[48]

---

[46] As quoted in Veerman, *supra* n. 23, 91.
[47] The Covenant of the League of Nations (1924). Marshall, *supra* n. 3, 106–108.
[48] *Ibid.*, 128.

The Declaration of the Rights of the Child,[49] also known as the Geneva Declaration, was adopted on 26 September 1924, becoming the first instrument of international law recognising children's rights.[50] However, while the Declaration's title and preamble use the term 'rights', the five substantive paragraphs do not mention this word at all. Instead, they use the term 'needs' and subsequently focus on measures to address these needs, ignoring the commitment to human rights suggested by the title. The Geneva Declaration mandates that certain needs of the child should be met by 'men and women of all nations', listing first the need of hungry children to be fed, followed by the need of sick children to be nursed, and the need to reclaim delinquent children.[51] It further asserts that children should be the first to receive relief in times of distress,[52] and that children must be put in a position where they can earn a livelihood while being protected against every form of exploitation.[53] The last paragraph states that children should be brought up in the consciousness that their talents must be devoted to the service of their fellow men.[54]

Using the language of needs rather than rights, the Declaration treats children as beneficiaries[55] or as 'recipients of treatment',[56] rather than as rights holders and as objects of international law. Geraldine Van Bueren rejects this assertation and claims that by linking children's needs to their rights, if only rhetorically, the Geneva Declaration created an international standard for children's rights.[57] Korczak was less sympathetic to the Geneva Declaration than was Van Bueren, rightly arguing that the Declaration reflects the conception of children as subjects of care and as persons in constant need of protection, and thus misses the opportunity to respect the agency of children. In addition, Korczak claims that since the Geneva Declaration does not assert the rights-bearing status of children themselves, it amounts to nothing more than 'an appeal to goodwill' of adults.[58] In line with the dominant perception of childhood at that time, the Geneva Declaration is primarily concerned with the child's future development. This conclusion is best demonstrated by its first Article, which reads: 'The child must be given the means requisite for its normal development, both materially and spiritually ... ' The Article

---

[49] League of Nations, Declaration of the Rights of the Child, O.J. Spec. Supp. 21, at 43 (1924).

[50] Veerman, *supra* n. 23, 155–156.

[51] League of Nations, Declaration of the Rights of the Child, 1924, Paragraph 2.

[52] *Ibid.*, Paragraph 3.   [53] *Ibid.*, Paragraph 4.   [54] *Ibid.*, Paragraph 5.

[55] Geraldine Van Bueren, *The International Law on the Rights of the Child* (Martinus Nijhoff, Dordrecht 1995) 7.

[56] *Ibid.*   [57] *Ibid.*, 8.   [58] Korczak, *The Child's Right to Respect, supra* n. 37, 34.

protects the child's 'normal development', which includes two elements: material and spiritual. Thus, children are entitled to have not a 'good' or 'healthy' process of growth, but rather a 'normal' one. The Declaration does not offer any qualifications as to what the result of this process should be (for example, 'optimum' or 'full' development). It also does not elaborate on the means required to fulfil the need for this 'normal' growth, but rather echoes developmental psychology in suggesting that there is a course of adequate or desirable 'normal' development that ought to be protected, in contrast to an abnormal, or distorted, development that might jeopardise the child's future.[59] This conceptualisation of development makes it clear that for the Declaration, the essence of childhood is the healthy transformation of a child into an adult, and the law needs to be part of the social endeavour that enables children to undergo this change.

Setting these conceptual limitations and biases aside, the importance of the Geneva Declaration when it comes to the right to development of children lies in the establishment, in its first paragraph, of the duty to protect child development. This suggests that the Declaration embraces the protection of child development as a core principle of international children's rights law, thereby positioning it as its main objective.

The next instrument in international children's rights law was the 1959 United Nations Declaration of the Rights of the Child. But before discussing this Declaration, there is a need to briefly review other developments in international human rights law that happened between the two Declarations – namely, the adoption of the Universal Declaration of Human Rights and the 1966 International Covenants. These instruments are important to the understanding and analysis of international children's rights law and its relationship to child development, not least due to their significant impact on the ways in which human rights – and the identity of the rights holder – have evolved in the United Nations human rights system.

Child Development and the Universal Declaration of Human Rights

In 1948, the newly established United Nations adopted the Universal Declaration of Human Rights (UDHR).[60] The UDHR protects civil and political rights, as well as social and economic rights.[61] It defines rights

---

[59] See Erica Burman, *Deconstructing Developmental Psychology* (3rd edition, Routledge, London 2017) 71–73.

[60] UN General Assembly, Universal Declaration of Human Rights (UDHR), adopted 10 December 1948, 217 A (III).

[61] For some background on the document and its drafting process, see Johannes Morsink, *The Universal Declaration of Human Rights: Origins, Drafting and Intent* (University of

holders as 'all members of the human family',[62] emphasising that 'all human beings are born free and equal in dignity and rights' and, therefore, 'everyone is entitled to all the rights and freedoms set forth in this Declaration'.[63] Presumably, this inclusive definition refers to children too.[64] But, unfortunately, children were rarely, if at all, seen as rights holders. Instead, they were seen as passive beneficiaries of the protection of the rights of families and, to a lesser extent, some rights of women. Article 25 (the right to an adequate standard of living) and Article 26 (the right to education) are two notable examples of the marginalisation of children. Article 25(1) reads:

> Everyone has the right to a standard of living adequate for the health and well-being of himself and of his family, including food, clothing, housing and medical care and necessary social services, and the right to security in the event of unemployment, sickness, disability, widowhood, old age or other lack of livelihood in circumstances beyond his control.[65]

While the language suggests that 'everyone' is a rights holder, evidently the rights holders are those men who head the household. These men – and only they – are entitled to the right to an adequate standard of living and to social security. It is through their largesse that other family members, namely women and children, benefit from this right. In other words, children may enjoy the fruits of the state offering a social security net, and thus may see their development needs met, but this objective will be achieved only if their fathers confer this right upon them. As to children who have no father, do not live in a traditional family unit, or have a father who is subject to discriminatory policies – for example, on the basis of civil status – it seems that they are not beneficiaries of this right.

Article 25(2) is one of the few places in the UDHR where children are explicitly mentioned. However, children are not perceived as rights holders. Instead, the Article merges the child's legal status with that of the mother, deeming that both mother and child are entitled to 'special care and assistance', and adding a limited non-discrimination clause by

---

Pennsylvania Press, Philadelphia 1999). Chapter 3 of the book is dedicated to equality, women's rights, and minorities' rights. However, the absence of children from the UDHR is not mentioned by Morsink. See pages 92–116.

[62] UDHR, *supra* n. 60, Preamble.   [63] UDHR, *supra* n. 60, Article 1.

[64] Hans-Joachim Heintze, 'Children's Rights within Human Rights Protection' in Michael Freeman and Philip Veerman (eds.), *The Ideologies of Children's Rights* (Martinus Nijhoff, Dordrecht 1992) 71–78, 72.

[65] UDHR, *supra*, n. 60.

stating that children who are born out of wedlock should enjoy the same protection as other children.[66] In that sense, Article 25 does not identify children as primary rights holders, but rather asks to remove one obstacle that prevents children from enjoying rights held by men – specifically, their fathers – and reinforces their image as vulnerable beings.

The second Article to explicitly mention children is UDHR Article 26(3), which protects the right to education.[67] Article 26 has an interesting composition. It begins by stating that 'everyone' has the right to education, but children are mentioned only in the context of parents having a right to 'choose the kind of education that shall be given to their children'. Thus, while children are the obvious holders and beneficiaries of this right, Article 26 – like Article 25 – considers children merely as passive or secondary beneficiaries of the parental right to education. Similar phrasing can be found in the United Nations Convention on the Rights of the Child, as will be discussed in Chapters 2 and 3. Another important aspect of the UDHR in that regard is Article 26(2), which defines the objective of education as the 'full development of the human personality'– thus setting a results-based test by which to assess the outcome of the educational process. Once again, this definition, while different from the one established by the Geneva Declaration, cements 'development', on a results-based test, as an objective. Although both concepts ('normal development' under the Geneva Declaration and 'full development' under the UDHR) are vague and entrenched in a narrow conceptualisation of child development, they nevertheless tell us something different about the child and about childhood. Furthermore, the definition of 'development' in the UDHR is broader, relating to the human personality in general rather than only to material or spiritual development.

The UDHR does not address specific issues that relate to children. It fails to explicitly recognise children as rights holders, even in the most obvious domains of their lives. The UDHR speaks about the need to advance human development, but remains silent about who is developing. It is against this perception of children as non-rights holders and as passive recipients of aid that the protection of child development and the

---

[66] For a commentary on Article 25, see Asbøjrn Eide and Wenche Barth Eide, 'Article 25' in Gudmundur Alfredsson and Asbøjrn Eide (eds.), *The Universal Declaration of Human Rights* (Martinus Nijhoff, The Hague 1999) 523–550.

[67] For a more detailed analysis of Article 26, see Pentti Arajärvi, 'Article 26' in Gudmundur Alfredsson and Asbøjrn Eide (eds.), *The Universal Declaration of Human Rights* (Martinus Nijhoff, The Hague 1999) 551–574.

right to development should be contextualised. Therefore, the progress that the UDHR generated in international human rights law has had less impact on children than on adults – or, more specifically, than on men.

1959 UN Declaration of the Rights of the Child

In 1950, soon after the adoption of the UDHR, the UN Social Commission asked the UN Secretary General to draft a declaration concerning the rights of the child.[68] Nine years later, in 1959, the General Assembly (UNGA) adopted the Declaration of the Rights of the Child.[69] Explaining the reasons for adopting this Declaration and its underpinning objectives, the Social Commission 'emphasized the need for special care of the rights of the child because of his immaturity in respect to a name, nationality, security, health, education and protection against all forms of exploitation *which might prejudice his development*'[70] (emphasis added). The child is thus perceived as an 'immature' person who is therefore vulnerable and in need of protection with regard to six key rights. Once those rights have been afforded 'special care', the child can develop and become an adult.

The original 1950 draft of the Declaration includes ten principles. Like the 1924 Declaration, the draft first addresses child development: 'The child shall be given the means necessary to enable him to *develop physically, mentally, morally, spiritually and socially in a healthy and normal manner* and in conditions of freedom and dignity'[71] (emphasis added). This principle introduces some new dimensions to the protection of child development. It refers to five aspects of child development (physical, mental, moral, spiritual, and social), two qualities of the developmental process (healthy and normal), and – for the first time – the conditions required for these objectives to be achieved (freedom and dignity).

Principles 4, 6, and 9 of the final version of the Declaration expand the commitment to protecting child development by introducing new dimensions to this objective. Principle 4 protects the child's right to social security. But, unlike Article 25 of the UDHR, it recognises children as rights holders, stating that the child 'shall be entitled to grow and

---

[68] UNHCHR, *Legislative History of the Convention on the Rights of the Child*, Volume I (United Nations, New York and Geneva, 2007) 4.

[69] UNGA, Declaration of the Rights of the Child, adopted by UN General Assembly Resolution 1386 (XIV) of 10 December 1959. For background on the drafting process, see Veerman, *supra* n. 23, 161–166.

[70] UNHCHR, *Legislative History of the Convention on the Rights of the Child*, *supra* n.68, 5.

[71] UNHCHR, *Legislative History of the Convention on the Rights of the Child*, *supra* n.68, 4.

develop in health'. By emphasising 'grow' and linking this to 'development', Principle 4 provides protection for the *process* of development, rather than its outcome, and identifies 'health' as the indicator for a successful process of growth. Principle 6 declares that the child 'needs love and understanding', as these are essential 'for the full and harmonious development of his personality'. This objective, similar to those that Korczak and Key suggested adopting, is not often found in human rights instruments. The principle describes the human desire for love as a need that should be protected as a human right, the fulfilment of which generates the process of 'full and harmonious development' of the child. As such, Principle 6 defines a broad – and somewhat vague – spectrum of development, one that ought to be both 'full' and 'harmonious'. The need for love and understanding, if read in conjunction with Principle 1, seems to be an attempt to coin the duty to acknowledge and respect children's agency and identity as rights holders.

Principle 9, corresponding with the fourth paragraph of the Geneva Declaration, states that the child shall 'in no case be caused or permitted to engage in any occupation or employment which would prejudice his health or education, or interfere with his *physical, mental or moral development*'[72] (emphasis added). This reflects a concern not only that work might be hazardous to children's health or education, but also that it could compromise three developmental aspects: physical, mental, and moral. Principle 9 is important for two reasons. First, it detaches the objective of promoting child development from the contexts of health, social security, and education, and acknowledges the distinct importance of supporting child development in various other contexts. Second, it expands the protection of child development to include three explicit components (physical development, mental development, and moral development) beyond the promise to support 'full' development. However, Principle 9 makes these distinctions only in relation to occupation or employment, and does not include other activities or situations that may also interfere with child development.

In 1959, Cuevas Cancino, the Rapporteur of the Declaration's Drafting Committee, presented the final text of the Declaration of the Rights of the Child to the UN General Assembly. In his speech, Cancino describes the normative grounds of the Declaration, emphasising that protecting child development in international law was one of the drafters' main objectives:

[72] *Ibid.*

> These rights are regarded as inherent in . . . a human being, that is to say,
> in a state of physical and moral growth . . . The draft Declaration dwells
> upon the ultimate contribution which the child will make to the human
> group to which he belongs . . . *The child is given rights so that he may
> become a complete and perfect human being* . . . It is not surprising that the
> draft Declaration should attach such importance to the spiritual factors
> which determine the *development* of the child . . . As a being in *the process
> of development*, the child requires special protection in that process; his
> development must be neither impeded nor forced into anti-social direc-
> tions[73] (emphasis added).

Further, on the issue of childhood and development, Cancino says that
the Declaration considers the child as an 'immature being' and therefore
'sets forth those rights which it regards as essential to the child's full
development'.[74]

It is not only the content but more especially the patronising tone of
this speech that reveals much about the drafters' perception of children,
childhood, children's rights, and child development. The speech portrays
a very clear image of children under this important instrument of
international children's rights law: the child is immature, and her course
of growth should be protected – especially her spiritual development. At
the end of this process, the expectation is that the child will become an
adult – or, more specifically, a 'complete and perfect' adult. Thus, the
child is seen not as a human being but, rather, as a human being in the
making. One ramification of this perception is that the 1959 Declaration
does not respect children as agents in their own right. Rather, it 'gives'
children some human rights so as to enable them to become 'complete
and perfect' human beings at their adulthood.

Principle 2 of the final version of the Declaration is another representation of these conceptions:

> The child shall enjoy special protection, and shall be given opportunities
> and facilities, by law and by other means, *to enable him to develop
> physically, mentally, morally, spiritually and socially in a healthy and
> normal manner* and in conditions of freedom and dignity. In the enact-
> ment of laws for this purpose, the best interests of the child shall be the
> paramount consideration[75] (emphasis added).

---

[73] UNHCHR, *Legislative History of the Convention on the Rights of the Child, supra*
n. 68, 21.

[74] *Ibid.*, 22.

[75] UN General Assembly, Declaration of the Rights of the Child, adopted by UN General
Assembly Resolution 1386 (XIV) of 10 December 1959.

Principle 2 defines a broader spectrum of development than was previously suggested. It declares what the goals of development are and what the development process should look like. While the first draft offered protection for six components of development (name, nationality, security, health, education, and protection against exploitation), Principle 2 delineates five aspects of child development (physical, mental, moral, spiritual, and social), tying them all to the principle of the 'best interests' of the child. This is the first time that the 'best-interests' principle is mentioned in an international document,[76] and it remains one of the rare occasions where it is connected to the issue of child development.

Reading Principles 2, 4, 6, and 9 of the UNDRC and Cancino's speech together demonstrates the implications of conceptualising children as the negative Others. The Declaration takes the position that since the child's purpose in life is to grow up, international children's rights law should protect the physical, mental, moral, spiritual, social, and full and harmonious development of children as a means of ensuring the outcome of this process. The endpoint of the developmental process, where the child turns into a 'fully developed' adult, is the objective, while the *process* of development, on its own merits, and children's agency are overlooked.

In the quest to understand why and how the child's right to development is perceived in international children's rights law, the Declaration is a useful source in clarifying some of the vagueness surrounding these issues. It specifies what components of child development ought to be promoted and it connects more aspects of the child's life to her course of growth. Read together, the 1924 and 1959 Declarations position the idea of children as developing human beings at the centre of international children's rights law, along with the need to protect a broad spectrum of child development and to ensure an ideal outcome of the developmental process. Both Declarations, at least in the context of the discussion about child development, subjugate the justification for protecting children's rights to the support of children's development.

The 1960s and the Emerging Recognition of Children's Autonomy

The 1959 UN Declaration of the Rights of the Child was adopted on the brink of the 1960s and the rise of the civil rights movement in the United States. At that time, women's rights, black people's rights, and

---

[76] Michael Freeman, *Article 3: The Best Interests of the Child* (Martinus Nijhoff, Leiden 2007) 15.

anticolonial movements gained impressive victories in promoting their agendas.[77] Some calls to recognise children's rights on the domestic level were also made,[78] but it is difficult to speak of any meaningful 'children's rights movement' during this time that had the same scale, in terms of visibility and influence, as those other human rights movements.

In the United States, the children's rights discourse penetrated legal domains that were previously exclusive to adults. A major change was granting children the same protection of their constitutional rights as , adults. According to Hilary Rodham, this approach mainly influenced criminal law, as demonstrated by the 1967 Supreme Court case of *In Re Gault*.[79] The case deals with the conviction of 15-year-old Gerald Gault. The Court, by upholding a liberal approach to nondiscrimination and giving no weight to any competency-based argument, ruled that there is no reason for denying children any of the rights promised to adults, as 'neither the Fourteenth Amendment nor the Bill of Rights is for adults alone'.[80] At the same time, the welfare approach was followed in other child-related laws, and more measures to protect children from abuse and neglect and to promote their well-being – mainly in the family domain – were introduced in many states and on the federal level. According to Rodham, the new legislation unveiled 'a blueprint for the child's fullest development'.[81] Rodham nonetheless argued that the new legislation and subsequent case law reflect a conceptual stagnation of childhood, rather than progress towards the recognition of children as rights holders. The status of children as civil rights holders is not recognised because these laws are essentially 'needs manifestos' that 'proclaim the rights of children to adequate nutrition, a healthy environment, continuous loving care, a sympathetic community, intellectual and emotional stimulation, and other prerequisites for healthy adulthood'.[82] Most claims were based on psychological and physical needs, and were not considered as legal rights.[83]

---

[77] Micheline R. Ishay, *The History of Human Rights* (University of California Press, Berkeley 2008) 191–205, 225–243.

[78] Veerman, *supra* n. 23, 113–124.   [79] *In Re Gault*, 387 U.S. 1 (1967).   [80] *Ibid.*, 13.

[81] Hillary Rodham, 'Children under the Law' (1973) 43 *Harvard Educational Review* 487, 494. For a review of the changing attitude towards children in US law during this time, see also Bruce C. Hafen, 'Children's Liberation and the New Egalitarianism: Some Reservations about Abandoning Youth to Their "Rights"' (1976) *Brigham Young University Law Review* 605.

[82] Rodham, *supra* n. 81.   [83] *Ibid.*

Rodham draws an important distinction between what adults see as children's needs and the legal manifestation of this perception. Under the welfare paradigm, the legal duty of parents to provide for their children's needs derives not from a recognition of children's human dignity and their entitlement to equal protection, but rather from a somewhat updated discourse of child salvation. Rodham further highlights the role that psychology plays, and the impact that it has on the formulation and interpretation of children's legal status.[84] Robert Geiser shares Rodham's view. Geiser's study analysed changes in mental health law during this period, and identified that 'children's rights are often given a developmental justification – that is, children need these rights satisfied in order to develop into physically and mentally healthy adults and to realise their full potential as human beings'.[85] These exponents of children's rights, Geiser suggests, 'prescribe a catalogue of the needs of children which must be met to ensure the development of children into productive citizens'.[86]

The influence that developmental psychology had on theory and positive law, as well as on the way in which the law imagines 'the child', is therefore rather clear. Geiser argues that protecting children's rights is understood as a means to an end, and that children's rights are not respected as being a result of the acknowledgement of children's agency. According to this approach, children's rights are the legal modification of children's welfare needs and of developmental psychology and are designed to facilitate the optimum development process. This stands in striking contrast to the changes in children's status in criminal law, which, as argued earlier, ignored any differences between children and adults in the context of procedural rights.

On the international level, the human rights movement saw some success with the adoption of two human rights treaties in 1966: the International Covenant on Civil and Political Rights (ICCPR)[87] and the International Covenant on Economic, Social and Cultural Rights (ICESCR).[88] These Covenants provide protection for the human rights

---

[84] Ibid.   [85] Geiser, supra n. 10, 1040.

[86] Ibid., 1044. For a review of the rise of children's rights in the United Kingdom during this time, see Bob Franklin (ed.), The Rights of Children (Basil Blackwell, Oxford 1986).

[87] International Covenant on Civil and Political Rights, adopted and opened to signature, ratification and accession by General Assembly Resolution 2200A (XXI) of 16 December 1996, entered into force on 23 March 1976.

[88] International Covenant on Economic, Social and Cultural Rights, adopted and opened to signature, ratification and accession by General Assembly Resolution 2200A (XXI) of 16 December 1966, entered into force on 3 January 1976.

of 'all' human beings, and – despite strong opposition during the drafting process[89] – both include specific clauses dedicated to children.

Common Article 3 of the ICCPR and the ICESCR protects the 'equal rights of men and women'. In addition, the ICCPR refers to 'all individuals' (Article 2) and to 'every human being' (Article 6) as rights holders. The ICCPR also declares that 'everyone shall have the right to recognition everywhere as a person before the law' (Article 16). Similarly to the language used by the UDHR, while these definitions may seem to include children, in practice, children – like other minority groups – were marginalised from this allegedly inclusive definition and were not seen as rights holders. For this reason, and in line with the view of children as needing protection, the Covenants dedicate specific provisions to the rights of women and children. In time, when it became evident that this attempt did not fulfil its promise, and as the image of both groups changed under the law, they become the subjects of specific human rights conventions: the UN Convention on the Elimination of All Forms of Discrimination against Women (1979) and the UN Convention on the Rights of the Child (1989).

ICCPR Article 24 recognises the child's right to nondiscrimination, the right to protection 'required by his status as a minor (in other words, due to the child's vulnerability), on the part of his family, society and the State', the right to be registered after birth, the right to a name, and the right to acquire a nationality.[90] In addition, four other Articles of the ICCPR mention children's rights. Article 6(5) protects the right to life and establishes that 'persons' below the age of 18 should not be sentenced to capital punishment. Articles 10(2)(b) and 14(4) address the rights of children in the context of criminal law, and Article 23 protects the right of 'men and women' to marry and includes some protection for children when their parents' marriage ends.

Although the provisions are more detailed than those in the UDHR, children's rights are still mentioned only in the context of traditional domains of childhood. Reflecting a liberal interpretation of nondiscrimination and a protectionist approach, they adopt and perpetuate a narrow approach towards children and rights. Unlike the UDHR, they do not refer, either explicitly or implicitly, to the developmental needs of children.

---

[89] Manfred Nowak, *U.N. Covenant on Civil and Political Rights – CCPR Commentary* (N.P. Engel, Kehl 1993) 422–434, 423.

[90] *Ibid.*

The ICESCR has even fewer references to children and their rights than does the ICCPR. One article that mentions children is Article 10(3), which deals with families and requires States Parties to recognise that:

> Special measures of protection and assistance should be taken on behalf of all children and young persons without any discrimination for reasons of parentage or other conditions. Children and young persons should be protected from economic and social exploitation. Their employment in work harmful to their morals or health or dangerous to life or likely to hamper their *normal development* should be punishable by law ...[91] (emphasis added).

In addition to protecting the right of children to nondiscrimination, Article 10(3) refers to the right to freedom from exploitation as a means of ensuring the 'normal' development of children. The text uses the same term as the Geneva Declaration, but it is not clear whether the child's 'normal development' refers to the process or the outcome of development. Nonetheless, unlike in the ICCPR, child development is clearly on the agenda and guides, at least to some extent, the attitude towards children. Article 13 of the ICESCR concerns the right to education[92] and recognises 'the right of everyone to education'. Like Article 26 of the UDHR, this Article does not explicitly name children as rights holders, and, as in Article 26, children are mentioned only in reference to the parental right to choose a child's education (Article 13(3)). The contribution of education to child development is overlooked in the text of this Article.

As neither children nor their rights receive significant attention in these two important Covenants, it is difficult to draw definite conclusions about the image of the child or the care for their development that the provisions reflect or ask to promote. Nevertheless, mentioning children as rights holders in a binding convention is not without significance. This in itself gives children visibility, recognising that they are rights holders in their own right and not only as extensions of their parents. To a limited extent, this recognition also demonstrates respect for their agency and signals a change to their image under international human rights law.

---

[91] ICESR, *supra* n. 88.
[92] For a comprehensive analysis of Article 13, see Klaus Dieter Beiter, *The Protection of the Right to Education by International Law* (Martinus Nijhoff, Leiden 2006) 459–569.

The Children's Liberation Movement

The children's liberation movement emerged in the United Kingdom and the United States in the late 1960s and early 1970s. After a little more than a decade of activity, it gradually faded away until it virtually vanished as a scholarly movement and lost the limited impact that it had, as the fields of childhood studies and children's rights began to be preoccupied with the UN Convention on the Rights of the Child.

The liberationists had an approach to children's rights and the legal treatment of child development that was remarkably different from anything that preceded it, or that came after. The movement offered new ways of conceptualising childhood and a new understanding of children's rights, shifting the attention away from the welfare paradigm. The liberationists generated some controversy and gained considerable criticism. Accused of promoting an irresponsible approach that leads to abandoning children to their rights,[93] they were attacked for being 'politically naïve, philosophically faulty and psychologically wrong'.[94] However, their rights-based approach, Martha Minow argues, is not as simplistic as it might at first seem. In fact, it enables advocates to 'argue for both more protection and more independence for different children, or for the same children in different circumstances'.[95] Regarding the issue arising from the relationship between child development, children's rights and the law, and the right to development, there is much to learn from this movement.

By and large, the child liberationists rejected the welfare paradigm, along with the idea that the capacity for 'rational' thinking is a necessary component in executing human rights – as advocated by the civil rights scholars. Instead, they argued in favour of respecting the equal rights of children.[96] According to Ann Palmeri, the suggestion that mental and cognitive capabilities are prerequisites for either being entitled to, or being able to exercise, rights (the 'will theory') is morally wrong – and, if it is used, it should not exclude children. If the will theory is upheld,

---

[93] Hafen, *supra* n. 81, 644–650.

[94] Michael Freeman, 'Children's Rights: Some Unanswered Questions and Some Unquestioned Answers' (1979–1980) 5 *Poly Law Review* 9, 15.

[95] Martha Minow, 'What Ever Happened to Children's Rights?' (1995–1996) 80 *Minnesota Law Review* 267, 273.

[96] See Annie Franklin and Bob Franklin, 'Growing Pains: The Developing Children's Rights Movement in the UK' in Jane Pilcher and Stephen Wagg (eds.), *Thatcher's Children?* (Falmer Press, London 1996) 94–113.

Palmeri claims, then children should be seen as having sufficient and necessary capacities to make an autonomous choice – or, at the bare minimum, to have as many capacities as adults.[97] In a similar vein, the usage of developmental psychology in conceptualising childhood was also rejected and was replaced with the argument that children should be considered as 'persons', and that 'childhood' should be seen as a stage in life with its own inherent significance and not merely as an apprenticeship. If society fails to recognise this, 'children will remain appendages of others and will be unable to develop in their own image'.[98]

As equal citizens, the child liberationists maintained, children should be free from the paternalistic control of their parents and the state, and should see their rights respected by law. In a view opposite to the welfare paradigm, parents were not seen as sources of comfort, and the nuclear family was not necessarily seen as a place where children can see their needs and interests protected. Not least, as A. S. Neill claims, 'the two enemies of children are ignorance of parents and unhappiness of marriages ... The problem is parents, always parental. Children are ruined by the complexes of their parents'.[99] John Holt, one of the prominent advocates of these ideas, uses even bolder terms. He suggests that children should have the same rights as adults, and the freedom to do anything that the law enables adults to do.[100] Richard Farson, whose work will be discussed below, makes a similar suggestion, arguing that society should have a 'single standard of morals and behaviour for children and adults'.[101] Revoking the differential treatment of children will eventually emancipate them, allowing children to be equal citizens.[102] However, Nan Berger, one of the first child liberationist

[97] Ann Palmeri, 'Childhood's End: Toward the Liberation of Children' in William Aiken and Hugh LaFollette (eds.), *Whose Child?* (Rowman and Littlefield, Totowa, New Jersey 1980) 105–124, 110; Katherine Hunt Federle, 'Looking Ahead: An Empowerment Perspective on the Rights of the Child' (1995) 689 *Temple Law Review* 1585, 1593. But see John Tobin on this issue: John Tobin, 'Justifying Children's Rights' (2013) 21 *International Journal of Children's Rights* 395.

[98] Nan Berger, 'The Child, the Law and the State' in Paul Adams *et al.* (eds.), *Children's Rights* (Elek Books, London 1971) 153–179.

[99] A. S. Neill, 'Freedom Works' in Paul Adams *et al.* (eds.), *Children's Rights* (Elek Books, London 1971) 127–152, 131–132.

[100] John Holt, *Escape from Childhood* (Penguin Books, Middlesex 1974) 19.

[101] Richard E. Farson, *Birthrights* (Macmillan, New York 1974) 27.

[102] For general background, see Veerman, *Rights of the Child, supra* n. 23, 133–152; Michael S. Wald, 'Children's Rights: A Framework for Analysis' (1979) 12 *University California Davis Law Review* 255. In the United Kingdom, liberationists came forward a decade later. See Bob Franklin, *supra* n. 86.

scholars, argues that dissolving discriminatory legislation is insufficient if the objective is to achieve full equality; it must be accompanied by a recognition of children's agency and their right to participation 'from a very early age'.[103]

Another implication of the revolt against the social order imposed upon children was the challenge to one of the crown jewels of the welfare paradigm: compulsory school attendance. According to Berger – and consistent with Key's approach in *The Century of the Child* – schools are used by society to oppress children's minds, to program children's future, and to make children dependent on their parents as much as possible.[104] Children, it is argued, should be liberated from schools so that they can pursue their own destiny.

Considering the core argument of the liberationists in the context of the right to development, the question of what is psychologically right or wrong resonates as the most important one. A subsequent question should therefore be what law can or should do in order to ensure the best, or least determinate, developmental outcome for children. The liberationists rejected the usage of developmental psychology as a criterion when discussing child law. From a constitutional point of view, Palmeri argues that there is no convincing way to define what 'developed enough' means or exactly when the 'end product' of the developmental process is achieved so that a person can be qualified as a rights holder.[105] This proposition undermines the core principles of international children's rights law as reflected and embedded in the 1924 and 1959 Declarations. However, it is not clear whether, if a more 'scientific' or 'satisfactory' criterion for determining 'sufficient capabilities' became available, Palmeri would accept this as a basis for the entitlement to rights. Somewhat anticipating this query, Palmeri further argues that if the notion of 'development' is considered important, then it should be expanded to apply to all ages,[106] so that everyone – children and adults alike – will be subject to the same regime. This approach, she believes, can create 'a world where people have the best characteristic[s] of both adults and children'.[107] One way or the other, if 'development' is the

[103] Berger, *supra* n. 98. See also Palmeri, *supra* n. 97.   [104] Berger, *supra* n. 98, 158–159.
[105] Palmeri, *supra* n. 97, 110.   [106] *Ibid.*, 119.
[107] *Ibid.*, 121. For more on the limitations of the developmental paradigm, see Arlene Skolnick, 'The Limits of Childhood: Conceptions of Child Development and Social Context' (1975) 39 *Law & Contemporary Problems* 38, 52–59.

wrong prism through which children's legal status should be analysed, then there is very little reason to discuss the child's right to development.

Robert Ollendorf, also a liberationist, has an opposite view about the use of developmental psychology.[108] For Ollendorf, developmental psychology offers analytical tools to analyse and to distinguish between childhood and adolescence. In sharp contrast to the other liberationists, he embraces the welfare paradigm and positions adolescence against the image of the child (which was created as a mirror image of adults) and claims that adolescence is the most important phase of human life.[109] He conceptualises adolescence as a time when the child is no longer dependent, immature and non-productive, and no longer a non-responsible sexual actor. Rather, the adolescent is almost an adult.[110] But, at the same time, Ollendorf rejects the capacities approach as a benchmark for acknowledging the human rights of children. He claims that the child should be able to determine 'on his own how he is going to learn, what he wants, what he rejects, what kind of art he likes, what kind of art he dislikes, what books he wants to read, in which way, if any, he wants to worship'.[111] Consequently, Ollendorf names four rights to which the adolescent child should be entitled in order to ensure her adequate development: the right to self-determination, the right to sexual freedom, the right to education, and the right to work.[112] Implementing these rights should 'ultimately' lead to the 'promise of a happier future'.[113] This is a rather interesting and, to some extent, incoherent proposition. On the one hand, Ollendorf asks to liberate high-school children and praise their current self. On the other hand, it seems that his main objective is to emancipate children at an earlier stage of their life, before they turn 18, thus perpetuating the division between adults and children. The essence of his argument is a call to lower the age of majority.

Paul Adams's theory can be situated in between the two somewhat extreme approaches that Palmeri and Ollendorf represent. Adams adopts a Freudian developmental model. He perceives childhood as a time of

---

[108] Robert Ollendorf, 'The Rights of Adolescents' in Paul Adams et al. (eds.), *Children's Rights* (Elek Books, London 1971) 91–126.

[109] Interestingly, Woodhead uses similar arguments to suggest that, from a developmental perspective, early childhood is the most important stage in the child's life: Martin Woodhead, 'Early Childhood Development: A Question of Rights' (2005) 37 *International Journal of Early Childhood* 80.

[110] Ollendorf, *supra* n. 108, 99.   [111] *Ibid.*, 120.   [112] *Ibid.*, 119–120.

[113] *Ibid.*, 126.

change and growth.[114] However, he rejects Palmeri's assertion, arguing that psychiatry and psychology can measure the 'true competence' of children. But Adams uses the developmental approach not as a rationale for denying children their rights, but rather as a justification for promoting the 'right to a healthy childhood'.[115] This right includes three dimensions: an objective dimension (competence and custodial stability); a neither entirely objective nor entirely subjective dimension (the entitlement to grow and learn, to live in a meaningful world, and to the opportunity for the 'unfolding of loving relations with other people'); and a subjective dimension (a 'favorable picture of self' and a 'sense of some unsocialised uniqueness').[116] Entrenched within development psychology, even the so-called 'objective' aspects of this approach are biased and subjective. Nonetheless, Adams sees children as rights holders. Their rights seem not only to serve their future selves, but also to provide them with pleasure during childhood. In that sense, Adams rejects Ollendorf's focus on older children's rights and his coopting of the adult/child division.

A more radical approach to the usage of child development in the context of childhood studies and child law has been introduced by John Holt in his seminal book *Escape from Childhood*.[117] Holt rejects the division between children and adults and between childhood and adulthood,[118] and challenges the perception of childhood as a time of happiness and of gradual development that should result in the creation of a mature adult: 'Childhood, as in Happy, Safe, Protected, Innocent Childhood, does not exist for many children. For many other children, however good it may be, childhood goes on far too long, and there is no gradual, sensible and painless way to grow out of it or leave it.'[119] Holt further claims that phrases such as 'a child needs to be allowed to be a child' are meaningless, since there is no such thing as a 'child'.[120] He also rejects the 'development' model as part of a rejection of all alleged unique characteristics of childhood.[121]

It is not only the 'being happy' nature of childhood that Holt dismisses, but also the perception that a child will gradually 'grow out' towards a desirable end in the form of 'adulthood'. Therefore, there is no justification for the law treating children differently from adults, and children should enjoy the exact same rights as adults. Holt lists 11 rights

---

[114] Paul Adams, 'The Infant, the Family and Society' in Paul Adams *et al.* (eds.), *Children's Rights* (Elek Books, London 1971) 51–90, 82–86.

[115] *Ibid.*, 89.   [116] *Ibid.*, 89–90.   [117] Holt, *supra* n. 100.   [118] *Ibid.*

[119] *Ibid.*, 23.   [120] *Ibid.*, 110–112.   [121] *Ibid.*, 77.

that he considers as the most important for children: the right to vote, the right to work, the right to own property, the right to a guaranteed income, the right to choose one's guardian, the right to travel, the right to drive, the right to control one's sex life, the right to use drugs, the right to total legal and financial responsibility, and the right to control one's learning. This list, which is in some ways similar to that of Key, perfectly symbolises the liberationists' approach. It not only makes the case for granting children the same rights as adults, including political rights, but primarily seeks to liberate children from many of the restraints they face in their daily lives. The list also challenges those who argue that lack of capabilities justifies denying some rights of children, if only in order to support their welfare or to protect them from potential wrongdoing. For this reason, the first right on Holt's list is the right to vote. This is perhaps the most important political right. It always has been – and still is – denied to children. Giving children the right to vote contradicts T. H. Marshall's claim that children cannot be citizens because they are 'citizens in making'.[122] Without the ability to vote, children will remain subject to policies determined by others,[123] thus perpetuating their inferior political status.

A slightly different approach towards law, and children's present and future, is offered by Joel Feinberg in his essay 'The Child's Right to an Open Future',[124] a title that already gives some idea about the entitlements of children. Feinberg asserts that children should have the same human rights as adults, but – unlike Holt – he does not argue that children can execute all of their rights, since they are 'quite different animals' from adults.[125] Feinberg tries to eradicate what he believes to be a misunderstanding of children's rights, and to offer a conceptual solution of his own. He suggests dividing human rights into three categories. The first category includes rights that adults and children share, such as the right to bodily integrity (Feinberg names this category 'A–C rights'); the second category includes rights that belong only to adults, such as the right to vote ('A rights'); and the final category

---

[122] T. H. Marshall, 'Citizenship and Social Class' in T. H. Marshall, *Citizenship and Social Class and Other Essays* (Cambridge University Press, Cambridge 1951) 1–86, 84.

[123] See Aoife Nolan, 'The Child as "Democratic Citizen": Challenging the "Participation Gap"'(2010) 4 *Public Law* 767.

[124] Joel Feinberg, 'The Child's Right to an Open Future' in William Aiken and Hugh LaFollette (eds.), *Whose Child?* (Rowman and Littlefield, Totowa, New Jersey 1980) 124–153.

[125] *Ibid.*, 126.

includes rights that are not particular to children but are characteristic of them ('C rights', or 'rights in trust').[126] Feinberg defines rights in trust as those rights that children cannot execute during the time of childhood, but are there as 'future options' that will be kept open until the child is a 'fully formed self-determining adult capable of deciding among them'.[127] As such, a right in trust fulfils the child's right to an open future.[128]

To explain his approach, Feinberg uses the example of the right in trust of a two-month-old baby to walk down the street. Despite lacking the physical capability to *exercise* this right, the child nevertheless *has* the right to walk freely down the street, and this right should not be forbidden in practice or dismissed in theory. If we fail to acknowledge the future usage of this right, we might end up cutting off the child's legs and arguing that this did not prevent the child from exhausting her right to walk at the present time. If we do so – and this is the key to Feinberg's theory – we undermine the child's right to walk in the future[129] (here Feinberg ignores the potential breach of the child's right to physical integrity in the present by this act):

> A right-in-trust cannot always be established by checking the child's present interests, a fortiori it cannot be established by determining the child's present desires of preferences. It is the adult he is to become who must exercise the choice, more exactly, the adult he will become if his basic options are kept open and his growth kept 'natural' or unforced. In any case, that adult does not exist yet, and perhaps he never will. But the child is *potentially* that adult, and it is that adult who is the person whose autonomy must be protected now (in advance).[130]

This theory therefore seems to require an evaluation of child development, thus inherently taking children to be insufficiently developed human beings. It seems that Feinberg seeks to endow the potential future adult that every child carries inside her with the opportunity to come into life and enjoy the entire spectrum of human rights. 'It is that adult who is the person whose autonomy must be protected now',[131] he claims. Feinberg is therefore willing to compromise some of the child's fundamental autonomy rights, since a 'child's future autonomy, as an adult, often requires preventing his free choice now'.[132] This proposition has an inherent theoretical difficulty, as Feinberg compromises the right to free choice, which is fundamental to a liberal theory of rights, in favour of the

---

[126] *Ibid.*, 125.   [127] *Ibid.*.   [128] *Ibid.*, 126.   [129] *Ibid.*, 127.   [130] *Ibid.*
[131] *Ibid.*   [132] *Ibid.*

ability to execute that right in the future. In that sense, his willingness to sacrifice the present in favour of a vague future is the clear manifestation of the human becomings approach to childhood.

Interestingly, Feinberg does not ground his approach in developmental psychology. Nonetheless, he does see a point where the process of development comes to an end – presumably, when the child achieves sufficient capacity and autonomy. Feinberg sees the endpoint of child-hood as a goal that requires protection throughout childhood. Achieving this goal is defined not only as an interest of the child, but also as a right 'because to some extent, the child's own good (self-fulfilment) depends on which interests the parents decide to create'.[133] This point draws a clear divide between Feinberg and other liberationists, who seek to disengage children's rights from parental rights. According to Feinberg, understanding some rights of children as rights in trust solves the tension that liberal discourses about capacities, rights, and autonomy create,[134] without rejecting their premise. Nonetheless, despite promising children the right to an open future, Feinberg does not suggest that children have a right to pursue their future in the form of either the right to develop-ment or the right to participation. For him, it seems that a right to development is the right to become a free and independent adult.

The most extreme liberationist, or emancipationist, approach was the suggestion that children's rights had not been advanced by the 1960s at all, not least because children were still not liberated from paternalistic views. In his 1974 book *Birthrights*,[135] Richard Farson argues that 'chil-dren's rights have actually diminished, for we have simply replaced ignorant domination of children with sophisticated domination'.[136] The solution for this continuing oppression is not via a slow change in the social and legal treatment of children, as Rodham suggests, but rather a fundamental change in the social structure. According to Farson, the existing situation should be replaced by a recognition of children as 'full' human beings. Farson argues that children have both the capabilities and the right to determine not only their future, but also their present. 'Children, like adults', he writes, 'should have the right to decide the matters which affect them most directly'.[137] The justifications for this view are based not on equality arguments, but rather on the assumption that 'liberation will help give children back their childhood'.[138] He thus rejects characterisations of childhood as either a time of joy and

---

[133] *Ibid.*, 148.   [134] *Ibid.*, 126–127.   [135] Farson, *supra* n. 101.   [136] *Ibid.*, 3.
[137] *Ibid.*, 27.   [138] *Ibid.*, 4.

innocence or a time of violence and cruelty,[139] instead suggesting that any social conception should be rejected in favour of the reinstitution of childhood as an autonomous space. (Re)creating this space for children requires adopting a comprehensive list of rights, which includes the right to self-determination,[140] the right to alternative home environments,[141] the right to responsive design,[142] the right to receive information,[143] the right to educate oneself,[144] the right to freedom from physical punishment,[145] the right to sexual freedom,[146] the right to economic power,[147] the right to political power,[148] and the right to justice.[149] This is a very different list from those of Holt and Feinberg. It does not perceive children as future adults, and therefore the right to grow up is not mentioned. In that sense, Farson's children are human 'beings', but they are not – and maybe never were – 'human becomings'.

The last issue that is worth discussing here is the question of the right of children to self-determination as the ultimate expression of their autonomy. For adults, the right to self-determination means the right to make autonomous decisions and to dictate one's own future. As we have seen, most of the liberationists reject the idea that a person's rights are subject to her capacities.[150] Sharon Bishop, for example, argues that 'the point of the right to self-determination is to enable people to work out their own way of life in response to their own assessments of current conditions and their own interests, capacities and needs'.[151] In relation to children, Bishop takes an approach similar to Feinberg's concept of rights-in-trust, suggesting that 'young persons should be treated in whatever ways give them the strength and imagination to make use of their right to self-determination autonomously when they reach maturity. Treating them in ways which are believed to do this is a way of respecting the right they will have when they reach maturity'.[152]

---

[139] *Ibid.*, 6.   [140] *Ibid.*, 26–41.   [141] *Ibid.*, 42–62.   [142] *Ibid.*, 82.
[143] *Ibid.*, 83–96.   [144] *Ibid.*, 97–112.   [145] *Ibid.*, 113–128.   [146] *Ibid.*, 129–153.
[147] *Ibid.*, 154–174.   [148] *Ibid.*, 175–190.   [149] *Ibid.*, 191–212.
[150] Federle makes an interesting differentiation between autonomy, capacity and power. She argues that capacity, rather than autonomy, should be the focus of conceptualising children's rights: Katherine Hunt Federle, 'Rights Flow Downhill' (1994) 2 *International Journal of Children's Rights* 343. See also Federle, 'Looking Ahead', *supra* n. 97.
[151] Sharon Bishop, 'Children, Autonomy, and the Right to Self-Determination' in William Aiken and Hugh LaFollette (eds.), *Whose Child?* (Rowman and Littlefield, Totowa, New Jersey 1980) 154–177, 163–164.
[152] *Ibid.*, 175.

This argument is positioned against the moral and philosophical idea of denying children's rights altogether and the call for full liberation. The idea of 'maturity' prevails, triumphing over other dimensions of the child's life. It emphasises the result of the developmental process as the main justification for acknowledging children's right to self-determination, overlooking the importance of recognising the rights of children during the time of childhood. However, it is not sufficiently clear whether it is the process of facilitating this future (that is, the process of development) that matters, or whether it is the result of the process (that is, being an adult) that counts in and of itself. One way or the other, it seems that those – like Farson – who refer to this right see significance in enabling the rights holder to enjoy some degree of self-determination and autonomy as a child, regardless of the contribution it may or may not make to the child in the future.

Despite the dismissal of utilising developmental psychology in the context of child law, there is still a need to ask what understanding of 'child development' is the most appropriate to employ in this context. The fact that children are growing up is nonetheless recognised by the liberationists. A separate set of questions concerns the levels of freedom or autonomy to exercise their rights that children should have in the course of their development, and whether the right to development should be seen as a vehicle to facilitate a process of emancipation. These questions remain unanswered by liberationist theories.

Conclusion

The end of the 1970s saw the children's rights movement in an odd situation. On the one hand, the legal presumption that children are human beings and, as such, cannot be treated as their parents' property, or merely as subjects of welfare policies, was fairly grounded. On the other hand, paternalism remained the dominant attitude and protection was the main objective of child law. While they were viewed as human rights holders, children were predominantly conceptualised under Durkheim's paradigm of the 'law of growth'. Law was utilised to support the social enterprise of enabling children to grow up and become competent adults.

Many of the changes in international human rights law during the twentieth century did not change the image of children. To a large extent, children did not enjoy the liberation process that other oppressed groups enjoyed. International human rights law continued to perceive the child as vulnerable, weak, and lacking the capacities of an adult. Its focus was on ensuring children's process of growth and protecting children from threatening elements that might jeopardise their transformation into independent adults. The child's traditional development was a source of concern and, therefore, required legal protection. The approaches of the liberationists, as well as Key and Korczak, were either actively rejected by the mainstream establishment or soon forgotten. International law adopted 'development' as its underlying narrative, focusing on the mission of 'saving the children'.

However, while 'child development' came to be a key concept, it gained no thorough analysis. Law presumably protected many components of development, but it was difficult to sketch a coherent picture of what it really meant. For example, what does 'normal development', to use the term in the Geneva Declaration, mean? Who defines what 'normal' is? How does it differ, if at all, from the various terms used by the 1959 Declaration of the Rights of the Child? Even if we accept the presumption that developmental psychology prevails, and that law ought to adopt this perspective on human life, we should ask which stream of psychology international human rights law has adopted, or which ought it adopt, and why. Needless to say, like many other disciplines, developmental psychology is neither homogeneous nor neutral and unbiased.[153] These questions have significance only if one doubts the premise that children's main remedy is to grow up.[154]

The next chapter continues to explore the role that child development occupies in international children's rights law, and how it was perceived and conceptualised at the drafting of the UN Convention on the Rights of the Child.

---

[153] For example, see Carol Gilligan's influential critique of the gender bias in developmental psychology: Carol Gilligan, *In a Different Voice* (Harvard University Press, Cambridge 1982). See also Sara Karkness, 'The Cultural Context of Child Development' (1980) 8 *New Directions of Child Development* 7.

[154] Onora O'Neill, 'Children's Rights and Children's Lives' (1988) 98 *Ethics* 445, 463.

2

Creating the Right to Development of Children

> The physical and mental nature of the child is identical everywhere ... the process of growth and adolescence takes a similar course in all children. Their physical and mental needs are also similar.
>
> Adam Lopatka, Chairperson of the Working Group on a Draft Convention on the Rights of the Child (1992)

As part of the twentieth birthday celebration of the 1959 UN Declaration on the Rights of the Child, the United Nations declared 1979 to be the International Year of the Child. The government of Poland took this opportunity to suggest a new Convention setting out the rights of the child. After a decade of negotiations, the UN General Assembly adopted the Convention on the Rights of the Child. The final version was radically different from the original draft, and one notable change – and one of the Convention's main innovations in international children's rights law – was the recognition of the child's right to development in a binding treaty.

This chapter looks at the genealogy of the child's right to development under Article 6(2) of the UN Convention on the Rights of the Child,[1] as well as the broad protection for child development that the Convention provides in other Articles. The chapter asks when, why, and how 'child development' became an issue of concern for human rights law and a fundamental principle of the Convention. Making the assumption that different conceptions of childhood lead to different interpretations of children's rights, the chapter also uses the drafting history to analyse the drafters' conception of childhood and asks how it contributes to the understanding of what the child's *right* to development can mean. This analysis does not aspire to ascertain the 'true' intentions of the drafters or

---

[1] UN Convention on the Rights of the Child 1989, adopted by General Assembly Resolution 44/25 of 20 November 1989, entered into force on 2 September 1990.

the 'true' meaning of the right under the Convention,[2] not least because I don't suggest that there is a single 'true' meaning. Nonetheless, and in line with Articles 31 and 32 of the Vienna Convention on the Law of Treaties, the analysis can help in exploring the potential meanings of the child's right to development in the Convention.[3]

The chapter begins with the first draft of the Convention, which was presented by Poland in 1978. It then follows the entire drafting process, which ended more than a decade later with the final text of the Convention being adopted by the UN General Assembly. The drafting is presented chronologically, tracking the progress of embedding the protection for child development in the Convention and examining the motivations that led to the creation of the right to development at a specific point in time. The information presented here is based on my own research at the UN Archive in Geneva. It includes the original draft of the Convention, the summaries of meetings of the Open-Ended Working Group (the forum composed of diplomats and professionals from nongovernmental organisations (NGOs) and UN agencies that drafted the Convention), and various memoranda and suggestions that were submitted to the Working Group before, during and after each drafting session by UN agencies and NGOs. The chapter also analyses *all* of the Open-Ended Working Group's reports. Some of these documents are now available online at the UN Library.

'We Should Have a Convention on the Rights of the Child': The First Draft of the Convention

In 1976, the UN General Assembly decided to commemorate the 20-year anniversary of the 1959 UN Declaration of the Rights of the Child by declaring 1979 the International Year of the Child.[4] The Government of Poland believed that this was the right time to advance the idea of adopting a convention on children's rights. On 18 January 1978, Ambassador Eugeniusz Wyzner of Poland submitted to the UN Commission on Human Rights (UNCHR) a draft for a Convention on the

---

[2] See Ronald Dworkin, 'Law as Interpretation' (1982) 9 *Critical Inquiry* 179, 196–199; Stanley Fish, 'Working on the Chain Gang: Interpretation in the Law and in Literary Criticism' (1982) 9 *Critical Inquiry* 201. See also Dennis Patterson, *Law and Truth* (Oxford University Press, Oxford 1996) 71–127.

[3] Vienna Convention on the Laws of Treaties (Done at Vienna on 23 May 1969, Entered into Force on 27 January 1980). *United Nations Treaty Series*, Vol. 1155, 331.

[4] General Assembly Resolution 31/169, 'International Year of the Child', adopted 21 December 1976.

Rights of the Child, asking that the draft be brought before the Commission during its 34th session.[5] Eleven years later, on 20 November 1989, the General Assembly adopted the Convention.

The draft was based on the 1959 Declaration of the Rights of the Child. It included 28 Articles, the first 10 of which were mostly identical to those found in the 1959 Declaration, dealing with substantial rights of the child. The remaining 18 Articles referred to the procedural and technical aspects of an international treaty. The 'question of a Convention on the Rights of the Child' was item number 22 on the agenda of the Commission on Human Rights for 13 February 1978.[6] Keba M'Baye, then the Chairperson of the Human Rights Commission, who would later play a key role in creating the right to development in 'general' international law,[7] led a short discussion that resulted in a decision to ask the UN Economic and Social Council to proceed with the process of adopting the suggested Convention.[8]

The Economic and Social Council accepted the Commission's recommendation[9] and asked the General Assembly (UNGA) to consider adopting the Convention.[10] One of the reasons for this decision was the Commission's awareness of the 'special need to assist children in the developing countries in a manner consistent with the goals of the new international economic order'.[11] This is one of the few places during the entire drafting process where some sort of awareness of developmental policies that tackle poverty and other economic disadvantages was evident. After some debates and initial consultation,[12] the Commission on Human Rights held another meeting on the topic on 7 March 1978.[13] Most of the discussion was dedicated to the question of timing rather

[5] UN Economic and Social Council (18 January 1978) UN Doc. E/CN.4/1284. Letter to the UN Commission on Human Rights (1978).

[6] UNCHR, 'Summary Record of the 1438th Meeting' (15 February 1978) UN Doc. E/CN.4/SR.1438.

[7] See Chapter 4.

[8] UNCHR, 'Question of a Convention on the Rights of the Child' (7 February 1978) UN Doc. E/CN.4/L.1366.

[9] Ibid.

[10] UNCHR, 'Question of a Convention on the Rights of the Child' (6 February–10 March 1978) UN Doc. E/1978/34/E/CN.4/1292, 4.

[11] Ibid.

[12] UN Economic and Social Council, 'Question of a Convention on the Rights of the Child' (23 February 1978) UN Doc. E/CN.4/NGO/225; UNCHR, 'Question of a Convention on the Rights of the Child' (6 February–10 March 1978).

[13] UNCHR, 'Summary Record of the 1471st Meeting' (13 March 1978) UN Doc. E/CN.4/SR.1471. The discussion concerning the convention on the rights of the child is taken from agenda item 22, supra n. 7.

than content, and arguments were made for and against adopting the Convention in 1979. Very few speakers referred to substantive issues, but one important comment made by the representative of Syria, Mawia Sheikh Fadli, is worthy of attention:

> The protection of the child should be one of the primary objectives of social and economic development strategy. The creation of a social climate favourable to the child would perhaps eliminate some of the problems which were obstacles to *the right to development*. . . .
>
> The privileged children had a right to leisure and to the *full development of their personality*, and to be protected against violence, cruelty, exploitation, drugs and the slave trade, while the underprivileged children of developing societies had *the right to life, to their daily bread, to shelter and to protection against underdevelopment*[14] (emphasis added).

This is the first and nearly the last instance that the term 'right to development' was used explicitly in the drafting process of the Convention. However, it refers to the then newly emerged 'general' right to development (see Chapter 4) without drawing a distinction about the potentially different meaning that the 'general' right might have if the human-rights holder is a child and not an adult. But with respect to child development, Sheikh Fadli presents a relatively clear vision concerning the Convention's objectives and the unique role that the right to development should have in relation to these aims. Drawing on differences in life experiences of children from different socioeconomic backgrounds, she claims that for poor children, the right to life and survival are of greater importance, while economically privileged children can enjoy a fuller life by being given the opportunity to develop. The Convention, she then claims, is an opportunity to create an international framework that can change this reality of inequality by providing all children with the opportunity to fully develop their personality. Sheikh Fadli did not utilise the logic of developmental psychology, nor did she refer only to an individual child's development. Rather, she addressed the social and economic conditions that affect – and, to a large extent, dictate – the child's life and future. She uses two dimensions of development, the individual development of the child and the socioeconomic development conditions of the child's environment, to argue that the latter influences the former and creates the necessary conditions for it to occur. This comment did not generate any meaningful discussion. From this point

---

[14] UNCHR, Summary Record of the 1471st Meeting, *supra* n. 12.

on, it was psychological development that underpinned the drafters' perception of child development and the discussion about development more broadly.

Protecting child development was further mentioned during a meeting held in December 1978.[15] The delegation from Bulgaria argued that the issue of child labour practices should be tackled by the new Convention because these practices are 'injurious to the health of children and prevent their proper development'.[16] With respect to the child's right to play and leisure, the delegation from France suggested that this right should not be confined to the context of formal education, because 'while educational games are to be encouraged, they should not be the only ones the child can play. For his full development, he also needs to involve himself in activities which are not necessarily part of a specific educational system'.[17] This suggests that 'full' development should be set as an objective, and that development happens in nonformal contexts too – and not only when the child is under an adult's supervision, guidance, and support.

The United Nations Educational, Scientific and Cultural Organization (UNESCO) claimed that the draft Convention did not 'accord sufficient importance to the right of the child to cultural development'.[18] The World Health Organization (WHO) was concerned about what it considered to be insufficient protection of children's well-being, arguing that the current draft was a retreat from the 1959 Declaration. To overcome this, the WHO suggested the addition of an explicit and detailed provision concerning the 'obligations of parents, both as individuals and as couples, of the family and the society, particularly in relation to the promotion of child growth and development in its threefold dimensions: physical, mental and emotional'.[19] The International Association of Youth Magistrates endorsed the draft for the 'well-formulated catalogue of minimum conditions for the mental, physical and educational well-being of the child'.[20] These comments conflate 'development' and 'well-being', and say very little about the meaning of different aspects

---

[15] UNCHR, 'Question of a Convention on the Rights of the Child' (1 February 1979) UN Doc. E/CN.4/1324/Add.1.

[16] *Ibid.*, 5.   [17] *Ibid.*, 7–8.

[18] UN High Commissioner for Human Rights(UNHCHR), *Legislative History of the Convention on the Rights of the Child – Volume I* (Office of the High Commissioner for Human Rights and Save the Children Sweden,, New York and Geneva 2007) 64.

[19] *Ibid.*, 64–65.   [20] *Ibid.*, 65.

of child development (such as physical development and mental development). Consequently, it is not possible to draw from this discussion any conclusion about the drafters' understanding of child development, what scientific knowledge should be used to understand this term, or how any of the objectives can be achieved. Notably, the process of expanding the protection for more and more components of child development was done in relation to different Articles of the Convention, but was not articulated at this stage – and not until 1987 – as an issue that might be addressed as a human right in and of itself.

Given the wide support for the idea of adopting a Convention dedicated to children's rights, an Open-Ended Working Group was established, and it was given the task of drafting the Convention. The Working Group held its first meetings in February and March 1979.

1979 Round of Discussions

The drafting group dedicated its first meeting to some conceptual discussions about the Convention.[21] One of the key objectives of the Convention that was often mentioned was the care for child development. Following Sheikh Fadli's earlier comment, several delegates made the observation that the Convention should pay attention to 'the status of children in developing countries suffering from malnutrition, hunger or poverty'[22] – not least because these conditions jeopardise children's lives and have a negative impact on their future.

Shortly after this round of discussions, in October 1979, Poland produced a new draft of the Convention, which mentioned child development in different ways under six Articles (Articles 3, 9, 13, 15, 17, and 19). These Articles read:

Article 3
> 2. The States Parties to the present Convention undertake to ensure the child such protection and care as his status requires, taking due account of the various stages of his *development* in family environment and in social relations, and, to this end, shall take necessary legislative measures.

---

[21] UNCHR, 'Report of the Open-Ended Working Group on a Draft Convention on the Rights of the Child' (12 March 1979) UN Doc. E/CN.4/L.1468.
[22] *Ibid.*, 2.

Article 9

Parents, guardians, State organs and social organizations shall protect the child against any harmful influence that mass media, and in particular the radio, film, television, printed materials and exhibitions, on account of their contents, may exert on his *mental and moral development.*

Article 13

1. It is recognized that the child shall be entitled to benefit from the highest attainable standard of health care for his *physical, mental and moral development,* and also, in the case of need, from medical and rehabilitation facilities.

Article 15

1. The States Parties to the present Convention recognize the right of every child to a standard of living adequate for his *healthy and normal physical, mental and moral development* in every phase of the child's *development.*
2. The parents shall, within their financial possibilities and powers, secure conditions of living necessary for a *normal growth* of the child.

Article 17

1. The States Parties to the present Convention recognize that the *bringing up* and education of the child should promote the *full development of his personality,* his respect for human rights and fundamental freedoms.

Article 19

2. The States Parties to the present Convention recognize that the child shall not be employed in any form of work harmful to his health or his *moral development,* or in work dangerous to his life or which would interfere with his *normal growth* ...[23] (emphasis added).

These six Articles give an indication of the ways in which the drafters conceptualised childhood, children's life, child development, and human rights. Article 9 takes the child's stage of development as a benchmark for establishing parental and state responsibilities, while Articles 13 and 15 seek to ensure that the child's health and standard of living will promote specific aspects of her development. Article 17 suggests that the aim of education is to promote the full development of the child's personality, and Article 19 seeks to protect children's 'normal growth' in the context of the labour market, deeming that children should not engage in work

---

[23] UNHCR, 'Report of the Open-Ended Working Group on a Draft Convention on the Rights of the Child' (12 March 1979) UN Doc E/CN.4/L.1468.

that can compromise their moral development. Article 9 is also protective in its nature, seeking to shield children from the immoral influences of the media and the risk that it poses to children's moral and mental development. In other words, these Articles refer to three aspects of development: mental, moral, and physical development, in addition to two qualifications of the developmental processes: healthy and full development.

This draft uses the terms 'development' and 'normal growth' without drawing any distinction between them. Presumably, both terms are used to describe a similar future where children can 'fully' develop, but the debates that followed this suggestion gave no indication as to what this future should look like, or why achieving it should be an objective of the Convention.

From this point onwards, and until the drafting process ended, the Open-Ended Working Group held annual sessions. Each session saw debates about some rights and, at the end, the group's chairperson published an official report summarising the session. The ways in which childhood, child development, and the aims of the Convention were conceptualised in the first draft did not change throughout the drafting process.

1980 and 1981 Rounds of Discussions

The discussions during the years 1980 and 1981[24] were dedicated to some conceptual questions, such as the definition of the 'child' under the Convention, the weight and references that the 1924 and 1959 Declarations should be given in the Convention's preamble, and questions surrounding parental responsibilities and the right of the child to have a name (today called 'the right to an identity'). None of the debates touched upon the issue of child development, and the impact that the Convention was likely to have on the legal protection of child development was not singled out as an issue worthy of attention.

1982 Round of Discussions

The 1982 session[25] was dedicated to discussing Articles 6, 9, 10, 11, and 12 of the 1979 draft, which address the child's right to parental care and

---

[24] UNCHR, 'Report of the Working Group on a Draft Convention on the Rights of the Child' (10 March 1980) UN Doc. E/CN.4/L.1542; UNCHR, 'Report of the Working Group on a Draft Convention on the Rights of the Child' (17 February 1981) UN Doc. E/CN.4/L.1975.

[25] UNHCHR, Legislative History of the Convention on the Rights of the Child, supra n. 17, 94; UNCHR, 'Report of the Working Group on a Draft Convention on the Rights of the Child' (8 March 1982) UN Doc. E/CN.4/1982/30/Add.1.

family environment, the right of children who seek refugee status or are recognised as refugees, and the rights of children with disabilities. In addition, some new Articles about the child's right to freedom of movement; the right to privacy; the right to freedom of thought, conscience and religion; and the right to freedom from abuse were also discussed.[26]

The debate about Article 9 (the right to information) marked the first substantive discussion on 'child development' undertaken by the drafters. Several delegates 'expressed concern' that exposure to 'too much' information might jeopardise the child's innocence. Therefore, it was suggested that 'States Parties to the Convention should have the obligation to protect children against any harmful influence that the contents of mass media may exert on their *mental and moral development*'[27] (emphasis added). The Holy See shared these concerns and suggested that the objectives of this clause be expanded to include protection for 'spiritual and social' development, in addition to the other two developmental domains already mentioned.[28]

The alleged perils of mass media echoed the social panic concerning a 'flood' of information that could bring 'childhood' to an end, as Neil Postman feared.[29] In other words, the sentiment was that some forms of information could threaten the mental and moral 'development' of the child, and thus bring to an end a specific fantasy about childhood and children. The assumption that media and information corrupt children's morality is not new, and it is raised with the introduction of every new communication technology. What is interesting here is the suggestion that those elements of child development should be protected, and that an international Convention is the right instrument to provide that protection – while ignoring the limited numbers of children who enjoy access to information.

The discussion about the right of children with disabilities was informed by apprehension concerning the future of such children. For example, the Canadian delegate, with the support of Australia, sought to include in the Convention a right to 'special protection and care' that will ensure the child 'the right to enjoy a decent life, as normal and full as

---

[26] UNCHR, 'Report of the Working Group on a Draft Convention on the Rights of the Child' (8 March 1982), *supra* n. 24, 71–72.

[27] *Ibid.*, 56.   [28] *Ibid.*

[29] Postman warned that exposing children to the mass media and to floods of information would bring childhood to an end: Neil Postman, *The Disappearance of Childhood* (Vintage Books, New York 1984).

possible'. The Canadian delegate further suggested including protection for the right of disabled children to employment, which would be 'designed to achieve the child's fullest possible social integration'.[30] Setting these objectives once again asserted the need to protect children's future ('a decent life') in accordance with the ambiguous standards of 'normal' and 'full' development. But this might also suggest that the right of a child with disability to enjoy 'a decent life' refers to the course of childhood too, and not only to the sort of life that this child will have in the future as an adult. The discussions shed no further light on the drafters' understanding of any of these aspects of child development.

1983 Round of Discussions

The discussions at this session[31] centred around the proposed rights of children who are separated from their parents (Article 6 of the draft); the right to freedom of thought, conscience and religion (Article 7 of the draft); and the rights of children with disabilities (Article 12 of the draft). Only the debate about Article 12 and the rights of children with disabilities touched upon the issue of child development. According to the travaux préparatoires, 'several delegates supported the view that wherever assistance is extended to a disabled child, it should be provided in a manner most conducive to that child's social integration and *individual development*'[32] (emphasis added). Canada took an active role in this debate, suggesting the addition of another clause concerning the services that children with disabilities should be entitled to receive:

> 3. Assistance extended shall be designed to ensure that the disabled child has access to and receives education, training, health care services, rehabilitation services, and preparation for employment, and enjoys recreation opportunities, in conditions most conducive to the child's fullest possible social integration and *individual development*.
> 4. The disabled child's special education needs and rehabilitation needs shall be provided in a manner most consistent with realizing the child's *fullest potential* . . .[33] (emphasis added).

---

[30] UNCHR, 'Report of the Working Group on a Draft Convention on the Rights of the Child' (8 March 1982), *supra* n. 24, 69–70.

[31] UNCHR, 'Report of the Working Group on a Draft Convention on the Rights of the Child' (25 March 1983) UN Doc. E/CN.4/1983/62.

[32] *Ibid.*, 14.   [33] *Ibid.*, 15–16.

In congruence with previous suggestions, the first of these clauses used the term 'individual development' in general terms, without specifying any aspect of development, and the second clause asked to ensure the realisation of the child's 'fullest potential'. Australia suggested a similar amendment, which on the one hand defined an objective of this clause as the achievement of the 'fullest possible social integration' of children with disabilities, but on the other hand omitted the commitment to support the 'individual development' of these children.[34] After the discussion on both suggestions had resulted in 'no agreement',[35] Canada suggested a revised version that extended the protection provided for child development to include the achievement of 'the fullest possible social integration and *individual, cultural and spiritual development*'[36] (emphasis added).

The discussion that followed, details of which are not available, resulted in an agreement for the text of Article 12(3). The agreed-upon version aimed to facilitate the provision of services that would enable a child with a disability to achieve 'the fullest possible social integration and *individual development*, including his *cultural and spiritual development*'[37] (emphasis added). This version, which is as ambiguous as those that preceded it, combined the child's individual developmental potential and two developmental aspects (cultural and spiritual) with the aim of achieving social integration. No discussions as to why these objectives should be listed, or what is required to achieve them, is mentioned. Nor does this version clarify the relationship between the child's development and supporting the realisation of the child's fullest potential.

1984 Round of Discussions

The 1984 round of discussions[38] focused on the right to freedom of thought, conscience, and religion (Article 7(bis) of the draft); the right to be protected from abuse (Article 8(bis) of the draft); the right to freedom of information (Article 9 of the draft); and the right to social security (Article 13 of the draft).

As with previous discussions, Article 9 and the right to freedom of information stimulated a heated debate – including, once again, concerns about the potential negative impact that information might have on child

---

[34] *Ibid.*   [35] *Ibid.*, 14.   [36] *Ibid.*, 16.   [37] *Ibid.*, 17.

[38] UNCHR, 'Report of the Working Group on a Draft Convention on the Rights of the Child' (23 February 1984) UN Doc. E/CN.4/1984/71.

development. Poland therefore suggested amending the Article in a way that would include a somewhat different protection for child development:

> 2. The States Parties shall also encourage parents and guardians to provide their children with appropriate protection if, on account of its contents, the disseminated information might negatively affect the *physical and moral development* of the child[39] (emphasis added).

The suggested amendment substituted the protection of moral and mental development with a protection of physical and moral development. This version generated another debate about media regulation, the flow of information within and outside state borders, and the potential for government intervention in disseminating content. However, no comments were made regarding the underlying assumption that information could have a negative impact on the child's physical and moral development, or about the potential positive effect that information might have on these, or other, developmental domains.

Two revised versions of Article 9 were then submitted, one by an informal ad hoc drafting group and the other by the Ukrainian SSR. Interestingly enough, the protection of child development was omitted from both versions. The ad hoc group's version replaced concern for 'development' with concern for the child's 'social, spiritual and moral *well-being* (emphasis added) and physical and mental health',[40] while the Ukrainian SSR's version sought to promote 'the health and welfare of the child, his social and cultural *upbringing*'[41] (emphasis added). In addition, this version sought to protect the child 'from material injuries to his physical or mental health or to his social, spiritual or moral *well-being*'[42] (emphasis added).

These two versions, which essentially replace 'development' with 'well-being' or 'upbringing', demonstrate once again that the drafters did not draw any distinction between these terms, thought that such a distinction already existed, or considered that their meaning was something that required further consideration. However, since no explanation was given concerning this choice of words, the last option seems most unlikely. Nonetheless, what can be inferred is the common desire of all drafters to protect the course of children's growth and to ensure some sort of imagined optimum result.

---

[39] *Ibid.*, 11.   [40] *Ibid.*, 12.   [41] *Ibid.*.   [42] *Ibid.*, 13.

More discussions followed, and the United States and the Ukrainian SSR jointly suggested a new version of Article 9. It read:

> The States Parties recognize the important function performed by the mass media and shall ensure that the child has access to information and material from a diversity of international and national sources, including those aimed at the promoting of his *social, spiritual and moral well-being and physical and mental health....*[43] (emphasis added).

None of the comments that followed, except for one made by the United Kingdom, were related to development, to children's well-being, or to children's upbringing. The United Kingdom referred to the distinction between 'well-being' and 'upbringing', arguing that 'anything injurious to a child's physical and mental health would be injurious to his well-being also'.[44] Thus, the UK argument presented a pyramid, with mental health and physical health at the base and well-being at the top. This structure identifies well-being as the ultimate object of protection of this Article. As illuminating as this analogy might be, it does not sufficiently clarify whether 'well-being' is identical or similar in any way to 'development', or whether 'good health' lays the foundation for the process of achieving 'well-being'.

1985 Round of Discussions

The 1985 session[45] saw extensive and lengthy discussions about child development in the context of the right to health (Article 12), the right to an adequate standard of living (Article 14), the right to education (Article 15) and the aims of education (Article 16), and the right to rest and leisure (Article 17). Article 12, which previously focused on the rights of children with disabilities, was now dedicated to the child's right to health. Child development was not mentioned in the first version of this Article, but after a lengthy discussion about questions of healthcare funding and how accessible health services should be for children, an NGO ad hoc working group suggested adding an additional paragraph concerning medical experiments:

> The States Parties to the present Convention shall undertake to protect children from any medical investigation or treatment detrimental to their

---

[43] *Ibid.*, 14.   [44] *Ibid.*, 16.
[45] UNCHR, 'Report of the Working Group on a Draft Convention on the Rights of the Child' (11 March 1985) UN Doc. E/CN.4/1985/L.1.

> *physical or psychological health and development*, and to take all appropriate and necessary measures to prevent children being subject to traditional practices harmful to their health[46] (emphasis added).

Unlike other clauses, this clause does not provide for the active promotion of development. Rather, it establishes negative protection against actions that might put the child's 'physical or psychological health and development' at risk. No suggestion is made at this point to link child development with the general right to health. The second half of the paragraph mentions traditional practices and takes them to be harmful to children's health, but it does not mention any impact on child development. The discussion that followed this suggestion did not mention 'child development'.

The debates about Article 14 and the right to an adequate standard of living are more significant. The discussions were based on a text proposed by the NGO ad hoc group, which reads as follows:

> The States Parties to the present Convention recognize the right of every child to a standard of living adequate to guarantee the child's *physical, mental, moral and social development*. The parent(s) or those responsible for the child have the primary responsibility to secure, within their financial possibilities and powers, the *conditions of living necessary for the healthy development* of the child . . .[47] (emphasis added).

There are several plausible interpretations of this Article. It can be read to protect two standards of living, rather than only one. The first standard is protected by a general right to an adequate standard of living, which guarantees four elements of child development. The second standard ought to ensure a fifth element of development, the 'healthy' development of the child, which it is the sole responsibility of parents to ensure. There is also the possibility that the drafters did not think of these as two different standards, and took 'healthy' development to have the same meaning as 'physical, mental, moral and social' development. Another possible explanation for this division is not the difference between the meaning of these developmental domains, but rather a desire to differentiate between the obligations of states and of parents. If this last possibility is the case, it seems that less attention was given to the content of the obligation vis-à-vis child development, compared to the different levels of obligations imposed on states and parents.

[46] *Ibid.*, 8.   [47] *Ibid.*

Even though the drafters had a relatively lengthy discussion on this right, the travaux préparatoires do not shed much light on these questions. Only the Holy See referred to the issue of child development, when it once again asked to add 'spiritual' development to the list of developmental components that should be protected by the child's standard of living.[48] This suggestion was rejected.[49]

The discussions on the right to education and on the aims of education (Articles 15 and 16, respectively, of the draft) also included some deliberations about the issue of child development. According to Article 15,[50] ensuring the child's right to education is necessary in order to promote the child's 'talents and abilities to their fullest potential, and to prepare the child for future life'. This clause does not explicitly address any components of child development, but rather focuses on two dimensions of the process of growing up: developing the child's talent and abilities. Article 15 sets forward-looking objectives for education, which are designed to generate the creation of maximum talent for each individual child. The drafters further debated the issues of the cost of education; whether children should be entitled to free education and, if so, for what period of time; and whether the state's financial resources should be taken into account in either formulating their obligations or implementing them. Other discussions touched upon the issues of the rights and duties of parents to ensure their children's education, and the duties of international cooperation with respect to education.[51]

The question of education and child development was addressed in the context of the discussion about the aims of education and Article 16. The Working Group was presented with five versions of Article 16, two of which refer to child development. The first version was the Canadian suggestion that defined the aim of education as to 'promote the development of the child's personality, talents and abilities to their fullest potential'.[52] The second version, introduced by the Baha'i International Community, included broader objectives for education:

[48] Ibid., 9. [49] Ibid.
[50] 'The States Parties to the present Convention shall guarantee to every child compulsory and cost-free education, at least at elementary school level, designed to assist the child to develop his or her talent and abilities to their fullest potential, and to prepare the child for future life ...' Ibid., 11.
[51] Ibid., 11–15. [52] Ibid., 16.

1. In addition to academic education, the child shall be entitled to receive guidance, training and education designed to promote his *social, spiritual and moral development and well-being.*
2. The fundamental objectives of such guidance, training and education shall be:
   (a) to promote the *harmonious development* of the personality of the child and the *realization of his full potential* . . .[53] (emphasis added).

While the Canadian version used familiar terms, such as 'talent' and 'fullest potential', the Baha'i version introduced several new ideas and terms. It took development and well-being as two complementary but nevertheless distinct terms, opting to promote the child's 'harmonious development' instead of autonomous elements of 'development'. It also aimed to create the conditions necessary to ensure the realisation of the 'full potential' of the child. The drafters were less than impressed by the innovative nature of this suggestion, and at the discussions that followed they did not address the issue of child development at all.[54]

The end of this round of discussions left the term 'child development' in a familiar state of conceptual ambiguity. Although the term 'development' was used by the drafters, and different components of child development were mentioned, the drafters nonetheless did not discuss the meaning or content of any of the terms, or explain their context. Even when the potential link between 'development' and 'well-being' was suggested, it was not unpacked in any meaningful way.

1986 Round of Discussions

Almost a dozen rights were discussed during the 1986 session,[55] including the right to nondiscrimination (Article 4(bis)), the right to leave the state (Article 6(bis)), the right to identity (Article 9(bis)), the rights of children who were removed from their family environment (Article 12(ter)), the educational and cultural rights of indigenous children (Article 16(bis)), the right to be protected from economic exploitation (Article 18), the measures needed to be taken against the use of narcotic drugs (Article 18(bis)), the right to freedom of association and assembly (Article 18(quarter)), the rights of children in criminal

---

[53] *Ibid.*   [54] *Ibid.*, 17–19.
[55] UNCHR, 'Report of the Working Group on a Draft Convention on the Rights of the Child' (13 March 1986) UN Doc. E/CN.4/1986/39.

procedures (Article 19), the rights of children in respect of international humanitarian law and during international armed conflict (Article 20), and the relationship between children's rights in domestic law and in the Convention (Article 21). While most of these clauses explicitly refer to child development, this issue was not addressed at all during the Working Group's discussions, save for two exceptions.

The first debate relevant to the issue of child development took place as part of the discussions on Article 18, which addressed the protection of children from economic exploitation. Poland suggested the following text: 'The child shall not be employed in any form of work harmful to the child's health or education or which will interfere with his *physical, mental or social development*'[56] (emphasis added). The drafters held an intensive debate about this suggestion. Despite the alleged impact that any form of work might have on child development, the reasons for such impacts were not discussed, let alone challenged. Only the Holy See referred to this issue and, as usual, seized the opportunity to suggest including 'spiritual' development to the list of developmental domains that might be endangered due to economic exploitation.[57] No further light was shed on the meaning of child development in this context, or on the motivation to protect it.

The next relevant discussion concerned Article 19, which dealt with the rights of children in the criminal justice system. Different versions of this Article were discussed, and all were aimed at ensuring the rehabilitation of juveniles. However, even though the drafters had debated issues concerning the 'full development' of children and the protection of their ability to develop to their fullest potential, and despite the somewhat obvious impact that incarceration has on children's future, neither the various drafts nor the debates that followed mentioned child development as an object of concern. The reference to child development can be found in the versions presented by Canada and Poland, which mention the child's level of development as a factor that should be considered when designing rehabilitation programs. The Polish text read as follows: 'The child subject to penal procedures shall be treated in a manner commensurate with his *phase of development*, with his reformation and social rehabilitation in view'[58] (emphasis added). And the Canadian version read: 'States Parties to the present Convention recognize the right of children accused or found guilty of infringing the penal law to be

---

[56] *Ibid.*, 13.   [57] *Ibid.*, 14.   [58] *Ibid.*, 18.

treated in a manner ... which takes into account their age and the desirability of promoting their rehabilitation'.[59] These suggestions were the prototype for what would later become the principle of 'evolving capacities' in the Convention. But, despite its significance, the drafters dedicated only a short discussion to the suggestions, with nothing substantial being said.

This round of discussions ended with 'child development' on the margin of the debates. In comparison to previous rounds, these discussions were exceptionally dull (or at least this is how they are reported), and it seems that either child development was not seen as important enough to warrant discussion, or the drafters did not feel any need to address the issue because it was self-evident. It seems that after more than five years of debates and discussions, there was no suggestion to discuss the meaning of child development in the context of the Convention, or why and how child development should be protected. Thus far, no suggestion had been made to refer to children's development as an issue of human rights.

1987 Round of Discussions

During the 1987 session,[60] a dozen rights and issues were discussed, including how to encourage children to read books (Article 9), the rights of children in alternative care, protecting children from harmful traditional practices (Article 12), the aims of education, the educational rights of children belonging to minorities or indigenous populations (Article 16), protecting children from sexual exploitation (Article 16(ter)), the prevention of the sale or traffic of children (Article 18(quinto)), parental rights and responsibilities (Articles 5(bis) and 14), the right to freedom of expression and association (Article 7(ter)), and the right to privacy (Article 7(ter)). The term 'development' was repeatedly mentioned, but was not considered to be an issue worth discussing in any meaningful way. Nonetheless, some of the discussions are worthy of attention.

The debate about the need and the measures required to protect children from economic and sexual exploitation continued in this session. France and the Netherlands suggested an Article that would protect children from 'all forms of exploitation, particularly sexual exploitation,

---

[59] *Ibid.*, 19.
[60] UNCHR, 'Report of the Working Group on a Draft Convention on the Rights of the Child' (23 February 1987) UN Doc. E/CN.4/1987/25.

as well as all degrading treatment and all acts prejudicial to the moral, spiritual, mental or physical integrity of the child'.[61] These words are similar to the language usually used in relation to child development, but in this version the object of concern is not child development but rather children's 'moral, spiritual, mental or physical integrity'. This is the first time that the term 'integrity' appears. Like 'well-being', the term 'integrity' was used as a substitute for the term 'child development', but no explanation or discussion about its meaning, or why it was preferable to use this ambiguous term instead of 'child development', was given by the travaux préparatoires.

Some delegates highlighted this opacity. The representative of the United Kingdom, for example, argued that the phrase 'acts prejudicial to the moral, spiritual, mental or physical integrity of the child' was 'too vague' and that 'more precise meaning would have to be given' to it.[62] The representatives of the United States, Venezuela, France, and the Netherlands (who introduced this suggestion) further claimed that the wording 'had no substantive legal meaning in the United States and in several other legal systems, and therefore could not be enforced'.[63] Eventually, the Working Group decided to replace the term 'integration' with 'welfare'. However, this change had little impact, since it did not resolve the fundamental problems regarding the meaning of this clause. 'Welfare', like 'integration', is at best a term calling for a definition and it is open to interpretation. Like 'integration' and 'well-being', the term 'welfare' has long been used in children's law – a longstanding aim of which is to promote children's welfare. Nonetheless, welfare was rarely seen as a matter of human rights,[64] and no discussions as to the advantages of caring for children's welfare in this context, or what that would entail, were held.

Another relevant discussion was held in relation to Article 5(bis), which deals with parental rights and responsibilities. The drafters debated the following text:

> Parents or legal guardians shall enjoy the primary rights and responsibilities for the care, *upbringing and development of the child*, having due regard for the importance of allowing the child to develop the skills and knowledge required for an *independent adulthood*[65] (emphasis added).

This is one of the rare occasions where the drafters explicitly say something meaningful about their views concerning the concept of childhood.

[61] *Ibid.*, 16.   [62] *Ibid.*, 17.   [63] *Ibid.*, 22–23.   [64] See Chapter 1.   [65] *Ibid.*, 24.

According to the text, the child is destined to grow up into 'an independent adulthood' and others have the responsibility to facilitate this objective. The discussion that followed touched upon the narratives of children's future, child development, and the perception of children as developing human beings.

Canada argued that its support for this provision depended on giving 'due regard for the evolving capacities of the child and for the child's need to mature into an independent adulthood'.[66] This comment is important for two reasons. First, it refers to a certain conception of childhood. Second, it presumes the evolving-capacities principle as an inherent characteristic of children. In other words, it takes development and change as the profound characteristics of children. Reading the text and the comments together sheds some light on the drafters' conception of childhood: it is a process of maturation, with the objective of creating a competent adult, and children's rights deserve special protection and prioritisation because of children's developmental potential and their vulnerabilities. The debate resulted in no decision being reached and the Working Group decided to postpone the conclusion to a later session.

The discussion concerning Article 7(ter) and the right to freedom of expression, the right to freedom of association, and the right to privacy saw more comments concerning the principle of evolving capacities. Reflecting its general stance during the Cold War era, the United States submitted a text that included a comprehensive definition and protection of these rights.[67] But nothing in the wording of that version either suggested that those rights should be restricted according to the child's stage of development (evolving capacities), or aimed to support any aspect of development. However, during 'a lengthy discussion',[68] the question of child development did arise. The representative of Australia was the first to ask why the provision did not refer to 'the evolving sense of responsibility of children'.[69] Sweden made a similar claim, suggesting the drafting of 'a separate article on the evolving capacities of the child'.[70]

The representative of Norway supported the United States's version, but, like the Australian representative, was concerned that there is 'a need for a general provision dealing with the evolving capacities of the child'.[71] Canada and Argentina shared this view. The USSR and China, on the other hand, objected to the inclusion of these rights, claiming that the focus on political rights neglected other important interests of the child,

---

[66] *Ibid.*, 25.   [67] *Ibid.*, 26.   [68] *Ibid.*, 27.   [69] *Ibid.*   [70] *Ibid.*   [71] *Ibid.*

such as economic and social rights. The representative from China also referred to the evolving-capacities argument, saying that 'the freedoms of association, peaceful assembly and privacy could not be enjoyed by children in the same way as they are enjoyed by adults because the intellect of a child was not as developed as that of an adult, and therefore a child could only engage in activities commensurate with its intellect'.[72] The association of capacities and intellect is unfortunate, but what is more important is the comparison of the undeveloped child to the developed adult, perpetuating the essence of the 'human becomings' model of childhood.

The end of the 1987 round of discussions left the protection of child development at a crossroads. On the one hand, protecting and promoting child development were seen as the aims of many of the Convention's rights, being relevant to many aspects – and rights – of children's lives and to children's ability to develop to their fullest potential. The conceptualisation of children as developing human beings underpins the drafters' idea of childhood in two different ways: development was either the expression of the process of growing up, or a point of reference in the form of the evolving-capacities principle. On the other hand, wide-ranging and alternative components of 'child development' were discussed, but their meanings were not addressed in any detail. The failure to engage with the meaning of 'child development' in itself was, in part, due to the fact that the term was intermixed with other concepts, such as 'well-being', 'upbringing', and 'integrity'. But, since the drafters clarified none of those terms either, their potential connection to 'child development' was not addressed.

After this round of discussions had concluded, and as part of the preparations for the next round, India submitted the following proposal for Article 1(bis) or 2(bis): 'The States Parties to the present Convention undertake to create an environment, within their capacities and constitutional processes, which ensures to the maximum extent possible, the survival and healthy development of the child'.[73] This was the first time that the terms 'survival' and 'development' were introduced as separate concepts. It established the explicit duty of States Parties to promote both children's survival and children's (healthy) development, not merely as objectives of other rights. This proposal was discussed the following year.

---

[72] *Ibid.*
[73] UNCHR, 'Pre-sessional Open-Ended Working Group on the Question of a Convention on the Rights of the Child, "Proposal Submitted By India"' (28 January 1988) UN Doc. E/CN.4/1988/WG1/WG.13.

1988 Round of Discussions

The 1988 round of discussions[74] was the penultimate session. During this round, the Working Group debated many of the Convention's rights, including the right to freedom of expression and information (Article 7a), the right to freedom of association and peaceful assembly (Article 7(ter)), the right to privacy (Article 7(quarter)), the right to health (Article 12(bis)), the right to physical and psychological recovery and social re-integration (Article 14), and rights during armed conflicts (Article 20). The issue of child development was mentioned in some of the debates, but none of the comments add more than what is already known. The most extensive discussion – and the one that is most relevant to the question of the right to development – is the discussion of India's proposal to adopt Article 1(bis) or 2(bis).

The conversation about this proposal was the first time that the drafters explicitly addressed the meaning of 'child development'. They also discussed the definition of 'survival' and explored the relationships between the concepts of 'survival' and 'child development', and between those two concepts and the 'right to life'. The significance of these debates justifies lengthy quotes from the travaux préparatoires. 'During the course of the debate', the travaux préparatoires report, 'several governmental representatives commented that the concept of survival was not legally defined, and one representative expressed the belief that it could even prove harmful to the concept of the right to development'.[75] Here, for the first time, the right to development is explicitly mentioned. But while the unidentified representatives were correct in their concern that the concept of survival lacked definition, it is interesting to note that a similar claim about the right to development was not made. One possible explanation is that the drafters did not think that the right to development lacked clarity, but the travaux préparatoires are silent about this point.

Following these comments, four alternative versions of an Article dealing with child survival and child development were proposed:

> [Version 1] The States Parties to the present Convention shall respect the *right of the child to survival*. The States Parties shall, within their capacities and constitutional processes, take all

---

[74] UNCHR, 'Report of the Working Group on a Draft Convention on the Rights of the Child' (6 April 1988) UN Doc. E/CN.4/1988/28.

[75] *Ibid.*, 5.

necessary measures to ensure, to the maximum extent possible, *the survival and healthy development* of the child.

[Version 2] The States Parties to the present Convention undertake to promote conditions which ensure, to the maximum extent possible, *the survival* of the child.

[Version 3] The States Parties to the present Convention undertake to create within the available resources the *psychosocial conditions* which will guarantee, to the maximum extent possible, *the life and the full development* of the child.

[Version 4] The States Parties to the present Convention undertake to promote *conditions* which guarantee *the life and healthy development* of the child[76] (emphasis added).

There are several interesting points here. First, the duty to ensure child survival is articulated as a duty arising from the fact that the child has a right to develop. Second, 'development' is mentioned in only three of the options and it is connected to survival – as in India's proposal – in only one of the options, while the other three detach the protection of child survival from the protection of child development. Third, two different adjectives are used to describe what sort of 'development' should be ensured by the Convention – it is either the child's 'healthy' development or the child's 'full' development. Fourth, one of the versions presents an obligation to ensure the child's 'full development', which should be facilitated by guaranteeing the 'psychosocial conditions' for this type of development.

The travaux préparatoires tell us that the observer for the United Nations International Children's Emergency Fund (UNICEF) 'explained what the Fund understood by survival',[77] but unfortunately, they do not elaborate on the content of this explanation. The travaux préparatoires then record that:

> The representative of India was of the view that the *right to survival* should be stressed[;] bearing in mind, as indicated by UNICEF, that many children died from preventable causes and that children could also survive in very poor conditions, the *right to survival* should be supplemented by the notion of healthy development[78] (emphasis added).

In other words, India sees little advantage in having a separate right to survival, as the objectives of such a right can be covered by protecting, on

---

[76] *Ibid.*, 5–6.   [77] *Ibid.*, 6.   [78] *Ibid.*

the one hand, the right to life (ensuring that children do not die from preventable causes) and, on the other hand, the right to development (caring for children's healthy development). It is therefore not surprising that the discussion that followed 'focused mainly on the definition of the concepts of survival, right to survival, right to development, and the child's development. The view was expressed that life and survival were complementary and were not mutually exclusive, and that survival could even mean the diminution of infant mortality'.[79]

This report sees some important distinctions between the right to life, the right to survival, and the right to development. It suggests, once again, that the drafters thought that child development could be protected as a right of the child. It also indicates that child survival has a broader meaning beyond the confined definition of ensuring that children will not die, arguably the domain of the yet-to-be-mentioned right to life. The short description of this discussion is rather surprising – and disappointing – given that other parts of the travaux préparatoires include lengthy discussions about the meanings of well-established rights such as freedom of expression and nondiscrimination, which supposedly are more straightforward and raise less controversy.

Following this hazy discussion, the Italian representative offered – probably for the first time – to add to the Convention a provision concerning children's right to life.[80] This suggestion was followed by a statement:

> The right to survival carried with it a more positive connotation than the right to life, it meant the right to have positive steps taken to prolong the life of the child. The view was further expressed that conditions should be defined in order to permit the exercise of the right to life, and not the right to mere survival. Two speakers stated that, despite the explanations that had been given on the word 'survival', they continue to have serious doubts about the inclusion of this concept in the convention.[81]

Here, the drafters draw a clearer distinction between the positive elements that the right to survival might include, and what is often thought to be a negative right – namely, the right to life. At this point, three revised versions of this Article were put to discussion:

> [Version 1] The States Parties to the present Convention undertake to promote conditions which protect, to the maximum extent possible, the *life* of the child.

---

[79] *Ibid.*   [80] *Ibid.*, 7.   [81] *Ibid.*, 6.

[Version 2] The States Parties to the present Convention undertake to promote conditions which ensure, to the maximum extent possible, the *survival and healthy development* of the child.

[Version 3] States Parties shall protect the *right to life* of children and ensure the *survival and healthy development* of children[82] (emphasis added).

Like the original Indian proposal, the second and third suggestions include protection of children's 'healthy development', and both bring 'survival' and 'healthy development' together. The right to life is mentioned as a separate issue in the first and third suggestions, with one referring to a 'right to life' and the other asking States Parties to 'protect' the child's life.

The travaux préparatoires then record that the discussion about this issue was concluded in this way:

> The Chairman-Rapporteur stated that the right to life had been omitted from the draft convention, and that the proposal made in Working Paper 13 was intended to remedy that shortcoming. The right to life, already enshrined in the International Covenants on Human Rights[,] should be included in the draft convention and listed as a priority before other rights of the child. The approach to the right to life in the Covenants was rather negative, while that of the convention should be positive and should take into account economic, social and cultural conditions.[83]

This was a major development. After nearly a decade of drafting, it was decided that the right to life should be included in the Convention, mainly due to the different and broader meaning that it has in the context of children's rights and lives. Unlike its interpretation at the time in international human rights law, it was decided that the right to life in international children's rights law should include some positive elements too, and should account for children's socioeconomic living conditions and their culture.[84] For some odd reason, nothing was said about the issues concerning survival and development, however.

In preparation for the final round of discussions, an ad hoc drafting group led by India introduced a new version of this clause:

---

[82] *Ibid.*, 6–7.   [83] *Ibid.*, 7.

[84] Compare with the current interpretation of the right to life under the International Convention on Civil and Political Rights (ICCPR), which includes some positive duties of State Parties, especially for children: UNCCPR, 'General Comment No. 36 (2018) on Article 6 of the International Covenant on Civil and Political Rights, on the Right to Life' (30 October 2018) UN Doc. CCPR/C/GC/36, paras. 21, 23 and 48.

1. The States Parties to the present Convention recognize that every child has the inherent right to life.
2. States Parties shall ensure, to the maximum extent possible, the survival and development of the child.[85]

India explained that this version tried to meet the following concerns that had been previously raised: '(a) the inherent right to life of the child, and (b) the focus on obligations for States parties to promote measures and conditions for the survival and development of the child'.[86] This explanation does nothing to clear up the ambiguity of either 'development' or 'survival' – a concern that was raised by the drafters themselves – or the potential overlap between the two. Another conclusion that can be drawn from this proposal and the discussions that led to it is that the proposal to protect child development and children's future is a clear embodiment of the human becomings model of childhood. There is a clear intention to protect children's healthy growth so that they can become competent and 'full' human beings.

The discussion about the revised Indian proposal focused primarily on the right to life,[87] but the travaux préparatoires give no details about this discussion and do not suggest that the drafters debated the meaning of the right to life, the right to survival, and the right to development; the differences among the three; or the pros and cons of including any of them in the Convention. This discussion was concluded with no further amendments to the text.[88] Given that the final text is similar to India's original proposal, it is safe to assume that the discussions resulted in the drafters being satisfied with the original version and the explanations that followed. If this is the case, one can wonder whether the initial concerns expressed by some of the delegates about the vague nature of the right to survival were met with convincing explanations. Another question is whether any of the drafters had a profound understanding of the meaning of any of these rights or their practical implications. The travaux préparatoires are silent about these issues.

1989 Round of Discussions

At the final meetings in 1989,[89] the Working Group discussed most of the Convention's rights. Child development was mentioned in relation to

[85] UNCHR, 'Report of the Working Group' (6 April 1988), *supra* n. 73.   [86] *Ibid.*
[87] *Ibid.*   [88] *Ibid.*
[89] UNCHR, 'Report of the Working Group on a Draft Convention on the Rights of the Child' (2 March 1989) UN Doc. E/CN.4/1989/48.

a few of the rights. The most relevant references were made during the debates concerning the adoption of Article 6 and the rights to life, survival, and development.

Two versions of Article 1(bis), which after a technical reading became Article 6,[90] were discussed in this final round. The first version was the one adopted at the end of the previous round of discussions. Venezuela presented a second version, which read:

> 1. For the purposes of the present Convention, 'child' means every human being up to the age of 18 years unless, under the law of his State he has attained the age of majority earlier.
> 2. The States Parties to the present Convention recognize that every child has the inherent right to life.
> 3. States Parties shall ensure to the maximum extent possible the healthy growth and development of the child.[91]

In this version, protecting child survival has been replaced with the protection of the child's 'healthy growth' and development. Consistent with its previous comments, the observer for the WHO objected to this change, claiming that 'the term "survival" had a special meaning within the United Nations context, especially for his organization and UNICEF'.[92] According to the WHO:

> 'Survival' included growth monitoring, oral rehydration and disease control, breastfeeding, immunization, child spacing, food and female literacy; the term 'growth' represented only a part of the concept of 'survival' and the change would be a step backwards from standards already accepted.[93]

This explanation sheds light on the understanding that some of the drafters had of the concepts of 'survival' and 'growth' and, inexplicitly, of development as well. This broad definition of 'survival' clarifies the difference between 'survival' and 'growth', and consequently between 'survival' and 'development'. Some of the elements that are considered part of the child's 'survival', such as literacy, were previously thought to be included in other parts of the Convention – especially in the aims of education and its contribution to child development. This explanation therefore raises the question of the differences between 'survival' and 'development' and what they might be.

---

[90] UNCHR, 'Draft Convention on the Rights of the Child, Working Paper Submitted by the Chairman, Text as Adopted at First Reading with Suggested Revisions' (24 November 1988) UN Doc. E/CN.4/1989/WG.1/WP.2.

[91] UNCHR, 'Report of the Working Group' (2 March 1989), *supra* n. 88, 17.   [92] *Ibid.*

[93] *Ibid.*

The comments made by the representatives of Australia, Norway, Italy, Sweden, and India, which supported the WHO's interpretation, might answer some of these questions. The representative of Italy said that:

> In the language of international organizations the two words 'survival' and 'development' had come to acquire the special meaning of ensuring the child's survival in order to realise the full development of his or her personality, both from the material and spiritual points of view.[94]

This is a very interesting articulation of the differences between survival and development, and of the overall objective of this clause (and the Convention). It reinforces the image of children as weak and in need of protection, and suggests that ensuring children's survival is a necessary step in protecting their 'full development', which in turn is the ultimate goal of childhood. In other words, it seems that the drafters aspired to ensure that every child gets the opportunity to physically grow up and to achieve her fullest potential.

The discussion ended with the Working Group adopting the following text as the final version of Article 6:

> 1. States Parties recognize that every child has the inherent right to life.
> 2. States Parties shall ensure to the maximum extent possible the survival and development of the child.[95]

'Child development' gained some additional rare attention in this round of discussions during the debate about the principle of the best interests of the child, when the representative of Venezuela addressed the potential links between the best interests principle and child development and commented:

> Although her [Venezuela's] delegation was not opposed to the phrase 'best interests of the child' being included in the final text, she however wished to draw attention to the subjectivity of the term, especially if the Convention contained no prior stipulation that the 'best interests of the child' were his all-round – *in other words, physical, mental, spiritual, moral and social – development*. That would mean leaving the interpretation of the 'best interests of the child' to the judgement of the person, institution or organization applying the rule. In the ensuing debate a number of delegations expressed satisfaction with the phrase and the representative of Venezuela therefore withdrew her suggestion[96] (emphasis added).

This is a rather striking statement. It suggests that while a concern was raised about the subjective nature of the principle of the best interests of

---

[94] *Ibid.*   [95] *Ibid.*, 18.   [96] *Ibid.*, 22.

the child, child development was used as an example for a clear and objective element of the Convention, which presumably should be the model for the best-interests principle to follow.

The Drafters' Perceptions about How to Best Protect Childhood's Trajectory

The analysis of the drafting process can illuminate the motivations for including a broad protection for child development, questions concerning the meaning of different aspects of child development and how they are affected by different rights of the child, and how Article 6 and its protection of life–survival–development can be understood.

But the first issue that requires attention is whether the drafters intended to include the child's right to development in the Convention. The answer to this question is not very clear. On the one hand, during the drafting process it was suggested several times that a 'right to development' should be mentioned. The final text of Article 6(2) does not explicitly mention a 'right to development', but rather proposes that States Parties shall ensure the 'survival and development of the child'. On the other hand, in a human rights treaty, what is the meaning of including this duty, and establishing this entitlement for children, if not to suggest that children can expect to have their right to survival and their right to development protected? The language is not insignificant, but the content of Article 6(2), as well as the obvious commitment to protecting child development, cannot lead to the conclusion that the Convention does not protect the right to development. In other words, even the drafting process – which carries only a limited weight in the interpretation of a treaty – suggests that the Convention does indeed protect children's right to development.

Embedding the Protection of 'Child Development' in the Convention

Despite the heterogeneous composition of the Open-Ended Working Group (in terms, for example, of the geographic spread and institutional affiliations of the delegates), most, if not all, of the references to child development during the drafting process stemmed from a conception of children as 'human becomings' and the subsequent need to ensure a healthy process of growth that should result in the successful transformation of the child into an adult. Thus, the protection of child development and of the right to development, and the commitments and duties that arise from that protection, are less open to challenges in the name of universalism, relativism, and cultural imperialism than are some of the other Articles in the Convention (for example, Article 23 and the issue of harmful traditional practices). Other conceptions of childhood, already debated in the literature and practised in law, did not seem to inform the discussions about child development. The discussions about Article 6 were conducted under a cloud of protectionist approaches to children and their rights, with the view that it is the future that matters most for children.

This view of childhood resulted in a wide and explicit protection of child development being embedded in five Articles of the Convention, in addition to Article 6(2) and its explicit protection of child development (and survival). In that sense, as Heather Montgomery claims, the Convention is designed to influence how children grow up, envisaging the child as 'an individual, autonomous being, an inheritor of liberal, humanist ideals of the Enlightenment'.[97]

It is, therefore, also clear why there were no meaningful discussions – or at least none that the travaux préparatoires report – about the meaning of child development. After all, why should one discuss a self-explanatory issue? But the presumption that child development is a term that does not require interpretation is wrong. Its ambiguity often led the drafters to mix it with other terms, such as children's 'well-being' and 'growth'. Likewise, the term 'well-being' is also open to interpretation and prima facie does not necessarily have the same meaning as 'child development'.[98]

Because of this approach, a new human right was introduced into the world of binding international human rights law: the right to development. This innovation continued the evolutionary narrative of international children's rights law – which began in 1924 – in protecting child development.[99] It also led to the protection of eight aspects of

---

[97] Heather Montgomery, *An Introduction to Childhood* (Wiley-Blackwell, West Sussex 2009) 6.

[98] Jane Aldgate, for example, suggests that the child well-being approach is composed of an ecological approach to children's physical and psychological wellness, strengths and attachment; Jane Aldgate, 'Child Well-Being, Child Development and Family Life' in Colette McAuley and Wendy Rose (eds.), *Child Well-Being* (Jessica Kingsley, London 2010) 21–38. For a more general discussion on the meaning of human well-being, see James Griffin, *Well-Being* (Clarendon Press, Oxford 1986).

[99] On events and narratives in international law, see Fleur Johns, 'Introduction' in Fleur Johns *et al.* (eds.), *Events: The Force of International Law* (Routledge, Oxford 2011) 1–17, 1–8.

child development – physical, mental, moral, social, cultural, spiritual, personality, and talent – being assimilated into five different Articles: Articles 18(1), 23(3), 27(1), 29(1)(a), and 32(1), which refer to parental responsibility, the child's right to health, the right to an adequate standard of living, the aims of education, and the right to freedom from economic exploitation, respectively, as summarised below.

Article 18(1)
States Parties shall use their best efforts to ensure recognition of the principle that both parents have common responsibilities for the upbringing and development of the child. Parents or, as the case may be, legal guardians, have the primary responsibility for the upbringing and development of the child. The best interests of the child will be their basic concern.

Article 23(3)
Recognizing the special needs of a disabled child, assistance extended in accordance with paragraph 2 of the present article shall be provided free of charge, whenever possible, taking into account the financial resources of the parents or others caring for the child, and shall be designed to ensure that the disabled child has effective access to and receives education, training, health care services, rehabilitation services, preparation for employment and recreation opportunities in a manner conducive to the child's achieving the fullest possible social integration and individual development, including his or her cultural and spiritual development.

Article 27(1)
States Parties recognize the right of every child to a standard of living adequate for the child's physical, mental, spiritual, moral and social development.

Article 29(1)
States Parties agree that the education of the child shall be directed to: (a) The development of the child's personality, talents and mental and physical abilities to their fullest potential . . .

Article 32(1)
States Parties recognize the right of the child to be protected from economic exploitation and from performing any work that is likely to be hazardous or to interfere with the child's education, or to be harmful to the child's health or physical, mental, spiritual, moral or social development.

The novelty of subjugating a human rights treaty to a developmentalist perception of childhood is also reflected in Article 5, which pins down the evolving-capacities principle. Determining that the rights of children will be respected 'in a manner consistent with the evolving capacities of the child'[100] makes a specific perception of childhood the guiding principle for the implementation of the Convention, which is thereby subject to children's 'development' stages.[101] This is a highly problematic restriction on children's agency.

The centrality of the developmentalist perception stands in contrast to the lack of any substantial or thorough analysis of the meaning of child development or the right to development, or of any subsequent questions that follow.[102] The analysis of the drafting process demonstrates that discussions were held concerning macro-level questions – such as what constitutes a component of development and what factors might impact 'development'. But micro-level questions – such as why the concern for child development should be articulated in human rights terms and what this innovation means for children – were rarely, if ever, addressed.

As the Working Group's Chairman Adam Lopatka explained (in an article published after the Convention had been adopted by the UN), the Convention was designed in order to protect a universal course of growth: 'The physical and mental nature of the child is identical everywhere ... the process of growth and adolescence takes a similar course in all children. Their physical and mental needs are also similar'.[103] This statement explains why none of the above questions were asked. If one considers all children to be identical – at least in their developmental needs – surely a concern for them, and for their future, should be articulated in terms of concern for their development. And 'development', so it seems, requires no further explanation. In other words, the false assumption that child development has a universal and singular meaning resulted in insufficient discussion about the diverse, rich, and contextual meaning of the term and the subsequent implications it can have on the interpretation of the Convention in general, and on its commitment to protecting child development in particular.

---

[100] Article 5.
[101] Gerison Lansdown, *The Evolving Capacities of the Child* (Save the Children and UNICEF, Innocenti Research Centre, Florence 2005) 16.
[102] This is true with the exception of the few comments made in the 1988 round of discussions.
[103] Adam Lopatka, 'The Rights of the Child Are Universal: The Perspective of the UN Convention on the Rights of the Child', in Michael Freeman and Phillip Veerman (eds.), *The Ideologies of Children's Rights* (Martinus Nijhoff, Dordrecht, 1992), 47–52, 49.

Article 6 and the Rights to Life, Survival, and Development

The right to development was introduced after a decade of discussions, at a time when different Articles already protected varieties of developmental domains, as part of a clause that also protected the right to life and the right to survival. These three rights can be understood as existing on one continuum, with the right to life at one end, the right to survival in the middle, and the right to development at the other end. The continuum represents two elements: states' obligations and the child's needs. The right to life is situated at the negative end of the continuum and relates to an immediate need: the need to live. The right to survival is situated at the positive end, and relates to the child's future growth. The continuum therefore covers the various needs of the child to live, to survive and to develop, and the correlating levels of obligations that these needs establish.

The right to life is situated at the negative end of the continuum because most of the obligations that it entails are negative – for example, ensuring that the child's life will not be taken arbitrarily. As Manfred Nowak asserts, the right to life under the Convention obligates States Parties to reduce the mortality rates of babies, to ensure adequate nutrition for children, to act against infanticide, and to reduce the number of homicides.[104] But, as we introduce more positive obligations into the sorts of duties that the right to life entails, we move on the continuum towards the place where the right to survival is located[105] – along with the entitlements that it mandates for children.

A thin line therefore distinguishes the right to life from the right to survival, and it is based on two criteria: the principle to protect (life per se, or the medium- or long-term physical survival of the child) and the obligations that it involves. Further up the continuum, there is yet another fine line that distinguishes between the right to survival and the right to development. This line can be based on the same criteria, distinguishing between the immediate physical survival of the child and the various developmental needs of the child – mental, moral, physical, or other – and the obligations that follow.

---

[104] Manfred Nowak, *Article 6: The Right to Life, Survival and Development* (Martinus Nijhoff, Leiden 2005) 18–35.

[105] See F. Menghistu, 'The Satisfaction of Survival Requirements' in B. G. Ramcharan (ed.), *The Right to Life in International Law* (Martinus Nijhoff, Dordrecht 1985) 63–83.

The right to survival, like the right to development, is another innovation of the Convention. According to the explanation given by the WHO during the drafting process, the right to survival means 'growth monitoring, oral rehydration and disease control, breastfeeding, immunization, child spacing, food and female literacy'.[106] Some of these goals overlap with the positive obligations that the right to life generates. Moreover, this interpretation does not sufficiently distinguish it from other rights of the child that the Convention protects, such as the right to health, the right to an adequate standard of living, and the right to education. Therefore, the question of why the drafters decided to enfold these issues together under the title of 'survival', and to designate a distinct obligation to fulfil them, remains open.

A possible answer to this question is that context makes a difference and symbolism is not without significance. Locating these obligations within the context of the life–survival–development continuum emphasises their importance to the child's future development. This context emphasises the pressing importance of protecting children's basic needs that are necessary for a healthy course of growth, and for providing equal opportunities to all children – the latter led the WHO to ask to include female literacy as part of this list of components.

This interpretation clarifies the importance not only of the right to survival, but also of the right to development, which is located at the positive end of the continuum. According to this line of analysis, the right to development is not about preventing a child from dying or providing the immediate needs required for her physical survival. Rather, the right to development addresses the long-terms needs of the child. The right is a forward-looking right that focuses on the child's course of growth and on the child's future. It aims to provide for the child's maturation process and for the adult that the child will eventually become.

Understanding Article 6 and the Right to Development

The right to development should be understood as a positive right that aims to ensure the child's transformation into an adult. Considering the travaux préparatoires and the text of the Convention, the right to development can be interpreted in five different ways. All of these options use the ambiguous term 'child development'.

---

[106] UNCHR, 'Report of the Working Group' (2 March 1989), *supra* n. 88, 17.

- The first option takes the right to development as a right that aims to protect the child's ability to reach the endpoint of the developmental process (that is, adulthood).
- In the second option, the right to development is the right that enables the process of growth itself.
- The third option combines the previous two, suggesting that the right to development can be understood as a right that facilitates the course of growth and the desirable outcome of fulfilling the child's potential as an adult.
- The fourth option is to claim that the right to development lacks any substantial and distinct meaning. According to this interpretation, this right has no added value or distinct meaning over other rights in the Convention, such as the rights to life, survival, health, an adequate standard of living, or play and leisure.
- The fifth option attempts to avoid these polarised views. This option substantiates Article 6 and delineates its distinct meaning, interpreting the right to development as the right of a child to have her material and nonmaterial needs that are required for a healthy process of growth met.

An obvious difficulty of this interpretation is that, to some extent, it brings us back to square one. This suggestion derives from the above-mentioned assumptions about children and development that under-pinned the drafting process. Therefore, in order to substantiate it and make it more concrete, there is a need to unfold the meaning of child development, to determine what its necessary components are, and to ascertain what constitutes 'healthy growth'. The unfolding process requires people to make some normative decisions. It requires them to acknowledge that the alleged universality of 'child development' is misleading, and that the term has various meanings in different disciplines and contexts.

Having said that, this interpretation does provide a distinct meaning for Article 6 and does justify its existence. It represents more than a summary of the various developmental components that are protected by other Articles of the Convention. It requires us to take the individual child's future seriously, mandating that all of the child's needs in the course of childhood be met in order to ensure the fulfilment of childhood in the form of adulthood. Ultimately, this interpretation is informed by the human becomings model of childhood. Rejecting this model of childhood undermines the normative ground of this approach, leaving it without any substantial meaning.

The Convention and the Right to Development in 'General' International Law

The drafting process highlights the gap between the innovative nature of the Convention, with regard to the right to development, and 'general' international law. As will be discussed in Chapter 4, the period when the Convention was drafted – from 1978 to 1989 – was also the time when 'the right to development' was being intensively debated in international law. Moreover, just before India suggested including a right to development in the Convention, the UN General Assembly adopted the 1986 Declaration on the Right to Development. According to the travaux préparatoires, neither this Declaration nor the meaning of the 'general' right to development was ever mentioned by the drafters. I doubt that this omission was the result of a lack of awareness of these developments in general international law. A more plausible explanation is that the unquestioned belief in the 'law of growth' of children[107] – and the aspiration to protect that growth – led the drafters to ignore a new conception in international law, which had an identical title. Chapters 4 and 5 address this point in detail.

Conclusion

The drafting process of the 1989 UN Convention on the Rights of the Child lasted 11 years. The original draft was a replica of the 1959 Declaration, but the final Convention is much broader in content and scope. The Convention protects more rights of children, introduces a more complex structure of responsibilities and duties divided between different duty bearers, and creates a monitoring mechanism for its implementation. However, with respect to child development, the final text did not change the underlying narrative of international children's rights law concerning the conception of childhood. It upholds and embeds the human becomings model, resulting in a narrow conception of child development that, ironically, aims to ensure children's future but fails to sufficiently respect their agency – a failure that undercuts the core principle of human rights law. The 1989 Convention, like the 1924 and 1959 Declarations, attempts to protect and actively promote child development. The novelty of the Convention in this regard is not the protection that it provides to children's development, but rather the creation of

---

[107] See Chapter 1.

a right to development and the wide protection that the Convention gives to a number of elements of the right – such as physical, emotional, spiritual, and cultural development.

As argued in Chapter 1, the perception of children as developing human beings and the comprehensive protection for their development were key components of international children's rights law before the creation of the 1989 Convention. Therefore, we can assume that the Convention's drafters not only shared a conviction that there was a need to protect children's development, but also understood the practical implications of transforming this idea into a human right. The right to development is presumed to have been included in the Convention for a good reason, although it is not explicitly protected in any of the previous international declarations on children's rights or in any 'general' human rights treaties. The travaux préparatoires shed light on the drafters' intentions and their understanding of this right, and can serve as a valuable resource in assessing the scope and practicality of the right.

The drafting process included very few substantive discussions on either the right to development or the perception of children as developing human beings. Although these terms (mainly 'child development' and, to a lesser degree, 'the right to development') were used consistently, their meanings were rarely discussed. As this chapter has demonstrated, despite the lack of attention given to the 'right to development' during the drafting process, it is possible to unlock the potential of Article 6 and to draw conclusions about the potential meanings of the right to development.

The Convention is not a declaration, but rather a binding treaty that ought to be implemented by all its parties. For this reason, the process of interpretation takes place in parallel to the implementation process. The next chapter focuses on this dual process by analysing the interpretation by the Convention's monitoring mechanism of the right to development, the UN Committee on the Rights of the Child.

3

The Interpretation of the Right to Development by the UN Committee on the Rights of the Child

> The Committee expects States to interpret 'development' in its broadest sense as a holistic concept, embracing the child's physical, mental, spiritual, moral, psychological and social development. Implementation measures should be aimed at achieving the optimal development for all children.
>
> UN Committee on the Rights of the Child, General Comment No. 5
> (2003)

This chapter analyses the UN Committee on the Rights of the Child's (the Committee) interpretation of the right to development. The chapter asks a set of questions, including how the Committee conceptualises the term 'child development', how 'child development' features in the interpretation of the right to development and other rights in the Convention, what the risk factors are that undermine the right to development, and what measures should be taken to promote and protect the right to development. The chapter examines all the Concluding Observations issued by the Committee between 1993, when it began reviewing States Parties' implementation reports, and 2016, as well as all the General Comments that it had published by December 2017. This amounts to nearly 500 Concluding Observations and 23 General Comments.

The analysis is presented in a way that follows a child's chronological development, using the prism of the life cycle from birth until the child reaches legal adulthood at the age of 18 (Article 1). It begins by addressing structural challenges to the realisation of child development and to the right to development, such as discrimination and its effects, before moving to look at the relationship between aspects of children's identities such as gender and (dis)ability and the right to development. The analysis moves to discuss the issue of early childhood development and children's socioeconomic rights, focusing on the relationship between child development and the rights to education and health. It then discusses the issue of child labour, before concluding the chapter.

As the monitoring body of the UN Convention on the Rights of the Child (the Convention), the Committee receives information from a wide range of sources, primarily from States Parties but also from UN agencies and civil society actors in each country. It is the institution most likely to have a comprehensive perspective about the state of the world's children (excluding the 75 million children living in the United States, which is the only country in the world that as of 2019 has not ratified the Convention). This volume of data, as distorted, biased, and incomplete as it may be, provides the Committee with a broad perspective on the challenges and obstacles faced in implementing the Convention in different cultural, political, financial, and social contexts.[1] Analysing 25 years of monitoring of the Convention's protection for child development and the right to development can tell us how the right to development has been treated, and what States Parties are expected to do in order to improve their protection and deliver on their duties with respect to this fundamental feature of the Convention.

The analysis considers the importance of protecting child development under the Convention, as established in the previous chapter, and the Committee's own view that the child's right to development should be interpreted in a broad and holistic way and should be considered as one of the Convention's four guiding principles.[2] Methodologically, the analysis takes a child-centred approach. This means that it reads the Committee's comments, recommendations, suggestions and interpretations of various Articles while positioning children, their rights, and their lives at the centre of the analysis.[3] It asks that the Committee's views be considered, as much as possible, in the context of children's lives, rather than analysing the text of the Committee's jurisprudence in the abstract.

---

[1] Gerison Lansdown, 'The Reporting Process under the Convention on the Rights of the Child' in Philip Alston and James Crawford (eds.), *The Future of UN Human Rights Treaty Monitoring* (Cambridge University Press, Cambridge 2000) 113–128. For a comparison of the monitoring processes of other UN treaty bodies, see Christian Tomuschat, "The Work of Expert Bodies: Examination of States Reports" in *Human Rights: Between Idealism and Realism* (2nd edition, Oxford University Press, Oxford 2008) 175–191.

[2] UNCRC, 'General Comment No. 5 (2003): General Measures of Implementation of the Convention on the Rights of the Child' (27 November 2003) CRC/GC/2003/5.

[3] *C.f.* Noam Peleg, 'Marginalisation by the Court: The Case of Roma Children and the European Court of Human Rights' (2018) 18 *Human Rights Law Review* 111. Also see Helen Stalford and Kathryn Hollingsworth, 'Judging Children's Rights: Tendencies, Tensions, Constraints' in Helen Stalford et al. (eds.) *Rewriting Children's Rights Judgments* (Hart 2017) 17–52.

The analysis is not free from methodological limitations and conceptual problems, and two of these are worth mentioning. First, the analysis presents a summary of the Committee's work, which, for convenience, I refer to as 'jurisprudence'. To some extent, the analysis does not sufficiently account for changes in the Committee's jurisprudence over the years, and especially since 2013, as it moves between presenting a changing narrative to the current position on certain issues. Second, the analysis might not present all the nuances of the Committee's jurisprudence and, in some circumstances, it might take a specific comment out of context (usually when the facts surrounding a certain comment, which was made at a specific time and place, are not mentioned). As the aim of this analysis is not to provide a historical overview of the Committee's jurisprudence, but rather to understand its position, the analysis is presented mostly in summary form, rather than as an evolving narrative. But, where relevant, the analysis addresses changes and trends in the Committee's interpretation.

The Committee, in its first 20 years of operation, reflected and perpetuated the dominant conception of children as 'human becomings' and has struggled, at least until recently, with thinking about children as 'human beings'. In doing so, I argue, the Committee seems to subjugate many of the Convention's rights to the promotion of 'full' or 'optimum' development for children, but without saying much about the meaning of this objective, or about the meaning of child development, or how the distinct right to development might be interpreted. From 2013 onwards, a slow shift can be identified. The Committee began to show more respect for children's agency, and it acknowledged that the right to development should be addressed independently of other rights and separately from the objective of promoting the child's development. But thus far the Committee has not provided a concrete interpretation of this right, essentially enabling States Parties to develop their own understanding of it – and, in practice, enabling duty bearers to ignore their commitment to protecting and promoting this right.

The Committee's Reporting Guidelines and the Right to Development

It is to be expected that there will be many references to the right to development in the Committee's jurisprudence – not only because this is one of the rights under the Convention, but also because the Committee itself has been asking States Parties to report about it, and about child development-related issues, in its reporting guidelines. This sort of request can be found as early as the first guidelines for reporting, which were published in 1991.[4] In these initial reporting guidelines, States Parties are asked to report about Article 6 and the right to life, survival, and development as part of their report concerning the 'general principles' of the Convention. Additional information concerning Article 6 (2) and the right to survival and development was requested in the context of information about 'basic health and welfare'. In the 2005 revised guidelines, which seek to frame the implementation of the Convention as a 'holistic' process that conceptualises children's rights as 'indivisible and interrelated',[5] the request to report about the right to development is featured in the context of the general principles of the Convention, as well as in the contexts of children's basic health and welfare.

Nonetheless, a closer look at the guidelines shows that the Committee's request for information about Article 6 focuses on the right to life and to a limited extent on the right to survival (for example, by asking for data about the death penalty and suicide rates among children),[6] while no specific requests for information about child development are made. Another revision of the guidelines from 2010 saw no significant changes in that regard. Information concerning the right to life continued to dominate Article 6, and the only new addition in this space was the request to address early childhood development in the context of education and 'general measures of implementation'.[7] The most recent guidelines from 2015 include the same requests with respect to the realisation of the right to education.[8] Requests for further information about child

---

[4] UNCRC, 'General Guidelines Regarding the Form and Content of Initial Reports to Be Submitted by States Parties under Article 44, Paragraph (1) (a), of the Convention' (30 October 1991) UN Doc. CRC/C/5; UNCRC, 'General Guidelines Regarding the Form and Content of Periodic Reports to Be Submitted by States Parties under Article 44, Paragraph (1) (b), of the Convention' (29 November 2005) UN Doc. CRC/C/58/Rev.1 (Revised Guidelines); UNCRC, 'Treaty-Specific Guidelines Regarding the Form and Content of Periodic Reports to Be Submitted by States Parties under Article 44, Paragraph 1 (b), of the Convention on the Rights of the Child' (25 November 2010) UN Doc. CRC/C/58/Rev.2 (2010 Guidelines); UNCRC, 'Treaty-Specific Guidelines Regarding the Form and Content of Periodic Reports to be Submitted by States Parties under Article 44, paragraph 1 (b), of the Convention on the Rights of the Child' (3 March 2015) UN Doc. CRC/C/58/Rev.3 (2015 Guidelines).

[5] UNCRC 2005, Revised Guidelines, *supra* n. 4, para. 3.   [6] *Ibid.*, para. 23.

[7] UNCRC, 2010 Guidelines, *supra* n. 4, paras. 3 and 22.

[8] UNCRC, 2015 Guidelines, *supra* n. 4.

development can be found in the context of the other four Articles that mention child development, namely Articles 18, 23, 27, and 32, as well as in other contexts where the Committee thinks that child development might be an issue of concern – for example, when reporting about basic health (Article 24) and, again, welfare-related issues.[9] The guidelines, including their most recent version, give the impression that the Committee prioritises the care for child development over the right to development. The qualification of the latter as a right under the Convention, or as a guiding principle of the Convention, carries, in that sense, very little weight. One immediate implication of these guidelines is that States Parties are not expected to specifically address the status of the right to development in their jurisdiction. This, in turn, can lead to very little information about this right being provided to the Committee, which curtails its ability to effectively monitor the protection provided for this right, and, on a different level, limits its ability to develop meaningful jurisprudence about it.

The Committee's Perspectives on the Right to Development

The right to development – or Article 6(2) – was not mentioned[10] in any of the first Concluding Observations published in 1993–1994. Child development was only rarely referenced, mostly with regard to unsupervised births, which can put the child's life at risk,[11] or addressing the impact on children of insufficient nutritious food.[12] In the following years, the Committee's scope significantly expanded in two ways. First, a linkage was established between most of the Convention's rights and child development, exceeding the five Articles that explicitly mention

---

[9] *Ibid.*, para. 36.

[10] See, for example: UNCRC, 'Concluding Observations: Sweden' (18 February 1993) UN Doc. CRC/C/15/Add.2; UNCRC, 'Concluding Observations: Viet Nam' (18 February 1993) UN Doc. CRC/C/15/Add.3; UNCRC, 'Concluding Observations: Russian Federation' (18 February 1993) UN Doc. CRC/C/15/Add.4; UNCRC, 'Concluding Observations: Egypt' (18 February 1993) UN Doc. CRC/C/15/Add.5; UNCRC, 'Concluding Observations: Sudan' (18 October 1993) UN Doc. CRC/C/15/Add.10; UNCRC, 'Concluding Observations: France' (25 April 1994) UN Doc. CRC/C/15/Add.20; UNCRC, 'Concluding Observations: Honduras' (24 October 1994) UN Doc. CRC/C/15/Add.24; UNCRC, 'Concluding Observations: Indonesia' (24 October 1994) UN Doc. CRC/C/15/Add.25.

[11] UNCRC, 'Concluding Observations: Bolivia' (18 February 1993) UN Doc. CRC/C/15/Add.1, para. 10.

[12] UNCRC, 'Concluding Observations: Honduras' (1994), *supra* n. 10, para. 15.

child development. Second, the right to development was mentioned as a distinct right of children that ought to be protected.

Nondiscrimination

Article 2 of the Convention protects the right to nondiscrimination, and, like Article 6, is one of the Convention's four guiding principles.[13] Neither the text of this article, nor its drafting history 2[14] suggests a connection between the right to nondiscrimination and child development or to the right to development. Nevertheless, since 2000, the Committee has made such a connection, concluding that a violation of the right to nondiscrimination undermines child development and the right to development as well.

The Committee concludes that discrimination leads to 'harassments'[15] and 'racial hatred and xenophobia',[16] and that discriminatory practices deny children access to public services – especially housing, health services, and education.[17] This, in turn, deprives children of the necessary support for their physical, mental, and moral development, as well as for their personal talent. On many occasions, the Committee suggests that discrimination has a negative effect on child development[18] and that it constitutes a violation of children's right to survival and development.[19]

---

[13] UNCRC, 'General Comment No. 5', *supra* n. 2.

[14] See Chapter 2; also see UNHCHR, *Legislative History of the Convention on the Rights of the Child* – Volume 1 (United Nations, New York and Geneva 2007) 314–334.

[15] UNCRC, 'Concluding Observations: Croatia' (3 November 2004) UN Doc. CRC/C/15/Add.243, para. 21.

[16] UNCRC, 'Concluding Observations: Germany' (26 February 2004) UN Doc. CRC/C/15/Add.226, para. 23.

[17] UNCRC, 'Concluding Observations: Canada' (20 June 1995) UN Doc. CRC/C/15/Add.37, para. 17; UNCRC, 'Concluding Observations: Senegal' (27 November 1995) UN Doc. CRC/C/15/Add.44, para. 12; UNCRC, 'Concluding Observations: Czech Republic' (27 October 1997) UN Doc. CRC/C/15/Add.81, para. 15.

[18] For example, UNCRC, 'Concluding Observations: Sierra Leone' (24 February 2000) UN Doc. CRC/C/15/Add.116, para. 40; UNCRC, 'Concluding Observations: Croatia' (2004), *supra* n. 15, para. 21; UNCRC, 'Concluding Observations: Germany' (2004), *supra* n. 16, para. 23; UNCRC, 'Concluding Observations: France' (30 June 2004) UN Doc. CRC/C/15/Add.240, para. 16.

[19] For example, UNCRC, 'Concluding Observations: Burundi' (16 October 2000) UN Doc. CRC/C/15/Add.133, para. 77; UNCRC, 'Concluding Observations: Cameroon' (6 November 2001) UN Doc. CRC/C/15/Add.164, para. 69; UNCRC, 'Concluding Observations: Sudan' (9 October 2002) UN Doc. CRC/C/15/Add.190, para. 46; UNCRC, 'Concluding Observations: Bangladesh' (18 June 1997) UN Doc. CRC/15/C/Add.74, para. 79; UNCRC, 'Concluding Observations: India' (26 February 2004) UN Doc. CRC/C/15/

Elimination of discrimination is, therefore, essential in ensuring the realisation of the right to development.

The Committee gives special attention to vulnerable groups of children who are often subject to social practices and/or political policies of discrimination, including girls,[20] children of ethnic minorities,[21] aboriginal[22] and indigenous children,[23] children born out of wedlock,[24] children from lower-income groups, rural children, child refugees, working children, displaced children,[25] children in street situations,[26] child

---

Add.228, para. 81; UNCRC, 'Concluding Observations: Myanmar' (30 June 2004) UN Doc. CRC/C/15/Add.237, para. 79; UNCRC, 'Concluding Observations: Rwanda' (1 July 2004) UN Doc. CRC/C/15/Add.234, para. 75; UNCRC, 'Concluding Observations: Yemen' (21 September 2005) UN Doc. CRC/C/15/Add.267, para. 81.

[20] UNCRC, 'Concluding Observations: Sri Lanka' (21 June 1995) UN Doc. CRC/C/15/Add.40, para. 12; UNCRC, 'Concluding Observations: Senegal' (1995) supra n. 17, para. 12; UNCRC, 'Concluding Observations: Angola' (11 October 2010) UN Doc. CRC/C/CO/2-4, paras. 53–54; UNCRC, 'Concluding Observations: Brunei Darussalam' (24 February 2016) UN Doc. CRC/C/BRN/CO/2-3, para. 25; UNCRC, 'Concluding Observations: Peru' (2 March 2016) UN Doc. CRC/C/PER/CO/4-5, para. 27.

[21] UNCRC, 'Concluding Observations: United Kingdom' (15 February 1995) UN Doc. CRC/C/15/Add.34, para. 13; UNCRC, 'Concluding Observations: Czech Republic' (1997), supra n. 17, para. 15; UNCRC, 'Concluding Observations: Bangladesh' (1997), supra n. 19, para. 15; UNCRC, 'Concluding Observations: Cameroon' (2001), supra n. 19, para. 69; UNCRC, 'Concluding Observations: Bangladesh' (27 July 2003) UN Doc. CRC/C/15/Add.221, para. 79; UNCRC, 'Concluding Observations: India' (2004), supra n. 19, para. 81; UNCRC, 'Concluding Observations: Republic of Serbia' (20 June 2008) UN Doc. CRC/C/SRB/CO/1, para. 75; UNCRC, 'Concluding Observations: Brunei Darussalam' (2016), supra n. 20, para. 25.

[22] UNCRC, 'Concluding Observations: Canada' (1995), supra n. 17, para. 17.

[23] UNCRC, 'General Comment No. 11 (2009): Indigenous Children and Their Rights under the Convention' (12 February 2009) UN Doc. CRC/C/GC/11; UNCRC, 'Concluding Observations: Burundi' (1 October 2010) UN Doc. CRC/C/BDI/CO/2, paras. 78–79; UNCRC, 'Concluding Observations: Guatemala' (1 October 2010) UN Doc. CRC/C/GTM/CO/3-4, para. 101; UNCRC, 'Concluding Observations: Peru' (2016), supra n. 20, para. 27.

[24] UNCRC, 'Concluding Observations: Sri Lanka' (1995), supra n. 20, para. 12; UNCRC, 'Concluding Observations: Senegal' (1995), supra n. 17, para. 12; UNCRC, 'Concluding Observations: Bangladesh' (1997), supra n. 19, para. 15.

[25] UNCRC, 'Concluding Observations: Sri Lanka' (1995), supra n. 20, para. 12; UNCRC, 'Concluding Observations: Myanmar' (2004), supra n. 19, para. 79; UNCRC, 'Concluding Observations: India' (2004), supra n. 19, para. 81; UNCRC, 'Concluding Observations: Rwanda' (2004), supra n. 19, para. 75; UNCRC, 'Concluding Observations: Yemen' (2005), supra n. 19, para. 81; UNCRC, 'Concluding Observations: Brunei Darussalam' (2016) supra n. 20, para. 25; UNCRC, 'Concluding Observations: Kenya' (21 March 2016) UN Doc. CRC/C/KEN/CO/3-5, para. 21.

[26] UNCRC, 'General Comment No. 21 (2017) on Children in Street Situations' (21 June 2017) UN Doc. UNCRC/C/GC/21; UNCRC, 'Concluding Observations: Pakistan' (11 July

victims of sexual exploitation,[27] children in the context of migration,[28] and stateless children.[29]

Specific attention is given to discrimination against three groups of children: girls (as well as gender-based discrimination more broadly), children with disabilities, and indigenous children. With respect to gender-based discrimination, the Committee highlights the younger marriage age for girls compared to boys as a practice that has a negative impact on the 'health, education and social development' of girls.[30] Pregnancy of young girls is also flagged as a risk factor for their development (this issue will be further discussed below),[31] as is domestic labour.[32]

As to children with disabilities, the Committee identifies some specific practices – including mistreatment and inadequate diagnostic systems,[33] as well as discrimination, that result in a lack of, or insufficient access to, health services, schools,[34] education programs,[35] and other facilities and

2016) UN Doc. CRC/C/PAK/CO/5, para. 74; UNCRC, 'Concluding Observations: Peru' (2016), *supra* n. 20, para. 68.

[27] UNCRC, 'Concluding Observations: Bangladesh' (1997), *supra* n. 19, para. 15.

[28] UNCMW and UNCRC, 'Joint General Comment No. 3 (2017) of the Committee on the Protection of the Rights of All Migrant Workers and Members of Their Families and No. 22 (2017) of the Committee on the Rights of the Child on the General Principles Regarding the Human Rights of Children in the Context of International Migration' (16 November 2017) UN Docs. CMW/C/GC/3–CRC/C/GC/22; UNCMW and UNCRC, 'Joint General Comment No. 4 (2017) of the Committee on the Protection of the Rights of All Migrant Workers and Members of Their Families and No. 23 (2017) of the Committee on the Rights of the Child on State Obligations Regarding the Human Rights of Children in the Context of International Migration in Countries of Origin, Transit, Destination and Return' (16 November 2017) UN Docs. CMW/C/GC/4-CRC/C/GC/23.

[29] UNCRC, 'Concluding Observations: Thailand' (17 March 2006) UN Doc. CRC/C/THA/CO/2, para. 33; UNCRC, 'Concluding Observations: Dominican Republic' (11 February 2008) UN Doc. CRC/C/DOM/CO/2, para. 77.

[30] For example, see UNCRC, 'Concluding Observations: Nicaragua' (20 June 1995) UN Doc. CRC/C/15/Add.36, para. 13; UNCRC, 'Concluding Observations: India' (2004), *supra* n. 19, para. 60.

[31] UNCRC, 'Concluding Observations: Holy See' (25 February 2014) UN Doc. CRC/C/VAT/CO/2, para. 57; UNCRC, 'Concluding Observations: Democratic Republic of Congo' (28 February 2017) UN Doc. CRC/C/COD/CO/3–5, para. 36.

[32] UNCRC, 'Concluding Observations: Democratic Republic of Congo' (2017), *supra* n. 31, para. 42.

[33] UNCRC, 'Concluding Observations: Russian Federation' (10 November 1999) UN Doc. CRC/C/15/Add.110, para. 40.

[34] UNCRC, 'Concluding Observations: Estonia' (17 March 2003) UN Doc. CRC/C/15/Add.196, para. 39.

[35] UNCRC, 'Concluding Observations: Sudan' (2002), *supra* n. 19, para. 46; UNCRC, 'Concluding Observations: Estonia' (2003), *supra* n. 34; UNCRC, 'Concluding

programs that meet their needs[36] – as having a negative effect on their 'development' in general,[37] and on their cultural development in particular.[38]

In General Comment No. 9,[39] the Committee emphasises that social discrimination and stigmatisation lead to the 'marginalisation and exclusion' of children with disabilities, which 'may even threaten their survival and development if it goes as far as physical or mental violence'.[40] The Committee further adds that the 'spiritual, emotional and cultural development and well-being of children with disabilities are very often overlooked',[41] and therefore suggests establishing 'programmes and activities designed for the child's cultural development and spiritual well-being'.[42] However, only towards the end of the General Comment does the Committee mention the right to development, stating that discrimination against children with disabilities not only poses a risk to their development, but can also result in the violation of numerous rights – including the right to development.[43] As to the objective of child development, the Committee makes a connection between the care for the development of

Observations: India' (2004), *supra* n. 19, para. 81; UNCRC, 'Concluding Observations: Republic of Congo' (20 October 2006) UN Doc. CRC/C/COG/CO/1, para. 56; UNCRC, 'Concluding Observations: Latvia' (28 June 2006) UN Doc. CRC/C/LTC/CO/2, para. 40; UNCRC, 'Concluding Observations: Uruguay' (5 July 2007) UN Doc. CRC/C/URY/CO/2, para. 48; UNCRC, 'Concluding Observations: Republic of Serbia' (2008), *supra* n. 21, para. 75. A recent study has found that in schools, children with disabilities are more likely to be victims of violence than are pupils who are not disabled. Lisa Jones et al., 'Prevalence and Risk of Violence against Children with Disabilities: A Systematic Review and Meta-analysis of Observational Studies' (2012) 380 *Lancet* 899–907.

[36] UNCRC, 'Concluding Observations: Djibouti' (28 June 2000) UN Doc. CRC/C/15/Add.131, para. 39; UNCRC, 'Concluding Observations: Comoros' (23 October 2000) UN Doc. CRC/C/15/Add.141, para. 37.

[37] UNCRC, 'Concluding Observations: New Zealand' (24 January 1997) UN Doc. CRC/C/15/Add.71, para. 5; UNCRC, 'Concluding Observations: Russian Federation' (1999), *supra* n. 33, para. 40; UNCRC, 'Concluding Observations: Djibouti' (2000), *supra* n. 36, para. 39; UNCRC, 'Concluding Observations: Comoros' (2000), *supra* n. 36, para. 37; UNCRC, 'Concluding Observations: Sudan' (2002), *supra* n. 19, para. 46; UNCRC, 'Concluding Observations: Estonia' (2003), *supra* n. 34, para. 39; UNCRC, 'Concluding Observations: Congo' (2006), *supra* n. 35, para. 56; UNCRC, 'Concluding Observations: Latvia' (2006), *supra* n. 35, para. 40.

[38] UNCRC, 'Concluding Observations: Uruguay' (2007), *supra* n. 35, para. 48.

[39] UNCRC, 'General Comment No. 9 (2006): The Rights of Children with Disabilities' (27 February 2007) UN Doc. CRC/C/GC/9.

[40] *Ibid.*, para. 8.   [41] *Ibid.*, para. 33.

[42] *Ibid.* See also UNCRC, 'Concluding Observations: Belgium' (18 June 2010) UN Doc. CRC/C/BEL/CO/3–4, para. 45.

[43] UNCRC, 'General Comment No. 9', *supra* n. 39, para. 32.

children with disabilities and the ability of these children to maximise their potential,[44] as well as their inclusion in society[45] and their 'enjoyment of a full and decent life and participation in the community'.[46] The care for these children's future development provides some qualitative description.

The third group of children mentioned in the Committee's work is indigenous children. General Comment No. 11 provides a comprehensive discussion about the rights of these children.[47] Similar recommendations are then repeated in Concluding Observations about countries with indigenous children, such as Canada, New Zealand, and Australia. At the outset, General Comment No. 11 makes the same remarks concerning discrimination and its impact on child development that have previously been made with respect to other marginalised groups of children.[48] But the novelty of this General Comment is the explicit references to the right to development that it makes. For example, the Committee expresses its concern that due to the particular vulnerability of indigenous children and the high level of poverty among them, discrimination could impact not only their 'survival and development', but also their right to an adequate standard of living.[49] Following Article 30 of the Convention, which protects the identity rights of indigenous children and children belonging to linguistic, religious, or cultural minorities, the Committee emphasises the need to protect the traditions and cultures of these children, 'particularly with reference to the protection and harmonious development of the child'.[50] In this context, the Committee adds that in cases where the child's community 'retain[s] a traditional lifestyle, the use of traditional land is of significant importance to their development and enjoyment of culture'.[51] Therefore, States Parties should guarantee that their policies concerning culture and land ensure 'children's right to life, survival and development to the maximum extent possible'.[52]

---

[44] UNCRC, 'Concluding Observations: New Zealand' (1997), *supra* n. 37, para. 5.

[45] UNCRC, 'Concluding Observations: Russian Federation' (1999), *supra* n. 33, para. 40; UNCRC, 'Concluding Observations: Djibouti' (2000), *supra* n. 36, para. 39; UNCRC, 'Concluding Observations: Comoros' (2000), *supra* n. 36, para. 37; UNCRC, 'Concluding Observations: Estonia' (2003), *supra* n. 34, para. 39; UNCRC, 'Concluding Observations: Latvia' (2006), *supra* n. 35, para. 40.

[46] UNCRC, 'Concluding Observations: Congo' (2006), *supra* n. 35, para. 56.

[47] UNCRC, 'General Comment No. 11', *supra* n. 23.   [48] *Ibid.*, para. 22.

[49] *Ibid.*, para. 34.   [50] *Ibid.*, para. 35.   [51] *Ibid.*   [52] *Ibid.*

It therefore seems that protecting the right to nondiscrimination is a precondition for realising child development and the right to development. In other words, protecting the right to nondiscrimination will enable children to have greater access to public goods and services. That, in turn, will promote their right to development. Protecting children's right to nondiscrimination also protects their human dignity, which facilitates the development of their personality. Conversely, disrespecting that right undermines children's personal development.

Birth Registration

Article 7 of the Convention concerns the right of every child to acquire a nationality, to be registered immediately after birth, and to have a name. While the Article does not connect these rights with the right to development, the Committee establishes such a relationship. It determines that having a birth certificate is a precondition for the realisation of the right to development, for two reasons. First, the absence of a national birth registration scheme has a negative impact on a child's identity. Second – and similar to the logic that guides the Committee's analysis of the right to nondiscrimination – without being registered at birth, children may be denied 'entitlements to basic health, education and social welfare'.[53] Therefore, as 'a first step in ensuring the rights to survival, development and access to quality services for all children (Art. 6), the Committee recommends that States Parties take all necessary measures to ensure that all children are registered at birth'[54] – especially among groups with below-average registration rates, such as minority children and those who live in rural areas.[55]

The connections between the child's knowledge about her origins and child development, and between the importance of access to education and health and development, add another dimension to the Committee's conception of child development. It seems that the Committee is concerned with the child's sense of self, and that it holds the view that education and health are important for child development. In this

[53] UNCRC, 'General Comment No. 11 (2009)', *supra* n. 23, para. 35.
[54] UNCRC, 'General Comment No. 7 (2005): Implementing Child Rights in Early Childhood' (20 September 2006) UN Doc. CRC/C/GC/7/Rev.1, para. 25.
[55] UNCRC, 'Concluding Observations: Fiji' (13 October 2014) UN Doc. CRC/C/FJI/CO/2-4, paras. 25–26; UNCRC, 'Concluding Observations: Ethiopia' (3 June 2015) UN Doc. CRC/C/ETH/CO/4–5, paras. 33–34.

context, however, the Committee does not make any distinction between measures that support child development and those that support the right to development in itself.

The Child's Family

The Convention reflects and enforces a Western model of the nuclear family by providing wide-ranging protection for the child's right to grow up in a household headed by two parents,[56] both of whom share the responsibility for their child's development.[57] In its discussions about parental responsibilities and child development, the Committee focuses on two issues: family structure and child-rearing.

When discussing events that preclude children from being raised by their two parents – such as death, natural disasters, armed conflicts, or the imprisonment of one parent – the Committee has emphasised the negative influence that such family structures will have on child development. Rapid references have been made to the negative impact that 'single parenthood'[58] and 'early parenthood' have on child development.[59] One household composition that the Committee is concerned about is polygamy.[60] It asks States Parties to 'undertake an in-depth and comprehensive study on impact of polygamy in order to find out whether polygamy has negative consequences on the upbringing and development of children'.[61] Notably, a distinction should be drawn between

---

[56] Articles 3, 5, 7, 9, 10, 14, 19, 21, 22, 23, 27, 29, and 40. See, for example, Article 9(3): 'States Parties shall respect the right of the child who is separated from one or both parents to maintain personal relations and direct contact with both parents . . .'; Article 18: 'States Parties shall use their best efforts to ensure recognition of the principle that both parents . . .'

[57] Article 18. But see a recent comment that might signal a change in this space: UNCRC, 'Concluding Observations: Slovakia' (20 July 2016) UN Doc. CRC/C/SVK/CO/3-5, para. 32.

[58] UNCRC, 'Concluding Observations: Spain' (24 October 1994) UN Doc. CRC/C/15/Add.28, para. 21; UNCRC, 'Concluding Observations: Barbados' (24 August 1999) UN Doc. CRC/C/15/Add.103, para. 20; see also UNCRC, 'Concluding Observations: Tajikistan' (5 February 2010) UN Doc. CRC/C/TJK/CO/2, para. 43.

[59] UNCRC, 'Concluding Observations: Spain' (1994), *supra n.* 58; UNCRC, 'Concluding Observations: Barbados' (1999), *supra n.* 58; UNCRC, 'Concluding Observations: Tajikistan' (2010), *supra n.* 58.

[60] UNCRC, 'Concluding Observations: Gabon' (8 July 2016) UN Doc. CRC/C/GAB/CO/2, para. 40.

[61] UNCRC, 'Concluding Observations: Djibouti' (7 October 2008) UN Doc. CRC/C/DJI/CO/2, para. 40.

household composition (in the case of single parenthood) and allegedly insufficient parental capacity (in the case of early parenthood), and their potential impact on child development, but it seems that the Committee does not do this.

The Committee rarely address the situation where, following parental separation, children grow up in two single-parent households. It is satisfied by saying that this situation 'can have a negative impact on [children's] harmonious development'.[62] Therefore, in cases of separation, States Parties need to assist 'both parents in the performance of their child-rearing responsibilities'.[63] The Committee also ignores the relationship between child development and children who are being brought up in non-Western family structures or in different kinship arrangements[64] – for example, children who are raised by members of their extended families, and not by their parents. This omission is rather surprising, given the Committee's own terms, which suggest the likelihood that these kinds of family structures affect child development.

Other questions that should be asked in light of the Committee's comments concerning the relationship between early parenthood, parental capacity and child development are questions about 'late parenthood' or a 'maximum' age (as opposed to a 'minimum' age) at which a person should become a parent. While it is easier to criticise the non-Western practice of 'early parenthood', it is more challenging and less politically convenient to have a discussion about the increasing number of adults in Europe and elsewhere who, with the help of reproduction technology, have children in the later stages of life. 'Late parenting' is socially acceptable. This acceptance is often seen as respecting people's autonomy, and as a reflection of much-welcomed changes in women's positionality in society – including in the labour market. But, from a children's rights point of view – and if parental age and parental capacity, and their influence on child development, are topics worth asking about – then a discussion about the ideal time frame during which adults should

---

[62] UNCRC, 'Concluding Observations: Paraguay' (6 November 2001) UN Doc. CRC/C/15/Add.166, para. 33.

[63] UNCRC, 'Concluding Observations: Spain' (1994), *supra* n. 58, para. 21; UNCRC, 'Concluding Observations: Czech Republic' (18 March 2003) UN Doc. CRC/C/15/Add.201, para. 42; UNCRC, 'Concluding Observations: Equatorial Guinea' (3 November 2004) UN Doc. CRC/C/15/Add.245, para. 41; UNCRC, 'Concluding Observations: Paraguay' (10 February 2010) UN Doc. CRC/C/PRY/CO/3, para. 30.

[64] General Comment No. 7 being the exception. See the discussion later in this chapter about early childhood development.

become parents is one worth having. The implication of not asking this question is that children who are born to people in a relatively later stage of life do not see their right to development addressed, or protected, by the Committee.

Deprivation of Family Environment and Child Development

A related issue concerns children who are deprived of a stable family environment. Various groupings of children have been identified by the Committee in this regard, including children who are abandoned by their families, children who have one parent or both parents imprisoned or living in other state institutions (such as hospitals), children who are themselves imprisoned or hospitalised, children who live in prison with their imprisoned parent, unaccompanied children, and children who are outside their country of origin. For all these groups of children, similar concerns have been made with regard to the short- and long-term effects that their family environment, or lack of it, may have on their development.

Abandoned children: This category includes children who find themselves deprived of a family environment for a variety of reasons – for example, the collapse of the nuclear family, immigration, or being runaway children (the last category overlaps with the question of children in street situations, which will be discussed later in the chapter). The Committee says that States Parties have a general duty to care for these children, including taking 'all available measures to establish alternative care centres' and monitoring and evaluating the progress of these children in order to ensure their 'adequate development'.[65]

Children who live in prison with their imprisoned parents: The Committee makes a similar recommendation, suggesting that States Parties have a duty to ensure that the living conditions of these children are 'adequate for the child's development'[66] and suitable for the child's 'needs for the harmonious development of his/her

---

[65] UNCRC, 'Concluding Observations: Yemen' (10 May 1999) UN Doc. CRC/C/15/Add.102, para. 23.

[66] UNCRC, 'Concluding Observations: Bolivia' (11 February 2005) UN Doc. CRC/C/15/Add.256, para. 40; UNCRC, 'Concluding Observations: Islamic Republic of Iran' (31 March 2005) UN Doc. CRC/C/15/Add.254, para. 52; UNCRC, 'Concluding Observations: Mexico' (2 June 2006) UN Doc. CRC/C/MEX/CO/3, para. 40; UNCRC, 'Concluding Observations: The Plurinational State of Bolivia' (16 October 2009) UN Doc. CRC/C/BOL/CO/4, para. 65.

personality',[67] and, more comprehensively, that living conditions for children who are in prison with their mothers are 'adequate for the child's physical, mental, moral and social development'.[68] A more specific duty requires States to ensure that these children are not 'deprived of their right to [the] health and education which is appropriate for their physiological and psychological development'.[69] In the case of young children, their living conditions should be 'adequate for the child's early development'.[70] Although children who live with one or both incarcerated parents do maintain a relationship with the parent or parents, the Committee is of the opinion that this physical proximity is not enough and that this form of living can have negative consequences on child development. Therefore, States Parties should establish institutional alternatives, such as foster families, as an alternative to sending these children to live in prison.[71] This kind of mechanism needs a placement process, which should also support child development.[72]

Imprisoned children and children who live in other institutions: States Parties have the duty to take 'into account the state of development' of any children deprived of their liberty because they are either imprisoned or held in a detention centre due to their civil status (migration, statelessness, or asylum-seeking),[73] and to ensure that the 'adequate development' of these children is constantly monitored and evaluated.[74] The conditions at detention centres should meet children's mental and physical health needs and should accommodate

---

[67] UNCRC, 'Concluding Observations: Nepal' (21 September 2005) UN Doc. CRC/C/15/Add.261, para. 52.

[68] UNCRC, 'Concluding Observations: Republic of Moldova' (20 October 2017) UN Doc. CRC/C/MDA/CO/4–5, para. 27.

[69] UNCRC, 'Concluding Observations: Burundi' (2010), *supra* n. 23, para. 62.

[70] UNCRC, 'Concluding Observations: Philippines' (21 September 2005) UN Doc. CRC/C/15/Add.259, para. 54.

[71] UNCRC, 'Concluding Observations: Bolivia' (26 October 1998) UN Doc. CRC/C/15/Add.95, para. 23; UNCRC, 'Concluding Observations: Bolivia' (2005), *supra* n. 66, para. 40.

[72] UNCRC, 'Concluding Observations: Lebanon' (8 June 2006) UN Doc. CRC/C/LBN/CO/2, para. 44.

[73] UNCRC, 'Concluding Observations: Austria' (January 2005) UN Doc. CRC/C/15/Add.251, para 48.

[74] UNCRC, 'Concluding Observations: Nicaragua' (24 August 1999) UN Doc. CRC/C/15/Add.108, para. 31; UNCRC, 'Concluding Observations: Zimbabwe' (7 March 2016) UN Doc. CRC/C/ZWE/CO/2, para. 55.

their 'overall development'.[75] But the better solution for these children is developing alternative institutional care, which should be designed and operated in a way that promotes the child's 'harmonious development and preparation for responsible participation in society'.[76]

Children who are imprisoned for their own crimes: The Committee divides the care for these children's development into two categories: their development while in prison, and their development upon release. In light of Articles 37 and 40 of the Convention, the Committee dedicates significant attention to the rights of imprisoned children,[77] including General Comment No. 10 (2007),[78] but does not say much about their right to development.

Health issues – including 'developmental, mental and reproductive health concerns and substance abuse'[79] – previously gained most of the attention in the context of discussing the rights of incarcerated juveniles, but in more recent times the Committee suggests that States Parties are under a duty to ensure 'that conditions in detention facilities are not contrary to the child's development'.[80] In addition, imprisoned children should receive educational opportunities that will 'remove any barriers to their positive development',[81] as well as support – including for their 'full development'.[82] These kinds of programs ought also to be available to

---

[75] UNCRC, 'Concluding Observations: Australia' (20 October 2005) UN Doc. CRC/C/15/Add.268, para. 62.

[76] UNCRC, 'Concluding Observations: Uruguay' (30 October 1996) UN Doc. CRC/C/15/Add.62, para. 23.

[77] See, for example, UNCRC, 'Concluding Observations: Madagascar' (24 October 1994) UN Doc. CRC/C/15/Add.26, para. 22; UNCRC, 'Concluding Observations: Philippines' (15 February 1995) UN Doc. CRC/C/15/Add.29, para. 8; UNCRC, 'Concluding Observations: Jamaica' (15 February 1995) UN Doc. CRC/C/15/Add.32, para. 17; UNCRC, 'Concluding Observations: Honduras' (24 August 1999) UN Doc. CRC/C/15/Add.105, para. 35.

[78] UNCRC, 'General Comment No. 10 (2007): Children's Rights in Juvenile Justice' (25 April 2007) UN Doc. CRC/C/GC/10.

[79] UNCRC, 'Concluding Observations: Burkina Faso' (9 October 2002) UN Doc. CRC/C/15/Add.193, para. 40.

[80] UNCRC, 'Concluding Observations: Venezuela' (5 October 2007) UN Doc. CRC/C/VEN/CO/2, para. 77; UNCRC, 'Concluding Observations: Sierra Leone' (20 June 2008) UN Doc. CRC/C/SLE/CO/2, para. 77; UNCRC, 'Concluding Observations: Chad' (12 February 2009) UN Doc. CRC/C/TCD/CO/2, para. 86; UNCRC, 'Concluding Observations: Argentina' (11 June 2010) UN Doc. CRC/C/ARG/CO/3-4, para. 79.

[81] UNCRC, 'Concluding Observations: Denmark' (26 October 2017) UN Doc. CRC/C/DNK/CO/5, para. 27.

[82] UNCRC, 'Concluding Observations: China' (24 November 2005) UN Doc. CRC/C/CHN/CO/2, para. 93; UNCRC, 'Concluding Observations: Mongolia' (21 September 2005) UN

children upon their release from prison.[83] In General Comment No. 10, the Committee emphasises that 'one of the most important goals of the implementation of the CRC is to promote the full and harmonious development of the child's personality, talent, and mental and physical abilities',[84] adding that 'it goes without saying that delinquency has a very negative impact on the child's development'.[85] Recognising the importance of development, the Committee asks that policies responding to juvenile delinquency be designed in 'ways that support the child's development'.[86] In particular, and on the basis of Article 37(a), States Parties should consider the 'very negative consequences for the child's harmonious development' that imprisonment brings.[87]

Unaccompanied children and children who are outside their country of origin: The Committee's recommendations concerning the development of children in this category are similar to those we previously saw with respect to this category of children. In General Comment No. 6 (2005), the Committee determined that separated and unaccompanied children are 'vulnerable to various risks that affect their life, survival and development, such as trafficking for purposes of sexual or other exploitation or involvement in criminal activities which could result in harm to the child, or in extreme cases, in death. Accordingly, Article 6 necessitates vigilance by States parties in this regard, particularly when organized crime may be involved'.[88]

The Committee further suggests that States Parties should take 'practical measures' in order to 'protect children from the risks',[89] while taking into account their 'state of development'.[90] These measures should include, among other things, care for their accommodations[91] and an

---

Doc. CRC/C/15/Add.264, para. 68; UNCRC, 'Concluding Observations: Jordan' (29 September 2006) UN Doc. CRC/C/JOR/CO/3, para. 95; UNCRC, 'Concluding Observations: Kenya' (19 June 2007) UN Doc. CRC/C/KEN/CO/2, para. 68.

[83] UNCRC, 'Concluding Observations: China' (2005), *supra* n. 82; UNCRC, 'Concluding Observations: Mongolia' (2005), *supra* n. 82; UNCRC, 'Concluding Observations: Jordan' (2006), *supra* n. 82; UNCRC, 'Concluding Observations: Kenya' (2007), *supra* n. 82, para. 68.

[84] UNCRC, 'General Comment No. 10', *supra* n. 78, para. 16.   [85] *Ibid.*, para. 11.

[86] *Ibid.*   [87] *Ibid.*

[88] UNCRC, 'General Comment No. 6 (2005): Treatment of Unaccompanied and Separated Children Outside Their Country of Origin' (1 September 2005) UN Doc. CRC/GC/2005/6, para. 23.

[89] *Ibid*, para. 24.

[90] UNCRC, 'Concluding Observations: Austria' (2005), *supra* n. 73, para. 48.

[91] *Ibid*, para. 40.

adequate standard of living to ensure their 'physical, mental, spiritual and moral development'.[92] More recently, the Committee has updated its approach. Together with the Committee on the Protection of the Rights of All Migrant Workers and Members of Their Families, it has published two General Comments (Nos. 22 and 23) about the rights of children in the context of international migration.[93] Article 6, along with the right to development, receives unprecedented attention in General Comment No. 22. The discussion about Article 6 begins with an acknowledgement of the many challenges that migration poses to children's lives, survival, and development. In an explicit reference to the right to development, the General Comment notes:

> While migration can provide opportunities to improve living conditions and escape from abuses, migration processes can pose risks, including physical harm, psychological trauma, marginalization, discrimination, xenophobia and sexual and economic exploitation, family separation, immigration raids and detention. At the same time, the obstacles children may face in gaining access to education, adequate housing, sufficient safe food and water or health services can negatively affect the physical, mental, spiritual, moral and social development of migrant children and children of migrants.[94]

Due to these diverse risk factors and their potential broad and negative effect on five elements of child development, States Parties are expected to prevent and reduce 'migration-related risks faced by children, which may jeopardize a child's right to life, survival and development'.[95] An obligation to take positive steps arises from reading Article 6 together with Articles 2 and 27, and this includes ensuring that 'children in the context of international migration, regardless of their status or that of their parents, have a standard of living adequate for their physical, mental, spiritual and moral development'.[96]

The Committee is concerned with the impact that migration, which might result in the deprivation of a family environment, has on various aspects of development (physical, psychological, mental, and social) and on the quality of development ('harmonious', 'overall', and 'full'). However, neither these concerns, nor the consequent duties imposed on

---

[92] *Ibid*, para. 44.
[93] UNCMW and UNCRC, 'Joint General Comments No. 3 and No. 22', *supra* n. 28; UNCMW and UNCRC, 'Joint General Comments No. 4 and No. 23', *supra* n. 28.
[94] UNCMW and UNCRC, 'Joint General Comments No. 3 and No. 22', *supra* n. 28, para. 40.
[95] *Ibid.*, para. 42.   [96] *Ibid.*, para. 43.

States Parties, are formulated in terms of caring for the right to development. It is also clear that developmental psychology informs the Committee's position on this subject. While this is not in itself a problem, the difficulty lies with the ways in which this body of knowledge is used to interpret an international treaty. The question that should be asked at this stage is whether the ongoing emphasis on caring for child development, while overlooking the right to development, is the result of a conscious choice or of conceptual, normative and institutional limitations.

Child-Rearing Practices

Another matter that the Committee flags as an issue of concern in the context of children and their families is child-rearing practices and their impact on child development. Until the early 2010s, the Committee upheld traditional views on gender and parental roles, suggesting that the child's mother should be the main caregiver and the child's father should be the breadwinner. Subsequently, fathers are expected to be 'involved enough' in the upbringing of their child.[97] In the exceptional circumstances where mothers work outside the matrimonial home and the child is left at a nursery or in other child care arrangements, States Parties are asked to provide sufficient resources for these arrangements. Otherwise, the child's 'full physical, mental and intellectual development' may not be sufficiently supported.[98]

In accordance with Article 18, States Parties are expected to ensure that parents fulfil their obligations towards their children's development. At the same time, the Committee suggests that States Parties should not interfere with the autonomy of the nuclear family. It expresses concern about the 'excessive degree of State involvement in childcare to the detriment of the parental involvement, hindering psychosocial and cognitive development of children'.[99]

[97] UNCRC, 'Concluding Observations: Barbados' (1999), *supra* n. 58; UNCRC, 'Concluding Observations: Zambia' (2 July 2003) UN Doc. CRC/C/15/Add.206, para. 35; UNCRC, 'Concluding Observations: Nigeria' (13 April 2005) UN Doc. CRC/C/15/Add.257, para. 40. See also UNCRC, 'Concluding Observations: Democratic People's Republic of Korea' (23 October 2017) UN Doc. CRC/C/PRK/CO/5, para. 30.
[98] UNCRC, 'Concluding Observations: Nigeria' (2005), *supra* n. 97; see also UNCRC, 'Concluding Observations: Jamaica' (1995), *supra* n. 77, para. 24.
[99] UNCRC, 'Concluding Observations: Democratic People's Republic of Korea' (1 July 2004) UN Doc. CRC/C/15/Add.239, para. 38.

This attitude towards gender roles has begun to change, and fathers are now encouraged to participate beyond a minimal involvement in their children's lives. For example, States Parties are encouraged to strengthen their 'efforts to promote the common responsibilities of parents and to involve fathers continuously in their children's education and development'.[100] Similarly, General Comment No. 17 (2013) on the right of the child to rest, leisure, play, recreational activities, cultural life and the arts, and General Comment No. 20 (2016) on the implementation of the rights of the child during adolescence, refer to the duties of 'parents' to enable their children to develop in the respected contexts (via play, including cultural activities, music and peer play, or with special attention to the changing needs of children once they approach adulthood, including mental development and development of the personality).[101] The General Comments also establish the duties of States Parties to support 'parents' in these regards, including by providing education and training to parents who might not be aware of these developmental needs of their children.

Two child-rearing practices that the Committee asks States Parties to bring to an end – among other reasons, because of their negative impact on Article 6 rights, including the right to development – are corporal punishment and harmful traditional practices. While Article 19 of the Convention is silent on the relationship between child development and the right to bodily integrity, the Committee concludes time and again that violence has a negative effect on child development.[102] Corporal punishment is only one form of domestic abuse that can be inflicted by parents, siblings, or members of the extended family. Regardless of any 'justifications' that adults might have for this – suggesting, for example, that it is an accepted disciplinary action or a part of cultural or religious practice, or that it causes no harm – the Committee conclusively suggests that corporal punishment is prohibited under Article 19 and that it

---

[100] UNCRC, 'Concluding Observations: Democratic People's Republic of Korea' (2017), *supra* n. 97, para. 30.

[101] UNCRC, 'General Comment No. 17 (2013) on the Right of the Child to Rest, Leisure, Play, Recreational Activities, Cultural Life and the Arts (art. 31)' (17 April 2013) UN Doc. CRC/C/GC/17; UNCRC, 'General Comment No. 20 (2016) on the Implementation of the Rights of the Child during Adolescence' (6 December 2016) UN Doc. CRC/C/GC/20.

[102] UNCRC, 'Concluding Observations: Peru' (22 February 2000) UN Doc. CRC/C/15/Add.120, para. 10; UNCRC, 'Concluding Observations: Russian Federation' (23 November 2005) UN Doc. CRC/C/RUS/CO/3, para. 39.

violates children's right to dignity[103] and hinders their 'optimal development'.[104] It notes that other 'developmental and behavioural consequences' of violence against children include 'school non-attendance
and aggressive, antisocial, self-destructive and interpersonal destructive
behaviours. [These consequences] can lead, inter alia, to deterioration of
relationships, exclusion from school and conflict with the law. There is
also evidence that exposure to violence increases a child's risk of further
victimization and an accumulation of violent experiences, including later
intimate partner violence'.[105] The corresponding duties of States Parties
are clear: they need to outlaw corporal punishment and other forms of
violence against children. Making changes to legislation is not sufficient
to reduce, and eventually eradicate, corporal punishment; other measures
should be taken as well. These include conducting awareness-raising
campaigns[106] that promote 'positive, non-violent forms of discipline
and respect for children's right to human dignity and physical integrity'[107] and that educate the public, especially parents, about the 'negative
effects of corporal punishment on the development of children'.[108]

As for harmful traditional practices, Article 24(3) requires States Parties
to abolish 'traditional practices prejudicial to the health of children'. It fails
to mention the effects that such practices have on child development, or to
identify what those practices are.[109] Over the years, the Committee has
named many practices – including dowries,[110] early marriage,[111] forced

---

[103] UNCRC, 'Concluding Observations: Yemen' (1999), *supra* n. 65, para. 21.
[104] UNCRC, 'General Comment No. 13 (2011): The Right of the Child to Freedom from All
Forms of Violence' (18 April 2011) UN Doc. CRC/C/GC/13.
[105] *Ibid.*
[106] UNCRC, 'Concluding Observations: Vanuatu' (10 November 1999) UN Doc. CRC/C/
15/Add.111, para. 17; UNCRC, 'Concluding Observations: Peru' (2000), *supra* n. 102,
para. 22.
[107] UNCRC, 'Concluding Observations: New Zealand' (27 October 2003) UN Doc. CRC/C/
15/Add.216, para. 30.
[108] UNCRC, 'Concluding Observations: Australia' (2005), *supra* n. 75, para. 40.
[109] Lack of consensus during the drafting process led to the decision not to mention any
specific practice in Article 24. UNHCHR, *Legislative History of the Convention on the
Rights of the Child* – Volume 1, supra n. 14, 580–603. See also Sonia Harris-Short,
'International Human Rights Law: Imperialist, Inept and Ineffective? Cultural Relativism
and the UN Convention on the Rights of the Child' (2003) 25 *Human Rights Quarterly*
130, 136–146.
[110] UNCRC, 'Concluding Observations: Bangladesh' (1997), *supra* n. 19, para. 15.
[111] UNCRC, 'Concluding Observations: Cyprus' (7 June 1996) UN Doc. CRC/C/15/Add.59,
para. 16; UNCRC, 'Concluding Observations: Bangladesh' (1997), *supra* n. 19, para. 15;
UNCRC, 'Concluding Observations: Republic of Chad' (2009), *supra* 80, para. 62;
UNCRC, 'Concluding Observations: Qatar' (14 October 2009) UN Doc. CRC/C/QAT/

marriage,[112] female genital mutilation (FGM),[113] corporal punishment, amputation, scarring, burning and branding, infanticide, violent and degrading initiation rites, force feeding of girls, fattening, virginity testing,[114] 'honour' crimes, accusations of witchcraft, uvulectomy and teeth extraction.[115]

The Committee concludes that these practices are harmful not only to children's health,[116] as the Convention states, but also to their lives,[117] nutrition,[118] education,[119] survival and development.[120] Early marriage

---

CO/2, para. 55; UNCRC, 'Concluding Observations: Nigeria' (11 June 2010) UN Doc. CRC/C/NGA/CO/3-4, para. 65.

[112] UNCRC, 'Concluding Observations: Chad' (2009), *supra* n. 80, para. 62.

[113] UNCRC, 'Concluding Observations: Uganda' (23 November 2005) UN Doc. CRC/C/ UGA/CO/2, para. 56; UNCRC, 'Concluding Observations: Benin' (20 October 2006) UN Doc. CRC/C/BEN/CO/2, para. 54; UNCRC, 'Concluding Observations: United Republic of Tanzania' (21 June 2006) UN Doc. CRC/C/TZA/CO/2, para. 50; UNCRC, 'Concluding Observations: Kenya' (2007) *supra* n. 82, para. 53; UNCRC, 'Concluding Observations: Nigeria' (2010), *supra* n. 111, para. 66. Previously, the Committee referred to FGM as a harmful practice, but without determining that it impacts children's development. See UNCRC, 'Concluding Observations: Nigeria' (30 October 1996) UN Doc. CRC/C/ 15/Add.61 and UNCRC, 'Concluding Observations: Djibouti' (2000), *supra* n. 36.

[114] UNCRC, 'Concluding Observations: Benin' (24 August 1999) UN Doc. CRC/C/15/ Add.106, para. 16; UNCRC, 'Concluding Observations: Russian Federation' (2005), *supra* n. 102, para. 28; UNCRC, 'Concluding Observations: Benin' (2006), *supra* n. 113, para. 31; UNCRC, 'Concluding Observations: Maldives' (13 July 2007) UN Doc. CRC/C/MDV/CO/3, para. 42.

[115] UNCRC, 'General Comment No. 13', *supra* n. 104, para. 29.

[116] UNCRC, 'Concluding Observations: Bangladesh' (1997), *supra* n. 19, para. 15; UNCRC, 'Concluding Observations: United Republic of Tanzania' (9 July 2001) UN Doc. CRC/C/ 15/Add.156, para. 51; UNCRC, 'Concluding Observations: Kenya' (7 November 2001) UN Doc. CRC/C/15/Add.160, para. 48; UNCRC, 'Concluding Observations: India' (2004), *supra* n. 19, para. 59; UNCRC, 'Concluding Observations: Uganda' (2005), *supra* n. 113, para. 56; UNCRC, 'Concluding Observations: Benin' (2006), *supra* n. 113, para. 54; UNCRC, 'Concluding Observations: United Republic of Tanzania' (2006), *supra* n. 113, para. 51; UNCRC, 'Concluding Observations: Kenya' (2007), *supra* n. 82, para. 54; UNCRC, 'Concluding Observations: Chad' (2009), *supra* n. 80, para. 62; UNCRC, 'Concluding Observations: Qatar' (2009) *supra* n. 111, para. 55.

[117] UNCRC, 'Concluding Observations: Maldives' (2007), *supra* n. 114, para. 42.

[118] UNCRC, 'Concluding Observations: Bangladesh' (2003), *supra* n. 21, para. 15.

[119] *Ibid.*

[120] UNCRC, 'Concluding Observations: Cyprus' (1996), *supra* n. 111, para. 16; UNCRC, 'Concluding Observations: Central African Republic' (18 October 2000) UN Doc. CRC/ C/15/Add.138, para. 33; UNCRC, 'Concluding Observations: United Republic of Tanzania' (2001), *supra* n. 116, para. 51; UNCRC, 'Concluding Observations: Kenya' (2001), *supra* n. 116, para. 48; UNCRC, 'Concluding Observations: India' (2004), *supra* n. 19, para. 59; UNCRC, 'Concluding Observations: Uganda' (2005), *supra* n. 113, para. 56; UNCRC, 'Concluding Observations: Benin' (2006), *supra* n. 113, para. 54; UNCRC, 'Concluding Observations: Tanzania' (2006), *supra* n. 113, para. 51; UNCRC,

and FGM are explicitly defined as being 'harmful to the physical and psychological well-being of children'.[121]

As girls are more likely to be subjected to these practices,[122] States Parties are asked to empower them so that they can decide 'on their own body and their plans for education and their future and also to make the public aware of girls' right to be respected, protected and supported in their personal development'.[123] The Committee nevertheless emphasises that, on the whole, these practices have an impact on 'boys as well as girls'.[124]

This jurisprudence reflects a somewhat conservative idea of family life and child rearing. The Committee utilises developmental psychology when it comments about the influence of family structures and child rearing practices on child development. There is nothing wrong with this approach, but problems arise when some children and their rights are overlooked, when the roles of parents and States Parties vis-à-vis the right to development of children in diverse family contexts are rarely addressed, and when there is little guidance as to how the right to development should be protected and promoted.

'Concluding Observations: Kenya' (2007) *supra* n. 82, para. 54; UNCRC, 'Concluding Observations: Chad' (2009), *supra* n. 80, para. 62; UNCRC, 'Concluding Observations: Qatar' (2009), *supra* n. 111, para. 55.

[121] UNCRC, 'Concluding Observations: Nepal' (2005) *supra* n. 67, para. 68. But see General Comment No. 3, where the emphasis is on the damage it causes for girls: UNCRC, 'General Comment No. 3 (2003): HIV/AIDS and the Rights of the Child' (17 March 2003) UN Doc. CRC/GC/2003/3, para. 11. UNCRC, 'Concluding Observations: Qatar' (2009), *supra* n. 111, para. 55.

[122] UNCRC, 'Concluding Observations: Uganda' (2005), *supra* n. 113, para. 56; UNCRC, 'Concluding Observations: Benin' (2006), *supra* n.113, para. 54; UNCRC, 'Concluding Observations: Tanzania' (2006), *supra* n. 113, para. 51; UNCRC, 'Concluding Observations: Kenya' (2007), *supra* n. 82, para. 54; UNCRC, 'Concluding Observations: Chad' (2009), *supra* n. 80, para. 62; UNCRC, 'Concluding Observations: Qatar' (2009), *supra* n. 111, 55.

[123] UNCRC, 'Concluding Observations: Angola' (2010), *supra* n. 20, para. 54.

[124] UNCRC, 'Concluding Observations: Kenya' (2001), *supra* n. 116, para. 48; UNCRC, 'Concluding Observations: India' (2004), *supra* n. 19, para. 59. The Committee's General Comment No. 18 (2014), jointly published with the Committee on the Elimination of Discrimination against Women, elaborates on the definitions of what constitute 'harmful traditional practices', measures that ought to be taken to tackle them, and so on. But it does not mention 'child development' or the right to development even once. CEDAW and UNCRC, 'Joint General Recommendation No. 31 of the Committee on the Elimination of Discrimination against Women/General Comment No. 18 of the Committee on the Rights of the Child on Harmful Practices' (14 November 2014) UN Docs. CEDAW/C/GC/31–CRC/C/GC/18.

Early Childhood Development

The Committee considers early childhood as a critical moment 'for realising children's rights'.[125] It dedicates significant and ongoing attention to this issue, including publishing a General Comment (No. 7, 2005). The Committee holds the view that it is crucial to promote the child's development during the early years of her life. The period of rapid change and development is also the dominant prism through which the Committee describes what is essentially the essence of a baby's existence:

> Young children experience the most rapid period of growth and change during the human lifespan, in terms of their maturing bodies and nervous systems, increasing mobility, communication skills and intellectual capacities, and rapid shifts in their interests and abilities ...
>
> [They] form strong emotional attachments to their parents or other caregivers, from whom they seek and require nurturance, care, guidance and protection, in ways that are respectful of their individuality and growing capacities ...[126]

Here, the Committee is inexplicitly embracing John Bowlby's attachment theory.[127] In a rather uncommon manner, it explains the basis for taking this position:

> The Committee notes the growing body of theory and research which confirms that young children are best understood as social actors whose *survival, well-being and development* are dependent on and built around close relationships. These relationships are normally with a small number of key people, most often parents, members of the extended family and peers, as well as caregivers and other early childhood professionals. At the same time, research into the social and cultural dimensions of early childhood draws attention to the diverse ways in which *early development* is understood and enacted, including varying expectations of the young child and arrangements for his or her care and education. A feature of modern societies is that increasing numbers of young children are growing up in multicultural communities and in contexts marked by rapid social change, where beliefs and expectations about young children are also changing, including through greater recognition of their rights ... Finally, research has highlighted the particular risks to young children from malnutrition, disease, poverty, neglect, social exclusion and a range

---

[125] UNCRC, 'General Comment No. 7', *supra* n. 54, para. 6.   [126] *Ibid.*

[127] John Bowlby, *A Secure Base: Clinical Applications of Attachment Theory* (Routledge, London 1988); Joseph Goldstein, Anna Freud, Sonja Goldstein and Albert Solnit, *The Best Interests of the Child: The Least Detrimental Alternative* (Simon & Schuster, New York 1996).

of other adversities. It shows that proper prevention and intervention strategies during early childhood have the potential to impact positively on young children's *current well-being and future prospects*. Implementing child rights in early childhood is thus an effective way to help prevent personal, social and educational difficulties during middle childhood and adolescence ...[128] (emphasis added).

The care for children's development in the early years serves a dual purpose: it has a positive impact on children's current well-being but – and, it seems, more crucially – it also has a positive impact on children's future prospects, including preventing various difficulties in the later stages of their lives. The Committee then concludes that the early years of the child's life 'are the foundation for their physical and mental health, emotional security, cultural and personal identity, and developing competencies'.[129] Perhaps even more important is the Committee's assertion:

> Young children's experiences of growth and development vary according to their individual nature, as well as their gender, living conditions, family organization, care arrangements and education systems ...
>
> Young children's experiences of growth and development are powerfully shaped by cultural beliefs about their needs and proper treatment, and about their active role in family and community.[130]

This statement acknowledges that children are not a homogeneous group of human beings and that the intersection[131] of individual identities and living conditions, culture, care arrangements, and education shapes their experience of development. I therefore suggest that this conclusion should also be considered when addressing the right to development.

The Committee provides a somewhat rare observation about the ways it conceives of the relationship between child development, the right to development, and other rights of children:

> Ensuring *survival and physical health* are priorities, but States parties are reminded that article 6 encompasses *all aspects of development*, and that a young child's *health and psychosocial well-being* are in many respects interdependent ... The Committee reminds States parties (and others concerned) that the *right to survival and development* can only be

---

[128] UNCRC, 'General Comment No. 7', *supra* n. 54, para. 7.   [129] *Ibid*, para. 6.
[130] *Ibid*, para. 7.
[131] C.f. Nura Taefi, 'The Synthesis of Age and Gender: Intersectionality, International Human Rights Law and the Marginalisation of the Girl-Child' (2009) 17 *International Journal of Human Rights* 345; Pok Yin S. Chow, 'Has Intersectionality Reached Its Limits? Intersectionality in the UN Human Rights Treaty Body Practice and the Issue of Ambivalence' (2016) 16 *Human Rights Law Review* 453; Peleg, *supra* n. 3, 126–127.

implemented in a holistic manner, through the enforcement of all the other provisions of the Convention, including rights to health, adequate nutrition, social security, an adequate standard of living, a healthy and safe environment, education and play ... as well as through respect for the responsibilities of parents and the provision of assistance and quality services ...[132] (emphasis added).

These statements are important for two reasons. First, the Committee explicitly mentions Article 6 and the right to development, thus adding weight to an interpretation that supports such a reading of that Article. Second, the Committee presents a relatively comprehensive perspective concerning various dimensions of the child's life and the relationship between the Convention rights and the right to development. Specifically, the Committee states that protecting rights, such as the right to health or the right to education, is a prerequisite to the promotion of the right to development. Having said that, very little can be learned from this statement about whether the Committee identifies a distinct meaning of the right to development, or about the differences between protecting the right to development and protecting other rights of the child, or about the reasons not to consider the realisation of all these other rights as sufficient protection of child development. Another ambiguity in this explanation is the insufficient distinction drawn between child survival, child development, child well-being, and the child's future. Nor does the Committee explain the meaning of these four concepts, or the different complementary or overlapping obligations that they impose on duty bearers.

When discussing early childhood development in its Concluding Observations, the Committee tries to solidify its position and to establish a link between early childhood development and some rights of the child. However, unlike the approach the Committee takes in the General Comments, in the Concluding Observations it generally overlooks the right to development. Frequently, the Committee makes general statements about the significance of promoting early childhood development programs,[133] especially among low-income households,[134] and about the

---

[132] UNCRC, 'General Comment No. 7', *supra* 54, para. 10.
[133] UNCRC, 'Concluding Observations: Jamaica' (1995), *supra* n. 77, para. 24; UNCRC, 'Concluding Observations: Burkina Faso' (9 February 2010) UN Doc. CRC/C/BFA/CO/3-4, para. 65.
[134] UNCRC, 'Concluding Observations: Jordan' (28 June 2000) UN Doc. CRC/C/15/Add.125, para. 54.

need to educate parents about the importance of the programs.[135] Such programs, the Committee notes in the context of Article 6, should target reducing infant and under-five mortality rates, providing universal immunisation,[136] and combating low birthweight.[137] The Committee further states that early childhood development is threatened by diseases such as acute respiratory infection and diarrhoea,[138] chronic malnutrition[139] (which has 'serious consequences on health and psychological development'),[140] vitamin A deficiency,[141] anaemia, intestinal infectious diseases, bacterial infection, measles and pneumonia,[142] and malaria,[143] as well as poor sanitation and insufficient access to clean and safe drinking water.[144] It calls for 'increasing the usage of effectively treated mosquito nets',[145] maintaining sufficient numbers 'of trained health workers',[146]

---

[135] UNCRC, 'Concluding Observations: Paraguay' (2010), *supra* n. 63, para. 61; UNCRC, 'Concluding Observations: Paraguay' (2010), *supra* n. 63, para. 61.

[136] UNCRC, 'Concluding Observations: Nigeria' (2005), *supra* n. 97, para. 49; UNCRC, 'Concluding Observations: Togo' (31 March 2005) UN Doc. CRC/C/15/Add.255, para. 50.

[137] UNCRC, 'Concluding Observations: Hungary' (5 June 1998) UN Doc. CRC/C/15/Add.87, para. 2; UNCRC, 'Concluding Observations: Togo' (2005), *supra* n. 136, para. 50.

[138] UNCRC, 'Concluding Observations: South Africa' (23 February 2000) UN Doc. CRC/C/15/Add.122, para. 29; UNCRC, 'Concluding Observations: Haiti' (18 March 2003) UN Doc. CRC/C/15/Add.202, para. 44.

[139] UNCRC, 'Concluding Observations: Vanuatu' (1999), *supra* n. 106, para. 18; UNCRC, 'Concluding Observations: Cameroon' (2001), *supra* n. 19, para. 42; UNCRC, 'Concluding Observations: Burkina Faso' (2002), *supra* n. 79, para. 38; UNCRC, 'Concluding Observations: Madagascar' (27 October 2003) UN Doc. CRC/C/15/Add.218, paras. 47–48.

[140] UNCRC, 'Concluding Observations: Pakistan' (27 July 2003) UN Doc. CRC/C/15/Add.217, para. 53; UNCRC, 'Concluding Observations: Togo' (2005), *supra* n. 136, para. 50; UNCRC, 'Concluding Observations: Djibouti' (2008), *supra* n. 61, para. 30.

[141] UNCRC, 'Concluding Observations: Haiti' (2003), *supra* n. 138, para. 44.

[142] UNCRC, 'Concluding Observations: Nepal' (2005), *supra* n. 67, para. 60.

[143] UNCRC, 'Concluding Observations: Mali' (2 November 1999) UN Doc. CRC/C/15/Add.113, para. 26.

[144] UNCRC, 'Concluding Observations: Vanuatu' (1999), *supra* n. 106, para. 18; UNCRC, 'Concluding Observations: Ivory Coast' (9 July 2001) UN Doc. CRC/C/15/Add.155, paras. 38–39; UNCRC, 'Concluding Observations: Burkina Faso' (2002), *supra* n. 79, para. 38; UNCRC, 'Concluding Observations: Haiti' (2003), *supra* n. 138, para. 44; UNCRC, 'Concluding Observations: Swaziland' (16 October 2006) UN Doc. CRC/C/SWZ/CO/1, para. 52.

[145] UNCRC, 'Concluding Observations: Timor-Leste' (14 February 2008) UN Doc. CRC/C/TLS/CO/1, para. 59.

[146] UNCRC, 'Concluding Observations: Vanuatu' (1999), *supra* n. 106, para. 18; UNCRC, 'Concluding Observations: Marshall Islands' (19 November 2007) UN Doc. CRC/C/MHL/CO/2, para. 50.

increasing access to 'baby friendly hospitals that do not separate new born babies from their mothers after birth',[147] and ensuring equal access to health services, particularly in remote and rural areas.[148]

In recent years, the Committee has begun to emphasise the importance of preschool education for the promotion of child development,[149] thus expanding the scope of education beyond the primary school level included in the Convention.[150] Preschool programs should 'address early childhood development holistically',[151] should be designed 'in a culturally sensitive manner',[152] and – an addition since 2016 – should receive appropriate funding.[153] This sensitivity is further stressed with respect to children who need more assistance than others, including minority children, children with disabilities,[154] and children from low socioeconomic backgrounds.[155]

Although the Committee primarily uses a needs-based discourse in its analysis and recommendations, most of these needs can also be articulated in human rights terms. This is where the child's right to health, the right to social security, the right to an adequate standard of living, the right to education, the right to play and leisure, and the right to non-discrimination[156] all become relevant. As in its statements in General

---

[147] UNCRC, 'Concluding Observations: Republic Serbia' (2008), *supra* n. 21, para. 51.

[148] UNCRC, 'Concluding Observations: Hungary' (1998), *supra* n. 137, para. 18; UNCRC, 'Concluding Observations: Vanuatu' (1999), *supra* n. 106, para. 18; UNCRC, 'Concluding Observations: Colombia' (16 October 2000) UN Doc. CRC/C/15/Add.137, para. 45; UNCRC, 'Concluding Observations: Ivory Coast' (2001), *supra* n. 144, para. 38; UNCRC, 'Concluding Observations: Cameroon' (2001), *supra* n. 19, para. 42.

[149] UNCRC, 'Concluding Observations: Libya Arab Jamahiriya' (4 July 2003) UN Doc. CRC/C/15/Add.209, para. 39; UNCRC, 'Concluding Observations: Malaysia' (25 June 2007) UN Doc. CRC/C/MYS/CO/1, para. 79.

[150] Article 28(1)(a) recognises the right of children to education only at the primary school level.

[151] UNCRC, 'Concluding Observations: Bangladesh' (26 June 2009) UN Doc. CRC/C/BGD/CO/4, para. 75; UNCRC, 'Concluding Observations: Bolivia' (16 October 2009) UN Doc. CRC/C/BOL/CO/4, para. 68.

[152] UNCRC, 'Concluding Observations: Bolivia' (2009), *supra* n. 151, para. 68.

[153] UNCRC, 'Concluding Observations: Bulgaria' (21 November 2016) UN Doc. CRC/C/BGR/CO/3-5, para. 49; UNCRC, 'Concluding Observations: Gabon' (2016), *supra* n. 60, para. 45; UNCRC, 'Concluding Observations: Democratic People's Republic of Korea' (2017), *supra* n. 97.

[154] UNCRC, 'Concluding Observations: Bulgaria' (23 June 2008) UN Doc. CRC/C/BGR/CO/2, para. 58.

[155] UNCRC, 'Concluding Observations: Georgia' (23 June 2008) UN Doc. CRC/C/GEO/CO/3, para. 57.

[156] UNCRC, 'General Comment No. 7', *supra* n. 54, para. 10.

Comments Nos. 1 and 7,[157] the Committee takes the position that promoting these rights will promote children's early development. The questions of the relevancy of, and the relationship with, the right to development in this space remain unaddressed.

The Right to Health and Development

Article 24 protects the child's right to health. It stipulates a number of obligations – which include providing equal access to health care services, diminishing infant and child mortality, developing primary health care services, and ensuring prenatal and postnatal health care for mothers – for States Parties in order to ensure the realisation of this right.[158] Protecting or promoting child development is not explicitly mentioned as an objective of Article 24. However, as we already have seen, the Committee has made a link between the child's right to health and child development when referring to harmful traditional practices and the need to abolish discriminatory practices that preclude some children from having equal access to health care.

Early comments about the relationship among Article 24, child development, and the right to development include the negative impact on child development of factors such as air pollution and environmental degradation, lack of sanitation facilities, and problems with industrial waste management.[159] The Committee consolidated these comments and elaborated on this relationship more in General Comment No. 15 (2013), which aims to provide a comprehensive interpretation of Article 24.[160]

At the outset of General Comment No. 15, the Committee states that 'all children have the right to opportunities to survive, grow and develop, within the context of physical, emotional and social well-being, to each child's full potential'.[161] It restates this definition, suggesting that the

---

[157] UNCRC, 'General Comment No. 1 (2001) – Article 29 (1): The Aims of Education' (17 April 2001) UN Doc. CRC/GC/2001/1; UNCRC, 'General Comment No. 7', *supra* n. 54.

[158] Article 24(1)–(3).

[159] UNCRC, 'Concluding Observations: Bangladesh' (2003), *supra* n. 21, para. 53. UNCRC, 'Concluding Observations: Philippines' (2005), *supra* n. 70, para. 60; UNCRC, 'Concluding Observations: Uzbekistan' (2 June 2006) UN Doc. CRC/C/UZB/CO/2, para. 54; UNCRC, 'Concluding Observations: Thailand' (2006), *supra* n. 29, para. 55.

[160] UNCRC, 'General Comment No. 15 (2013) on the Right of the Child to the Enjoyment of the Highest Attainable Standard of Health (art. 24)' (17 April 2013) UN Doc. CRC/C/GC/15.

[161] *Ibid.*, para. 1.

right to health should be interpreted broadly to include the right of children 'to grow and develop to their full potential'.[162] This interpretation goes beyond the Convention's text, bringing survival, growth, and development together, signifying that the objective of the development process is to enable every child to achieve her potential:

> Not only is children's right to health important in and of itself, but also the realization of the right to health is indispensable for the enjoyment of all the other rights in the Convention. Moreover, achieving children's right to health is dependent on the realization of many other rights outlined in the Convention.[163]

Thus, the interdependency of Article 24 and other rights of the child, including the right to development, means that neither Article 24 nor Article 6 can be fully protected without defining what child development means in this context. This interpretation also suggests a circular relationship between the right to health and child development, where protecting the former is a necessary precondition to achieving the latter, while a healthy development is also a manifestation of good health.

The method of defining child development should include, according to General Comment No. 15, participatory consultations where children can discuss 'their health challenges, developmental needs and expectations'.[164] This is probably the first time that the Committee mainstreams Article 12 to the process of understanding the meaning of one of the Convention's rights, marking a huge step in respecting children's agency. It has since then been repeated in General Comment No. 14 on the meaning of the principle of the best interests of the child,[165] General Comment No. 20 on the rights of adolescents,[166] and General Comment No. 21 on the rights of children in street situations.[167]

The Committee gives considerable attention to two issues: children with HIV/AIDS and adolescent health, to which it dedicates two General

---

[162] *Ibid.*, para. 2.   [163] *Ibid.*, para. 7.   [164] *Ibid.*, para. 17.
[165] UNCRC, 'General Comment No. 14 (2013) on the Right of the Child to Have His or Her Best Interests Taken as a Primary Consideration (art. 3, para. 1)' (29 May 2013) UN Doc. CRC/C/GC/14.
[166] UNCRC, 'General Comment No. 20', *supra* n. 101.
[167] UNCRC, 'General Comment No. 21', *supra* n. 26.

Comments (Nos. 3 and 4, respectively),[168] in addition to General Comment No. 15 about the right to health.[169]

Children with HIV/AIDS

HIV/AIDS is a pandemic that affects the health of children who have contracted the disease, as well as children whose family members are afflicted. Therefore, the Committee suggests that HIV/AIDS affects all rights of children, including 'civil, political, economic, social and cultural'[170] rights. Consequently, the Convention's four guiding principles, including the right to development, should 'be the guiding themes in the consideration of HIV/AIDS at all levels of prevention, treatment, care and support'.[171] In addition to this general proclamation, the Committee further emphasises the need to address specific rights of children with HIV/AIDS, including:

> The right to access information and material aimed at the promotion of their social, spiritual and moral well-being and physical and mental health (Article 17); the right to preventive health care, sex education and family planning education and services (Article 24(f)); the right to an appropriate standard of living (Article 27); the right to privacy (Article 16); the right not to be separated from parents (Article 9); the right to be protected from violence (Article 19); the right to special protection and assistance by the State (Article 20); the rights of children with disabilities (Article 23); the right to health (Article 24); the right to social security, including social insurance (Article 26); the right to education and leisure (Articles 28 and 31); the right to be protected from economic and sexual exploitation and abuse, and from illicit use of narcotic drugs (Articles 32, 33, 34 and 36); the right to be protected from abduction, sale and trafficking as well as torture or other cruel, inhuman or degrading treatment or punishment (Articles 35 and 37); and the right to physical and psychological recovery and social reintegration (Article 39).[172]

---

[168] UNCRC, 'General Comment No. 3', *supra* n. 121; UNCRC, 'General Comment No. 4 (2003): Adolescent Health and Development in the Context of the Convention on the Rights of the Child' (1 July 2003) UN Doc. CRC/GC/2003/4. But see, for example, an exception to this general claim, where the Committee expresses concerns about the threat to children's health and development in Ukraine, due to the 'negative consequences of the Chernobyl nuclear plant disaster': UNCRC, 'Concluding Observations: Ukraine' (9 October 2002) UN Doc. CRC/C/15/Add.191, para. 6.

[169] UNCRC, 'General Comment No. 15', *supra* n. 160.

[170] UNCRC, 'General Comment No. 3', *supra* n. 121, para. 5; UNCRC, 'Concluding Observations: United Republic of Tanzania' (2001), *supra* n. 116, para. 30.

[171] UNCRC, 'General Comment No. 3', *supra* n. 121, para. 5.   [172] *Ibid.*, para. 6.

This elaborate list overlooks the care for child development and does not mention the right to development, despite the obvious impact that HIV/ AIDS has on both of these issues. Nevertheless, reflecting the description of Article 6 as representing a life–survival–development continuum,[173] the Committee states that 'children [with HIV/AIDS] have the right not to have their lives arbitrarily taken, as well as to benefit from economic and social policies that will allow them to survive into adulthood and develop in the broadest sense of the word'.[174] The end of the process, therefore, could not be clearer, nor could the embodiment in the Committee's work of the 'human becomings' conception of childhood.

Adolescent Health and Development

The Convention does not generally distinguish between children based on their age (with the exceptions of Articles 5 and 12, and the questions of the age of criminal responsibility and the requirement to join armed forces). However, in the early 2000s, the Committee began to give increased attention to adolescent rights – probably due to the realisation that at this stage in their lives, children face different challenges compared to adults, their needs are different, and, in the context of Article 6, both their developmental stage and their development needs are also different and therefore require special attention.

General Comment No. 4 (2003) is dedicated to 'adolescent health and development', thus establishing and discussing the relationship between health and development in multiple stages of a child's life. In this General Comment, the Committee uses Article 5 and the evolving-capacities principle, in conjunction with the human becomings model of childhood, as narratives of analysis. It describes adolescence as:

> [A] period characterized by rapid physical, cognitive and social changes, including sexual and reproductive maturation; the gradual building up of the capacity to assume adult behaviours and roles involving new responsi- bilities requiring new knowledge and skills. While adolescents are in general a healthy population group, adolescence also poses new challenges to health and development owing to their relative vulnerability and pressure from society, including peers, to adopt risky health behaviour ... The dynamic transition period to adulthood is also gener- ally a period of positive changes, prompted by the significant capacity of adolescents to learn rapidly, to experience new and diverse situations, to

---

[173] See Chapter 2.   [174] UNCRC, 'General Comment No. 3', *supra* n. 121, para. 11.

develop and use critical thinking, to familiarize themselves with freedom, to be creative and to socialize.[175]

The adolescent child is therefore situated in a unique mode of transition, as she is no longer a 'child' (that is, an incompetent and vulnerable infant or toddler) and she is on the edge of becoming an 'adult' (that is, a competent human being). This period of 'dynamic transition' requires, according to the Committee, interpreting Articles 6 and 24 'more broadly'[176] in order to 'ensure that adolescents do enjoy the highest attainable standard of health, develop in a well-balanced manner, and are adequately prepared to enter adulthood and assume a constructive role in their communities and in society at large'.[177] In other words, the Committee suggests that the reason for protecting children's rights, and safeguarding their development, is the ability of children to become socially functioning adults. The virtue of protecting the development process or the individual adolescent child in the present is glossed over.

The Committee further stipulates the risk factors to adolescent health and development, and, subsequently, the rights that should be protected in order to combat them, as part of the process of realising the right to development. These risk factors – some of which have already been mentioned in this chapter – include discrimination;[178] early marriage and pregnancy; injuries and death resulting from road traffic accidents; mental disorders and psychosocial illness, including depression, eating disorders, and self-destructive behaviour (which can sometimes lead to self-inflicted injuries and suicide); and 'honour' killings.[179] Guaranteeing adolescents' right to health and development requires tackling these risk factors, as well as 'the promotion and enforcement of the provisions and principles of the Convention, especially Articles 2–6, 12–17, 24, 28, 29 and 31'.[180] The Committee gives no further explanations for these determinations, beyond making a few general statements about the importance of respecting a certain right in order to realise the right to health and development.[181]

---

[175] UNCRC, 'General Comment No. 4', *supra* n. 168, para. 2.   [176] *Ibid.*, para. 4.
[177] *Ibid.*
[178] 'Adolescents who are subject to discrimination are more vulnerable to abuse, other types of violence and exploitation, and their health and development are put at greater risk': *ibid.*, para. 6.
[179] *Ibid.*, paras. 20–22, 24.   [180] *Ibid.*, para. 14.   [181] *Ibid.*, para. 8.

The issue of adolescent health gained scarce attention prior to the publication of General Comment No. 4,[182] and the issue of adolescent development was at the margins of these discussions.[183] But, after the publication of General Comment No. 4 in 2003, adolescent development features in many Concluding Observations, although the question of the right to development is rarely and randomly mentioned. When this right is mentioned, the Committee is likely to use exactly the same phrases that it employs in the General Comment.[184] A closer look suggests that, in some cases, the Committee makes additional observations about adolescent health and development. For example, the Committee concludes that in realising adolescent health, questions of sex, age and 'psychological development'[185] should be considered, and that the 'harmful effects of substance consumption on the physical, emotional and psychological development and wellbeing of children'[186] should be considered. (It is worth nothing that these are rare instances of the Committee explicitly referring to developmental psychology.) Likewise, mental health issues should also be considered, and assistance should be available to children 'in order to support their cognitive, social and emotional developmental needs'.[187]

The Committee's approach to adolescent development is interesting for several reasons. Probably the most important of these is the use of a

---

[182] See, for example, UNCRC, 'Concluding Observations: Ecuador' (26 October 1998) UN Doc. CRC/C/15/Add.93, para. 23; UNCRC, 'Concluding Observations: Kuwait' (26 October 1998) UN Doc. CRC/C/15/Add.96, para. 27.

[183] UNCRC, 'Concluding Observations: Jordan' (2000), *supra* n. 134, para. 47.

[184] See, for example, UNCRC, 'Concluding Observations: Morocco' (10 July 2003) UN Doc. CRC/C/15/Add.211, para. 46; UNCRC, 'Concluding Observations: Zambia' (2003), *supra* n. 97, para. 48; UNCRC, 'Concluding Observations: Antigua and Barbuda' (3 November 2004) UN Doc. CRC/C/15/Add.247, para. 53; UNCRC, 'Concluding Observations: Democratic People's Republic of Korea' (2004), *supra* n. 99, para. 52; UNCRC, 'Concluding Observations: Liberia' (1 July 2004) UN Doc. CRC/C/15/Add.236, para. 48; UNCRC, 'Concluding Observations: Rwanda' (2004), *supra* n. 19, para. 50; UNCRC, 'Concluding Observations: Benin' (2006), *supra* n. 113, para. 55; UNCRC, 'Concluding Observations: Swaziland' (2006), *supra* n. 144, para. 55; UNCRC, 'Concluding Observations: Colombia' (8 June 2006) UN Doc. CRC/C/COL/CO/3, para. 70; UNCRC, 'Concluding Observations: Tanzania' (2006), *supra* n. 113, para. 47; UNCRC, 'Concluding Observations: Kenya' (2007), *supra* n. 82, para. 50.

[185] UNCRC, 'Concluding Observations: Romania' (30 June 2009) UN Doc. CRC/C/ROM/CO/4, para. 69.

[186] UNCRC, 'Concluding Observations: Democratic People's Republic of Korea' (27 March 2009) UN Doc. CRC/C/PRK/CO/4, para. 62.

[187] UNCRC, 'Concluding Observations: Mongolia' (29 January 2010) UN Doc. CRC/C/MNG/CO/3–4, para. 55.

rights discourse in relation to development. Although the Committee usually speaks about child 'development' as a description of children's organic condition, in this case the Committee explicitly refers to the right to development and suggests why and how it should be protected. Nonetheless, the consistent analysis through the prism of the 'becomings' child continues. The Committee thus highlights the developmental needs of adolescents – especially in relation to their health – and elaborates on what sort of rights these needs imply, anticipating a developed human being living her life as an adult.

Poverty and Adequate Standard of Living

Article 27 is one of the five Articles of the Convention that include explicit reference to child development. It protects the child's right to an adequate standard of living, suggesting that this objective should ally with the child's 'physical, mental, spiritual, moral and social development'. As such, the right to an adequate standard of living is not only an important right in itself, but – similarly, for example, to the ways in which the Committee perceives the right to health – is also a vehicle for promoting five dimensions of development.[188] In its discussions about this right, the Committee focuses mostly on the relationship between the living conditions of poor children and the potential negative impact that these can have on child development.

In its jurisprudence, the Committee has focused on questions related to malnutrition and housing,[189] determining that eliminating poverty and malnutrition and improving food security[190] are needed to improve children's rights to survival, healthy development, education and well-being,[191]

---

[188] Compare to Article 25 of the Universal Declaration of Human Rights and Article 11 of the International Covenant on Economic, Social and Cultural Rights. These two articles protect the right to an adequate standard of living and include different specifications and aims. In these articles of 'general' international law, the right includes, inter alia, the right to food, clothing, and shelter. The impact of this desirable standard of living is not manifested in terms of the future benefit that the person will have.

[189] For example, UNCRC, 'Concluding Observations: Norway' (3 March 2010) UN Doc. CRC/C/NOR/CO/4, paras. 46–47.

[190] UNCRC, 'Concluding Observations: Sierra Leone' (2008), supra n. 80, para. 29.

[191] UNCRC, 'Concluding Observations: Honduras' (1994), supra n. 10, para. 15; UNCRC, 'Concluding Observations: Bangladesh' (1997), supra n. 19, para. 21; UNCRC, 'Concluding Observations: Austria' (7 May 1999) UN Doc. CRC/C/15/Add.98, para. 24; UNCRC, 'Concluding Observations: Ethiopia' (21 February 2000) UN Doc. CRC/C/15/Add.144, para. 33; UNCRC, 'Concluding Observations: Kenya' (2001), supra n. 116,

thus facilitating children's 'full'[192] and 'holistic development'[193] and improving their 'everyday quality of life'.[194] No details are given as to what these three objectives ('full', 'holistic' and 'quality of life') mean, or how they differ. The Committee suggests a number of times that, in order to begin the process of meeting these objectives, one course of action is to define a national poverty line (if such a definition does not already exist).[195] Policies and programs can then be designed in accordance with this definition.[196] Furthermore, and on more concrete terms, the Committee suggests that helping struggling families and tackling household poverty should be prioritised 'in order to ensure, to the maximum extent possible, the survival and development of all children',[197] and that such measures should be developed with the participation of children.[198]

Children in Street Situations

One group of children who do not enjoy the right to an adequate standard of living are those living in street situations. These children

para. 27; UNCRC, 'Concluding Observations: Australia' (2005), *supra* n. 75, para. 56; UNCRC, 'Concluding Observations: Ireland' (29 September 2006) UN Doc. CRC/C/IRL/CO/2, para. 57; UNCRC, 'Concluding Observations: Venezuela' (2007), *supra* n. 80, para. 65; UNCRC, 'Concluding Observations: Djibouti' (2008), *supra* n. 61, para. 71. It is worth mentioning that at the early stages of its work, the Committee used to 'express concerns' about children's poverty and its impact on their health and education, but without linking it to their development. See, for example, UNCRC, 'Concluding Observations: Bulgaria' (24 January 1997) UN Doc. CRC/C/15/Add.66, para. 16; UNCRC, 'Concluding Observations: Ethiopia' (24 January 1997) UN Doc. CRC/C/15/Add.67, para. 12. But see UNCRC, 'Concluding Observations: New Zealand' (21 October 2016) UN Doc. CRC/C/NZL/CO/5, para. 35.

[192] UNCRC, 'Concluding Observations: Spain' (29 September 2010) UN Doc. CRC/C/ESP/CO/3–4, para. 52.

[193] UNCRC, 'Concluding Observations: Sudan' (1 October 2010) UN Doc. CRC/C/SDN/CO/3-4, para. 60; UNCRC, 'Concluding Observations: Central African Republic' (8 March 2016) UN Doc. CRC/C/CAF/CO/2, para. 46.

[194] UNCRC, 'Concluding Observations: Latvia' (21 February 2000) UN Doc. CRC/C/15/Add.142, para. 42.

[195] UNCRC, 'Concluding Observations: Australia' (2005), *supra* n. 75, para. 56.

[196] UNCRC, 'Concluding Observations: Lithuania' (21 February 2000) UN Doc. CRC/C/15/Add.146, para. 42.

[197] UNCRC, 'Concluding Observations: Latvia' (21 February 2001) UN Doc. CRC/C/15/Add.142, para. 42. See also UNCRC, 'Concluding Observations: Georgia' (27 July 2003) UN Doc. CRC/C/15/Add.222, para. 54; UNCRC, 'Concluding Observations: Jamaica' (4 July 2003) UN Doc. CRC/C/15/Add.210, para. 46; UNCRC, 'Concluding Observations: Angola' (2010), *supra* n. 20, para. 58.

[198] UNCRC, 'Concluding Observations: Tajikistan' (2010), *supra* n. 58, para. 59.

suffer from a multidimensional violation of their rights, which inherently undermines the enjoyment of their right under Article 27 – but also, as will be discussed, their right to development. Most children in street situations are deprived of a family environment and are denied their rights to education, health, and freedom from economic exploitation and abuse (Articles 28–29, 24, and 32 respectively).[199] Therefore, States Parties are expected to provide this heterogeneous group of children with programs that will 'enhance their living conditions and improve their development'.[200] Some more concrete obligations require States Parties to care for their 'full development',[201] which includes providing for 'adequate nutrition, clothing, housing, health care and educational opportunities, including vocational and life-skills training',[202] and to provide access to 'rehabilitation services for physical, sexual and substance abuse', 'protection from police brutality', 'services for reconciliation with their families',[203] and 'official documents when necessary'.[204]

---

[199] UNCRC, 'Concluding Observations: Russian Federation' (1999), *supra* n. 33, para. 12; UNCRC, 'Concluding Observations: Colombia' (2000), *supra* n. 148, para. 34; UNCRC, 'Concluding Observations: Turkey' (9 July 2001) UN Doc. CRC/C/15/Add.152, para. 64; UNCRC, 'Concluding Observations: Republic of Moldova' (31 October 2002) UN Doc. CRC/C/15/Add.192, para. 48; UNCRC, 'Concluding Observations: Zambia' (2003), *supra* n. 97, para. 69; UNCRC, 'Concluding Observations: Estonia' (2003), *supra* n. 34, para. 45; UNCRC, 'Concluding Observations: India' (2004), *supra* n. 19, para. 77; UNCRC, 'Concluding Observations: Mongolia' (2002), *supra* n. 82, para. 63; UNCRC, 'Concluding Observations: Azerbaijan' (17 March 2006) UN Doc. CRC/C/AZE/CO/2, para. 64; UNCRC, 'Concluding Observations: Venezuela' (2007), *supra* n. 80, para. 73.

[200] UNCRC, 'Concluding Observations: The Former Yugoslav Republic of Macedonia' (11 June 2010) UN Doc. CRC/C/CO/2, para. 72.

[201] UNCRC, 'Concluding Observations: Turkey' (2001), *supra* n. 199, para. 65; UNCRC, 'Concluding Observations: Republic of Moldova' (2002), *supra* n. 199, para. 48; UNCRC, 'Concluding Observations: Zambia' (2003), *supra* n. 97, para. 69; UNCRC, 'Concluding Observations: Estonia' (2003), *supra* n. 34, para. 45; UNCRC, 'Concluding Observations: India' (2004), *supra* n. 19, para. 77; UNCRC, 'Concluding Observations: Mongolia' (2005), *supra* n. 82, para. 63; UNCRC, 'Concluding Observations: Burkina Faso' (29 January 2010) UN Doc. CRC/C/BFA/CO/3-4, para. 71; UNCRC, 'Concluding Observations: Paraguay' (2010), *supra* n. 63, para. 69; UNCRC, 'Concluding Observations: Pakistan' (2016), *supra* n. 26, para. 74; UNCRC, 'Concluding Observations: Senegal' (7 March 2016) UN Doc. CRC/C/SEN/CO/3-5, para. 68.

[202] UNCRC, 'Concluding Observations: Turkey' (2001), *supra* n. 199, para. 64.

[203] *Ibid.*, para. 64. See also UNCRC, 'Concluding Observations: Kuwait' (1998), *supra* n. 182, para. 25; UNCRC, 'Concluding Observations: Republic of Moldova' (2002), *supra* n. 199, para. 48; UNCRC, 'Concluding Observations: Zambia' (2003), *supra* n. 97, para. 69; UNCRC, 'Concluding Observations: Estonia' (2003), *supra* n. 34, para. 45; UNCRC, 'Concluding Observations: Mongolia' (2005), *supra* n. 82, para. 63; UNCRC, 'Concluding Observations: Azerbaijan' (2006), *supra* n. 199, para. 64.

[204] UNCRC, 'Concluding Observations: India' (2004), *supra* n. 19, para. 77.

The design process of these programs should include consultation with children in street situations – not only because this is their right under Article 12, but also because it has the potential to improve 'their development'.[205] The latter comment is one of the rare occasions on which the Committee articulates any connection between Articles 12 and 6.

General Comment No. 21 (2017) is dedicated to children in street situations. This detailed document represents a change in the Committee's approach to the balance between children's protection and the provision of rights.[206] Similarly, it also includes a change in the approach towards the right to development. Explicitly and directly commenting on Article 6, the Committee reiterates that 'child development' should be interpreted as a holistic concept,[207] and that interventions should 'support individual children in street situations to achieve their optimal development, maximizing their positive contribution to society'.[208] Thus, the Committee names the right to development, sets a personal 'optimum development' as an ambitious outcome for the process of development, and suggests that this objective also has a social benefit in the form of 'maximizing' the child's ability to contribute to society. In that sense, the objectives of – or reasons for – protecting the right to development are stipulated in similar terms to those used in Article 29 with respect to the objectives of education.

Education and Development

The importance of education to the positive outcome of child development is almost self-explanatory. As was shown in previous chapters, the relationship between these two rights, and domains, of children's lives has been established since the early days of children's rights law. It is therefore not surprising to see that child development occupies a significant part of Article 29, which defines the aims of education, and subsequently of the Committee's recommendations in this space. Conceiving of childhood as a time of change and growth, Article 29(1)(a) defines the first aim of education as 'the development of the child's personality, talent and mental and physical abilities to their fullest potential'. This is the only place in the Convention where the objective of development is

---

[205] UNCRC, 'Concluding Observations: Peru' (2016), *supra* n. 20, para. 68.
[206] UNCRC, 'General Comment No. 21', *supra* n. 26.
[207] UNCRC, 'General Comment No. 5', *supra* n. 2.
[208] UNCRC, 'General Comment No. 21', *supra* n. 26, para. 31.

defined. The issue of child development, as opposed to the right to development itself, also gained much more attention in this context.

Over the years, the Committee has created an extensive jurisprudence on the right to education. It comments on the ways in which this right should be made available to all children, elaborates on the objectives of education, delineates which aspects of child development are supported by education, and defines the duties that Articles 28 and 29, in conjunction with Article 6, impose upon States Parties. The Committee recommends that educational opportunities be available to children as early as possible, explaining 'the right to education during early childhood as beginning at birth and closely linked to young children's right to maximum development'.[209]

One of the core elements of the right to education is access to school.[210] Therefore, States Parties are obliged to ensure the school attendance of children, including actively promoting the attendance of girls and other disempowered groups.[211] Another element of accessibility that should be tackled is school drop-out rates, since absenteeism has a negative impact on children's 'development and future access to employment'.[212] A structural element of access to education – the physical availability of an education system – has begun to attract attention in recent years, with the Committee commenting on the obligation of States Parties to ensure access to education in remote and rural areas, in order to ensure, inter alia, 'quality early childhood development'.[213]

Making education available requires making it free of cost,[214] including eliminating fees for school books and other supplies. States Parties should also provide sufficient support to families with financial problems,

---

[209] UNCRC, 'General Comment No. 7', *supra* n. 54, para. 28. See also the discussion about early childhood and development.

[210] Realising that the right to education requires much more, mainly the four A's – availability, accessibility, acceptability and adaptability –the Committee has addressed these aspects as part of its monitoring the implementation of Article 28. I refer only to the links that the Committee made between the realisation of the right to education and development.

[211] UNCRC, 'Concluding Observations: Brazil' (3 November 2004) UN Doc. CRC/C/15/ Add.241, para. 58.

[212] UNCRC, 'Concluding Observations: Finland' (20 October 2005) UN Doc. CRC/C/15/ Add.272, para. 42.

[213] UNCRC, 'Concluding Observations: Bulgaria' (2016), *supra* n. 153, para. 49; UNCRC, 'Concluding Observations: Gabon' (2016), *supra* n. 60, para. 45. See also UNCRC, 'Concluding Observations: Georgia' (9 March 2017) UN Doc. CRC/C/GEO/CO/4, para. 36.

[214] Article 28(1)(a).

so that they can provide for the 'adequate educational development of their children'.[215]

Having considered access to education, we can turn now to the school environment. In that regard, the Committee concludes that schools should be free from violence, including bullying, since this practice affects children's 'psychological health, educational achievements and social development'.[216]

In its very first General Comment, published in 2001,[217] the Committee discusses the aims of education:

> These aims, set out in the five subparagraphs of article 29(1)[,] are all linked directly to the realization of the child's human dignity and rights, taking into account the child's *special developmental needs* and diverse evolving capacities. The aims are: *the holistic development of the full potential of the child* ...[218] (emphasis added).

'Education' goes far beyond formal schooling to include a 'broad range of life experiences and learning processes which enable children, individually and collectively, to develop their personalities, talents and abilities and to live a full and satisfying life within society'.[219] Adding a specific comment on the first aim of education, the Committee notes that:

> Article 29(1) ... insists upon a holistic approach to education which ensures that the educational opportunities made available reflect an appropriate balance between *promoting the physical, mental, spiritual and emotional aspects of education,* the intellectual, social and practical dimensions, and the childhood and lifelong aspects. The overall objective of education is to maximize the child's ability and opportunity to participate fully and responsibly in a free society. It should be emphasized that the type of teaching that is focused primarily on accumulation of knowledge, prompting competition and leading to an excessive burden of work on children, may *seriously hamper the harmonious development of the child to the fullest potential of his or her abilities and talents*[220] (emphasis added).

Protecting the child's right to education is therefore a major precondition for the ability of the child to enjoy harmonious development and to

---

[215] UNCRC, 'Concluding Observations: Nicaragua' (21 September 2005) UN Doc. CRC/C/15/Add.265, para. 58.

[216] UNCRC, 'Concluding Observations: Australia' (2005), *supra* n. 75, para. 60.

[217] UNCRC, 'General Comment No. 1', *supra* n. 157.   [218] *Ibid.*   [219] *Ibid.*

[220] *Ibid.* See also UNCRC, 'Concluding Observations: Romania' (18 March 2003) UN Doc. CRC/C/15/Add.199, para. 53.

realise her fullest potential and talent. This definition also looks at two dimensions of development: the process ('harmonious') and its outcome ('fullest potential and talents'). The Committee, however, does not mention the right to development in this context, once again leaving open the question of whether there is a difference between caring for child development and caring for the right to development.

It is with these perceptions that the Committee monitors the implementation of Articles 28 and 29. The Committee, by restating Article 29 (1), continually emphasises that education should be directed towards the development 'of the child's personality, talent and mental and physical abilities to their fullest potential'.[221] It adds that school curricula should address 'all-round development',[222] 'focus on the personal development . . . of students',[223] and promote children's 'cognitive, social and emotional development'.[224] Nevertheless, while encouraging students to achieve their potential, the Committee asks schools not to create an atmosphere that is too competitive between pupils, since such an environment can place 'additional burdens on children and may hamper the development of the child to her or his fullest potential'[225] and may expose children 'to developmental disorders'.[226] This tension, as well as long school hours, can also prevent children from spending time pursuing 'leisure, physical activities and rest', thereby frustrating their development.[227] These statements reinforce the claim that the Committee's perception of child development is entrenched in mainstream developmental psychology and a Western perception of childhood. Although the Committee seeks to advance the development of children's potential, it

---

[221] See, for example, UNCRC, 'Concluding Observations: Slovakia' (23 October 2000) UN Doc. CRC/C/15/Add.140, para. 46.

[222] UNCRC, 'Concluding Observations: China' (2005), *supra* n. 82, para. 77.

[223] UNCRC, 'Concluding Observations: Macedonia' (23 February 2000) UN Doc. CRC/C/15/Add.118, para. 45.

[224] UNCRC, 'Concluding Observations: Poland' (30 October 2002) UN Doc. CRC/C/15/Add.194, para. 45.

[225] UNCRC, 'Concluding Observations: Thailand' (2006), *supra* n. 29, para. 64.

[226] UNCRC, 'Concluding Observations: Japan' (24 June 1998) UN Doc. CRC/C/15/Add.90, para. 22; UNCRC, 'Concluding Observations: Singapore' (27 July 2003) UN Doc. CRC/C/15/Add.220, para. 42; UNCRC, 'Concluding Observations: Republic of Korea' (18 March 2003) UN Doc. CRC/C/15/Add.197, para. 52; UNCRC, 'Concluding Observations: Japan' (26 February 2004) UN Doc. CRC/C/15/Add.231, para. 49; UNCRC, 'Concluding Observations: Thailand' (2006), *supra* n. 29, para. 65.

[227] UNCRC, 'Concluding Observations: Japan' (1998), *supra* n. 226, para. 22.

flinches from educational practices that 'push' the child too much and thus pose a risk to the fragile process of development.

Until 2013, the right to rest and leisure, as protected in Article 31, was rarely mentioned and the Committee's jurisprudence was rather slim. The few comments about this right, nonetheless, emphasise its importance in supporting child development.[228] States Parties are therefore asked to take into consideration 'the physical and psychological development of the child'[229] when planning leisure and cultural activities, which, in turn, also support 'the physical and psychological development of the child'.[230] The Committee further emphasises that early childhood play,[231] peer play, and the time and quality of a child's play with her with parents[232] are important to the child's emotional and social development.

General Comment No. 17 (2013) marks a change in this regard. It has the explicit objective of raising awareness of the importance of the right to play and leisure, while also providing some concrete context and a clearer interpretation.[233] The General Comment reiterates the previous comments made about the relationship between this right and child development, and further emphasises that play is a 'fundamental and vital dimension of the pleasure of childhood, as well as an essential component of physical, social, cognitive, emotional and spiritual development'.[234] This statement is followed by a rather rare explanation in which the Committee grounds its position in 'research', saying that 'play is also central to children's spontaneous drive for development, and that it performs a significant role in the development of the brain, particularly in the early years'.[235] The Committee adds that play is essential for children's ability to create a 'culture of childhood' through a range of activities, 'from games in school and in the playground to urban activities such as playing marbles, free running, street art and so on'.[236] In the context of Article 31, child development therefore seems to occupy a

---

[228] UNCRC, 'Concluding Observations: Mauritania' (6 November 2001) UN Doc. CRC/C/15/Add.159, para. 46.

[229] UNCRC, 'Concluding Observations: Benin' (2006), *supra* n. 113, para. 64; UNCRC, 'Concluding Observations: Lithuania' (17 March 2006) UN Doc. CRC/C/LTU/CO/2, para. 59.

[230] UNCRC, 'Concluding Observations: Lithuania' (2001), *supra* n. 196, para. 46.

[231] UNCRC, 'Concluding Observations: Belize' (10 May 1999) UN Doc. CRC/C/15/Add.99, para. 23.

[232] *Ibid.*; UNCRC, 'Concluding Observations: Mauritania' (2001), *supra* n. 228, para. 46.

[233] UNCRC, 'General Comment No. 17', *supra* n. 101.   [234] *Ibid.*, para. 14.

[235] *Ibid.*, para. 9.   [236] *Ibid.*, para. 12.

twofold role: the child's age and level of development ought to be considered when designing appropriate play and leisure activities, and, at the same time, play and leisure activities should be designed to promote children's 'optimum development'. The child's age should be taken into account when shaping play and leisure activities:

> As children grow older, their needs and wants evolve from settings that afford play opportunities to places offering opportunities to socialize, be with peers or be alone. [Children] will also explore progressively more opportunities involving risk-taking and challenge. These experiences are developmentally necessary for adolescents, and contribute to their discovery of identity and belonging.[237]

Another aspect of the Convention that has a close proximity to both education and child development is access to information and exposure to the media. Article 17 recognises the child's right to receive information, stating that it is important for children's 'social, spiritual and moral well-being and physical and mental health'. However, the Committee holds the view that exposure to information should be restricted if the media abuses children to the 'detriment of their personality and status as minors',[238] or when exposure to certain materials – especially 'violence and pornography'[239] – can injure 'their well-being and development'.[240] This concern is reflected in the duty of States Parties to take measures that will enable children to access information, especially in libraries,[241] that can promote their 'development and physical and mental health',[242] as well as their 'cultural development'.[243]

---

[237] Ibid., para. 14.

[238] UNCRC, 'Concluding Observations: Nicaragua' (1995), supra n. 30, para. 17.

[239] UNCRC, 'Concluding Observations: Federated States of Micronesia' (4 February 1998) UN Doc. CRC/C/15/Add.86, para. 16; UNCRC, 'Concluding Observations: Canada' (1995), supra n. 17, para. 15; UNCRC, 'Concluding Observations: Trinidad and Tobago' (10 October 1997) UN Doc. CRC/C/15/Add.82, para. 15; UNCRC, 'Concluding Observations: Lithuania' (2001), supra n. 196, para. 28; UNCRC, 'Concluding Observations: Kazakhstan' (19 June 2007) UN Doc. CRC/C/KAZ/CO/3, para. 32; UNCRC, 'Concluding Observations: Mongolia' (2010), supra n. 17, para. 35.

[240] UNCRC, 'Concluding Observations: Nicaragua' (1995), supra n. 30, para. 17.

[241] UNCRC, 'Concluding Observations: The Democratic Republic of Congo' (2006), supra n. 35, para. 35.

[242] UNCRC, 'Concluding Observations: Marshall Islands' (16 October 2000) UN Doc. CRC/C/15/Add.139, para. 34; UNCRC, 'Concluding Observations: Spain' (2010), supra n. 192, paras. 31–33.

[243] UNCRC, 'Concluding Observations: Lebanon' (7 June 1996) UN Doc. CRC/C/15/Add.54, para. 36.

It is therefore clear that the Committee perceives education and the right to education as fundamental factors in promoting children's harmonious development and the realisation of their 'maximum' potential. But it is only early childhood education opportunities that the Committee has linked to the child's right to development, while in general it overlooks the articulation of the care for child development as a human right.

Armed Conflicts

Children can be affected by armed conflicts in several ways – all of which have direct and indirect and short- and long-term effects on their development and, consequently, on their right to development. Children might be forcibly recruited to armed groups (either by official state armies or by other militias), thereby suffering injury or death, and may lose family members or become refugees. Armed conflicts also have immense and immediate impacts on access to healthcare and education services[244] – two rights that, as discussed earlier, are essential prerequisites to the realisation of the right to development.

In light of Articles 38 and 39 of the Convention, the Committee focuses its jurisprudence in this space on children who are victims of wars, broadly defined, and on child soldiers. In this context, it is worth mentioning that, since 2002, the rights of child soldiers are primarily discussed during discussions about the implementation of the Optional Protocol on the Involvement of Children in Armed Conflict,[245] which are not reviewed in this book.

The Committee is mostly concerned with the impact that 'an atmosphere of violence' has on children's 'development and right to life'[246] – or, using a slightly different wording, with the impact that armed conflicts have on children's rights to survival and development.[247]

---

[244] See, for example, UNCRC, 'Concluding Observations: Ecuador' (29 January 2010) UN Doc. CRC/C/ECU/CO/4, para. 68.

[245] GA Resolution A/RES/54/263 (20 May 2000), entered into force on 12 February 2002.

[246] UNCRC, 'Concluding Observations: Peru' (2000), *supra* n. 102, para. 18.

[247] UNCRC, 'Concluding Observations: India' (23 February 2000) UN Doc. CRC/C/15/ Add.115, para. 63; UNCRC, 'Concluding Observations: Burundi' (2000), *supra* n. 19, para. 30; UNCRC, 'Concluding Observations: Democratic Republic of Congo' (9 July 2001) UN Doc. CRC/C/15/Add.153, para. 26; UNCRC, 'Concluding Observations: India' (2004), *supra* n. 19, para. 68; UNCRC, 'Concluding Observations: Algeria' (12 October 2005) UN Doc. CRC/C/15/Add.269, para. 70; UNCRC, 'Concluding Observations: Democratic Republic of the Congo' (10 February 2009) UN Doc. CRC/C/COD/ CO/2, para. 33; UNCRC, 'Concluding Observations: Pakistan' (15 October 2009) UN

Particular attention is given to the effects of land mines, which the Committee sees as a 'threat ... to the survival and development of children'.[248] Troubled by the 'psychological trauma'[249] that armed conflicts inflict on children, the Committee asks States Parties to ensure the protection and rehabilitation of children. Children therefore should receive 'adequate assistance and counselling for their rehabilitation, physical and psychological recovery and social integration'.[250] The discussion about children and armed conflict is rather unique in the sense that it explicitly mentions the right to development, and not only child development, as an issue. But no discussion about its meaning follows.

Child Labour and Economic Exploitation

Article 32 is one of the five Articles in the Convention that explicitly identify the protection of child development as one of their objectives. It names the same five aspects of child development that are mentioned in Article 27. Article 32 respects the right of children to be protected 'from economic exploitation and from performing any work that is likely to be hazardous or to interfere with the child's education, or to be harmful to the child's health and physical, mental, spiritual, moral or social development'. It is worth noting that the language does not define what child labour means (for example, it does not differentiate between domestic labour and nondomestic labour), nor does it suggest that children should not engage in any form of work.

In General Comment No. 11 (2009), the Committee defines child labour as 'work that deprives children of their childhood, their potential and dignity and that is harmful to their physical and mental development'.[251] Understanding this definition and developing proper implementation measures require unpacking the meaning of 'childhood', which, as discussed in Chapter 1, is not a concept with a universal or

---

Doc. CRC/C/PAK/CO/3-4, para. 35; UNCRC, 'Concluding Observations: The Philippines' (22 October 2009) UN Doc. CRC/C/PHL/CO/3-4, para. 32; UNCRC, 'Concluding Observations: Nigeria' (2010), *supra* n. 111, para. 80.

[248] UNCRC, 'Concluding Observations: Iraq' (26 October 1998) UN Doc. CRC/C/15/Add.94, para. 28; UNCRC, 'Concluding Observations: Angola' (3 November 2004) UN Doc. CRC/C/15/Add.246, para. 62; UNCRC, 'Concluding Observations: Jordan' (2006), *supra* n. 82, para. 77.

[249] UNCRC, 'Concluding Observations: Colombia' (2000), *supra* n. 148, para. 34.

[250] UNCRC, 'Concluding Observations: Angola' (2005), *supra* n. 247, para. 71.

[251] UNCRC, 'General Comment No. 11', *supra* n. 23, para. 69.

singular meaning. The definition also highlights, once again, the Committee's inclination to care for the child's future as an adult, while paying less attention to the experience of children, or their development, during the course of their childhood. Notably, this definition does not draw a distinction between domestic labour and other forms of labour, despite the fact that the regulation of these two sites might require different measures and face different challenges – including a call to respect cultures in which children are expected to perform domestic duties. In a more recent attempt to articulate a clearer interpretation of Article 32 and to contextualise the phenomenon of child labour in a broader approach to children's rights, the Committee seems to suggest, or even welcome, some forms of child labour in a later stage of childhood – that is, adolescence. General Comment No. 21 (2017), for example, urges States Parties not to criminalise 'begging or unlicensed trading', as this can lead children to engage 'in worse forms of survival behaviours, such as commercial sex exploitation'.[252] The Committee thus creates a hierarchy of different forms of labour. It recognises that for children in street situations, labour is a means of survival rather than a matter of choice.

In the Concluding Observations, the Committee replicates the Convention's text, calling upon States Parties to 'combat economic exploitation' that can be 'harmful to the child's health or physical, mental, spiritual, moral or social development'.[253] On more concrete terms, it asks States Parties to 'provide for a minimum age or minimum ages for admission for employment',[254] and to regulate the working hours and working conditions of children.

Turning its attention to the domestic context and children's positionality within their families, the Committee asks States Parties to pay attention to the 'conditions of children working within their families, in

---

[252] UNCRC, 'General Comment No. 20', *supra* n. 101, para. 59.

[253] UNCRC, 'Concluding Observations: Laos' (10 October 1997) UN Doc. CRC/C/15/Add.78, para. 50; UNCRC, 'Concluding Observations: Federated States of Micronesia' (1998), *supra* n. 239, para. 39; UNCRC, 'Concluding Observations: Fiji' (24 June 1998) UN Doc. CRC/C/15.Add.89, para. 42; UNCRC, 'Concluding Observations: Costa Rica' (24 February 2000) UN Doc. CRC/C/15/Add.117, para. 26; UNCRC, 'Concluding Observations: Central African Republic' (2000), *supra* n. 120, para. 78; UNCRC, 'Concluding Observations: Ukraine' (2002), *supra* n. 168, para. 65; UNCRC, 'Concluding Observations: Czech Republic' (2003), *supra* n. 63, para. 59; UNCRC, 'Concluding Observations: Ghana' (17 March 2006) UN Doc. CRC/C/GHA/CO/2, para. 65.

[254] Article 32(2)(a).

order to protect them fully'.[255] Long working hours are another issue of concern due to the negative impact that they have not only on school attendance, as Article 32 suggests, but also on the child's 'development'[256] or 'full and harmonious development'.[257] The Committee also calls on States Parties to narrow the gap between the age at which compulsory education ends and the minimum legal age for access to employment,[258] as this gap opens the door for illegal employment practices, which, in turn, can expose children to situations of abuse and exploitation. The jurisprudence focuses on the impact of labour on various aspects of child development, but it is silent about the relevance of the right to development in this context.

Ignoring the Elephant in the Room

More than 25 years of monitoring the various ways in which States Parties have addressed their duty to protect the right to development of children have resulted in a long and detailed, but nonetheless somewhat vague, index that connects almost every aspect of a child's life and many of the Convention's rights to various domains of child development and to the right to development. But, essentially, the functionality of this index is a suggestion that child development will be protected and promoted when other rights of the child – not necessarily the right to development itself – will also be protected.

The index, as this chapter argues, tells us very little about the distinct meaning of the right to development, compared to other rights of the child, or what children can expect in terms of means provided to protect this right. Likewise, the emphasis on the various duties arising from the obligation to protect child development highlights the absence of a meaningful body of jurisprudence concerning the right to development.

---

[255] UNCRC, 'Concluding Observations: Fiji' (1998), *supra* n. 253, para. 42; UNCRC, 'Concluding Observations: Malaysia' (2007), *supra* n. 149, para. 91.

[256] UNCRC, 'Concluding Observations: Central African Republic' (2000), *supra* n. 120, para. 78; UNCRC, 'Concluding Observations: Cameroon' (2001), *supra* n. 19, para. 58; UNCRC, 'Concluding Observations: Republic of Moldova' (2002), *supra* n. 199, para. 43; UNCRC, 'Concluding Observations: Madagascar' (2003), *supra* n. 139, para. 59; UNCRC, 'Concluding Observations: Nigeria' (2005), *supra* n. 97, para. 75.

[257] UNCRC, 'Concluding Observations: Jamaica' (2003), *supra* n. 197, para. 51.

[258] UNCRC, 'Concluding Observations: Nicaragua' (1995), *supra* n. 30, para. 14; UNCRC, 'Concluding Observations: Senegal' (1995), *supra* n. 17, para. 11; UNCRC, 'Concluding Observations: Iraq' (1998), *supra* n. 248, para. 26; UNCRC, 'Concluding Observations: Madagascar' (2003), *supra* n. 139, para. 59.

In that sense, the fact that the right to development remains in the shadows of the Committee's work mirrors its treatment in the Convention's drafting process.

Overlooking the right to development while focusing on 'child development', or specific aspects of it, or on the other two rights protected by Article 6 (the right to life and the right to survival), is evident in the Committee's work. As discussed at the beginning of this chapter, the Committee's reporting guidelines ask States Parties to elaborate on the steps taken for implementing the Convention's guiding principles, including the rights to life, survival, and development. Likewise, since 2005, the Concluding Observations and General Comments are based on unified formats that include a section concerning the implementation of these general principles. However, while most of the Concluding Observations and General Comments refer to Article 6, only a handful of them explicitly refer to the right to development (though in growing numbers and with much more consistency since 2013).

The Committee's jurisprudence about the right to development is lacking in consistency regarding the treatment of the right to development. I argue that the main reason for this is an unsounded conception of child development and the corresponding meaning of protecting it as a human right of children. Although including any elaborate discussions about the various meanings of child development in the Concluding Observations exceeds the function of these documents, we might expect to see some discussion about this issue in the General Comments – or even see a General Comment that is dedicated to this right, which the Committee itself identifies as one of the Convention's four guiding principles.

In its work, the Committee refers to different domains of child development, such as mental, physical, and social development, as well as to more descriptive terms, such as the 'full' or 'harmonious' development of the child. But it does not explain their meaning, or how they relate to human rights language, discourse and mechanisms. In its references to child development, the Committee either highlights the risk factors that can damage different domains of child development, or suggests how these domains should be protected and supported. This is where the conceptual ambiguity – similar to the one we saw in the drafting process of the Convention – arises: the meanings of these domains of child development are not self-evident, and the meanings vary based on context and the discipline one chooses to employ. Moreover, even within a single discipline – for example, developmental psychology – there can be different understandings of 'child development'. As noted in previous chapters, Anna Freud's approach to child development – including what constitutes a healthy process of development and what sort of events in the child's life can damage it – is different from, for example, that of Piaget. Needless to say, the difference in meaning leads to different means that are required to support 'development'. Therefore, when the Committee speaks of the need to support children's mental development – to take one recommendation as an example – this recommendation can only be followed when a definition of this term is provided or where a consensus or shared understanding exists. But the Committee does not say how it understands the term 'child development', and since no consensus about its meaning exists in other approaches in psychology too, it essentially invites States Parties to develop a local interpretation. The problem with this approach is that it opens the door for misunderstanding a key component of the Convention. In reality, the approach has led to an even more troubling result: by and large, States Parties ignore the right to development altogether.

The analysis in this chapter illustrates that the Committee interprets many of the Convention's rights, in relation to child development, in one of two ways. In one approach, it takes the protection of right X – for example, the right to be registered at birth – as a precondition necessary for protecting one or more aspects of child development: in other words, the right to development cannot be fully protected unless the child is registered after birth. In the other approach, it views the protection of right Y – for example, the right to education – as an integral element of protecting one or more aspects of child development. In other words, protecting the right to education, while serving its own independent and separate objectives, also contributes, in parallel, to the realisation of the right to development.

There is no single occasion when the Committee clarifies what the right to development stands for, or what it should stand for; what it protects (for example, the process of development, the outcome of it, or perhaps both); what its aims are; or what, if any, its added values are in comparison to other rights of the Convention. I believe that this ambiguity is the result of two factors. The first has already been discussed, and it is the conceptual ambiguity of the term 'child development'. The second is because the Committee's work is informed by the traditional binary conception of childhood as a time of 'becomings', and is incapable of departing from this 'romantic developmentalism'[259] approach.

---

[259]   Alison Diduck, *Law's Families* (LexisNexis, London 2003) 79.

Therefore, the Committee is mostly concerned with the care for children's future and consequently subjugates most of the Convention's rights to support 'child development'.

Another implication of interpreting the Convention in light of the human becomings approach is the denial of children's agency. Although a relationship between most of the Convention's rights to child development is established – including rights that are not explicitly mentioned in the Convention, such as the right to freedom of movement[260] – two rights are notably missing from this analysis: the right to freedom of expression and the right to participation (Articles 13 and 12, respectively).[261] With some rare exceptions – and despite the effort to broaden the interpretation and to embody the importance of the right of children to participate in all aspects of their lives[262] – the Committee overlooks these two rights, one of which is also a guiding principle of the Convention, when discussing the right to development.[263] This contributes to the perpetuation of the image of children as passive human beings who have only one goal in life: to grow up and become adults.[264]

With the exception of the right to nondiscrimination, most of the causality between supporting child development and the Convention's rights is made with respect to socioeconomic rights, and not civil and political rights. This is a problematic lacuna, given that the development of the child's personality, for example, is supported when the child exercises her right to freedom of speech. But considering the insufficient respect given to children's agency in the context of their own development, it is not surprising that autonomy rights are glossed over. If, indeed, a child is only a human becoming, then her autonomy rights

---

[260] UNCRC, 'Concluding Observations: United Kingdom' (20 October 2008) UN Doc. CRC/C/GBR/CO/4, para. 35.

[261] With the exception of stating that ensuring the right to participation is needed 'in order to empower children to their fullest development and dignity'. UNCRC, 'Concluding Observations: Dominican Republic' (21 February 2000) UN Doc. CRC/C/15/Add.150, para. 25. Similar statements can be found in General Comment No. 12: UNCRC, 'General Comment No. 12 (2009): The Right of the Child to Be Heard' (20 July 2009) UN Doc. CRC/C/GC/12.

[262] UNCRC, 'General Comment No. 17', *supra* n. 101; UNCRC, 'General Comment No. 20', *supra* n. 101; UNCRC, 'General Comment No. 21', *supra* n. 26.

[263] The right to participation. See UNCRC, 'General Comment No. 5', *supra* n. 2.

[264] This conclusion also meets the interpretation of the right to development derived from the drafting process of the Convention: see Chapter 2. The Committee has had many failures with respect to the right to participation: see Aoife Nolan, 'The Child as a "Democratic Citizen": Challenging the "Participation Gap"' (2010) 4 *Public Law* 767, 782.

will become relevant or operational only when she grows up and becomes an adult – or perhaps at adolescence, the stage when children are closer in their imagined capacities and capabilities to the prototype adult. This approach to civil and political rights and the right to development was introduced at length in December 2016, when the Committee published General Comment No. 20 on the rights of the child during adolescence.[265] There, the Committee takes the view that adolescents should be consulted with and should be given the opportunity to participate in discussions concerning questions of education, especially dropping out of school, as well as issues relating to adolescent-headed households and the importance of the right to play and leisure time. However, while adolescent development and the right to development are mentioned in General Comment No. 20, no connection between the right to participation and the right to development is made.

Utilising the human becomings approach to childhood also explains the Committee's repeated emphasis on protecting children's 'full' development, in addition to their emotional, physical, social, mental, and psychological development, which are the objectives set by the Convention itself. Providing as broad as possible a protection to children's course of growth has led the Committee – as it earlier led the Convention's drafters – to synthesise the protection of 'child development' with the protection of children's 'well-being' and their 'full potential'. The Committee conflates these three concepts, although all three have different (with some potentially overlapping) meanings.

The long index reviewed here also raises the question of the merit of defining Article 6, including the right to development, as one of the Convention's guiding principles. Although the particular roles of the other three guiding principles have become increasingly clear,[266] the Committee has been unsuccessful in articulating a similarly distinct meaning for the right to development.

The question that should therefore be asked is this: Is there any real substance to the right to development? Perhaps, due to the Convention's aim of supporting children's journey into their future selves as adults, the Committee is right in subjugating the Convention to support as many

---

[265] UNCRC, 'General Comment No. 20', *supra* n. 101.

[266] Karl Hanson and Laura Lundy, 'Does Exactly What It Says on the Tin? A Critical Analysis and Alternative Conceptualisation of the So-Called "General Principles" of the Convention on the Rights of the Child' (2017) 25 *International Journal of Children's Rights* 285.

domains of child development as possible – essentially suggesting that this will lead to sufficient protection of this characteristic of children. Such a conclusion ignores the existence of the right to development as a distinct right, and ignores the added value that it can have in achieving this objective. The next chapter will explore some options that have the potential to remedy some of the problems that have been identified with the current treatment of the right to development.

Conclusion

As with the Convention, the Committee's jurisprudence does not sufficiently distinguish between child development and the child's right to development. The Committee's interpretation of the Convention provides broad protection for child development, but it does not explicitly clarify what child development means, and its jurisprudence lacks any coherent interpretation of the child's right to development. Thus, the committee is failing to accomplish what has been described by its former chairperson, Jaap Doek, to be its 'core activity'[267] – namely, to monitor the implementation of the Convention.

Derived from a range of psychosociological conceptions of 'development', the Committee's jurisprudence amounts to a detailed, but nevertheless biased, catalogue of how to raise a child while caring for her development. This catalogue creates the impression that the jurisprudence is substantial. But the Committee finds it difficult to translate its aspiration to protect children as 'becoming' human beings (and, therefore, their development) into the actual protection of their legal right to development. Despite its clear intentions, the Committee's interpretation does not provide any holistic concept of the right to development, but rather constitutes, at most, a very detailed catalogue of the steps necessary to protect the elusive concept of 'child development'.

---

[267] Jaap E. Doek, 'The CRC: Dynamics and Directions of Monitoring Its Implementation' in Antonella Invernizzi and Jane Williams (eds.), *The Human Rights of Children* (Ashgate Falmer, London 2011) 99–116, 99.

4

Exploring the Meanings of Human and Child Development

> Giving temporary freedom to a child does not always mean that the child will have freedom in future, and similarly, restricting the temporary freedom of a child may well expend the freedom that the child will have in the future. We, therefore, have to consider the freedom for a child in a lifelong perspective.
>
> Madoka Saito (2003)

This chapter compares and analyses three options for understanding human and child development and the potential to utilise them in developing a more coherent and concrete interpretation of the child's right to development.

The chapter is divided into three parts. The first part analyses the meaning of 'human development' under the right to development in 'general' international law.[1] In this part, I suggest adopting key principles of this right when interpreting the Convention on the Rights of the Child, including the distinction between the process of development and its outcomes, and the respect for people's agency and participation rights as part of realising their right to development. The second part studies the capability approach, presenting the concept of 'development as freedom', the importance of agency in developing one's capabilities, and the different ways to concretise, quantify, and contextualise people's capabilities. Here, I discuss the feasibility of adapting the capability approach as well as the applicability of basic capabilities lists to children, in the legal analysis of the child's right to development. I further suggest that children, like adults, should be conceived of as being entitled to develop in the capability approach's sense of the word. The third part looks at the

---

[1] The term 'general' international human rights law refers to human rights instruments such as the Universal Declaration on Human Rights or the 1966 Covenants, which are not group specific (unlike the Convention on the Rights of the Child or the Convention on the Elimination of All Forms of Discrimination against Women). In this chapter, unless otherwise specified, whenever the term 'right to development' is mentioned, it refers to the general right to development and not to the child's right to development.

various ways in which research into child indicators conceptualises and measures child development and well-being. In the third part, I ask whether the different indices that were developed over the years, with their various underpinned narratives of childhood, can be framed in children's human rights terms and utilised in the interpretation of the child's right to development.

This comparison makes it possible to draw on the experiences of utilising the terms 'human development' and 'child development' in law in similar domains, despite the different legal contexts in which these past exercises were conducted and their potentially different objectives.

The general right to development and the capability approach were created, to different extents, as responses to political conceptions that envisaged 'development' in terms of poverty elimination and bringing prosperity to the 'underdeveloped' world.[2] Based on liberal economic theories, 'development' was conceived of as being synonymous with an increase in per capita gross national product, advancing the notion that economic growth will trickle down and improve the economic conditions of all parts of the population.[3] 'Development' has been the foundation of Western international aid programs since the end of the Second World War, channelling billions of US dollars to 'underdeveloped' countries.[4] It has been criticised for focusing on systems rather than on people, perceiving the latter as means rather than ends. Feminist critique has highlighted the gender bias of this approach, arguing that it ignores women's role in society in general, and in the economy and labour market in particular.[5] Other critical approaches have claimed that

---

[2] As described by Harry Truman, the president of the United States, in his inaugural address on 20 January 1949.

[3] William A. Lewis, *The Theory of Economic Growth* (Routledge, London 2007; originally published 1950) 9–10, 420–421.

[4] David Hulme and Mark Turner, *Sociology and Development* (Harvester Wheatsheaf, New York 1990) 3–5; L. Amede Obiora, 'Beyond the Rhetoric of a Right to Development' (1996) 18 *Law & Policy* 355, 361.

[5] The first feminist critique on development was published in 1970 by Ester Boserup. See Ester Boserup, *Women's Role in Economic Development* (revised edition, Earthscan, London 2007; originally published 1970). See also Jane S. Jaquette and Kathleen Staudt, 'Women, Gender and Development' in Jane S. Jaquette and Gale Summerfield (eds.), *Women and Gender Equality in Development Theory and Practice* (Duke University Press, Durham and London 2006) 17–52; Naila Kabeer, *Reserved Realities: Gender Hierarchies in Development Thought* (Verso, London 1994) 76–77; Janet Mason, *Gender and Development* (2nd edition, Routledge, London 2011) 11; Cecile Jackson, 'Rescue Gender from the Poverty Trap' in Cecile Jackson and Ruth Pearson (eds.), *Feminist Visions of Development: Gender Analysis and Policy* (Routledge, London 1998) 39–64, 43–36.

'development' and 'aid' constitute new forms of imperialism and coloni-alism.[6] Such discussions are not the sort that you tend to find in children's rights scholarship. Nonetheless – and despite the fact that children were not, by and large, seen as rights holders under the general right to development, or thought of in the context of the capability approach – looking at this legal instrument (the general right to devel-opment), moral theory (the capability approach), and social science scholarship (child indicator movement) can be beneficial to our investi-gation of the child's right to development, as it broadens the discussion beyond the confinement of the Convention on the Rights of the Child and contemporary children's rights scholarship.[7] In particular, it teaches us about previous experiences of defining human development in con-crete terms, about the efforts of accommodating and utilising this term in international human rights law, and about developing concrete measures of implementation.

The Right to Development in General International Law

This part discusses the creation of the right to development in general international law, before discussing four issues: first, the meaning of the term 'human development'; second, the distinction between the process and outcomes of development; third, the respect for agency and the right to participation as integral parts of realising the right to development; and fourth, the differences between the collective and the individual aspects of this right. It will then consider what the general right to development can contribute to the analysis of the child's right to development.

The Creation of the General Right to Development

The right to development was not explicitly included in the primary post–Second World War international human rights law instruments,

---

[6] Arturo Escobar, *Encountering Development* (Princeton University Press, Princeton 1995). See also Uma Kothari, who describes the transition from colonial to development admin-istration: Uma Kothari, 'From Colonial Administration to Development Studies: A Post-Colonial Critique on the History of Development Studies' in Uma Kothari (ed.), *A Radical History of Development Studies* (Zed Books, New York 2005) 47–66; William Easterly, *The White Man's Burden* (Oxford University Press, Oxford 2006). See also Cheryl McEwan, *Postcolonialism and Development* (Routledge, New York 2009); Ivan D. Illich, *Celebration of Awareness: A Call for Institutional Revolution* (Calder & Boyars, London 1969).

[7] Ann Quennerstedt, 'Children's Rights Research Moving into the Future – Challenges on the Way Forward' (2013) 21 *International Journal of Children's Rights* 233.

namely the Universal Declaration of Human Rights and the 1966 Covenants. None of these documents makes an explicit reference to a right called 'the right to development', although arguably they plant the seeds for future recognition of it by protecting socioeconomic rights and ideas concerning freedom and self-determination.[8] The suggestion to create an explicit right to development in international human rights law was first introduced in 1972 in a speech given by Keba M'Baye, the former vice president of the International Court of Justice.[9] Against an 'on-going experience of decolonialization'[10] in Africa and other parts of the world, M'Baye suggested creating the right to development as a means of integrating 'an emancipatory ideal of development into international human rights law'.[11] This idea was supported by critical scholars and activists working in international aid and development, who felt a need to ground their work in international law as a means of reducing its dependency on the goodwill of governments – which, in turn, had no legal obligation to support and facilitate the work of these agencies.[12]

In 1977, M'Baye, by then the chairperson of the UN Commission on Human Rights, continued to roll what Peter Uvin termed the 'snowball' of the right to development,[13] leading the Commission to launch a study about the 'international dimensions of the right to development as a human right'.[14] Not surprisingly, the study concluded with the

---

[8] Philip Alston, 'The Shortcomings of a "Garfield the Cat" Approach to the Right to Development' (1985) 15 *California Western International Law Journal* 510. See also Dinah Shelton, 'A Response to Donnelly and Alston' (1985) 15 *California Western International Law Journal* 524, 526. The understanding of development as a commitment of international solidarity is also reflected in Article 4 of the Convention on the Rights of the Child. See Wouter Vandenhole, 'Economic, Social and Cultural Rights in the CRC: Is There a Legal Obligation to Cooperate Internationally for Development?' (2009) 17 *International Journal of Children's Rights* 23.

[9] Arjun Sengupta, 'Realizing the Right to Development' (2000) 31 *Development and Change* 553, 555; Peter Uvin, *Human Rights and Development* (Kumarian Press, Sterling, Virginia 2004) 40–41.

[10] Paul H. Brietzke, 'Consorting with the Chameleon, or Realizing the Right to Development' (1985) 15 *California Western International Law Journal* 560, 582.

[11] *Ibid.*

[12] Paul J. Nelson and Ellen Dorsey, 'At the Nexus of Human Rights and Development: New Methods and Strategies of Global NGOs' (2003) 31 *World Development* 2013.

[13] Uvin, *supra* n. 9, 40.

[14] UN Commission on Human Rights, Resolution 4 (XXXIII) of 21 February 1977, UN Doc. E/CN.4/RES/4(XXXIII).

recommendation to acknowledge this right.[15] The Commission on Human Rights followed this recommendation with a series of debates about the meaning of the right to development, its connection to 'development' policies, and its relationship to other human rights.[16] On the positive level, these debates resulted in the adoption of the Declaration on the Right to Development by the General Assembly in 1986,[17] which essentially created this right.[18]It is worth noting that the adoption process, as well as the many academic debates about this right, took place in parallel to the drafting process of the Convention on the Rights of the Child. Despite the coincidence in time, the 1986 Declaration is silent about children, and children are considered neither as right holders nor as beneficiaries of the general right to development.[19] In 1993, four years after the adoption of the Convention on the Rights of the Child, the Vienna Declaration and Programme of Action reaffirmed the 1986 Declaration's recognition of development as a human right.[20] The Vienna Declaration explicitly acknowledges children as holders of the general right to development,[21] and the potential implications of this recognition are discussed below.

The Meaning of 'Human Development' and the 'Right to Development'

The 1986 Declaration defines the terms 'human development' and the 'right to development' as 'an inalienable human right by virtue of which

---

[15] On third-generation human rights, see Philip Alston, 'A Third Generation of Solidarity Rights: Progressive Development or Obfuscation on International Human Rights Law?' (1982) 29 *Netherlands International Law Review* 307.

[16] See, for example, Philip Alston, 'Making Space for New Human Rights: The Case of the Right to Development' (1988) 1 *Harvard Human Rights Yearbook* 3; Stephen Marks, 'The Human Right to Development: Between Rhetoric and Reality' (2004) 17 *Harvard Human Rights Journal* 137, 138–141. See also Margot Salomon, *Global Responsibility for Human Rights* (Oxford University Press, Oxford 2007) 64–109; Daniel J. Whelan, *Indivisible Human Rights* (University of Pennsylvania Press, Philadelphia 2010) 167–168.

[17] Adopted by General Assembly Resolution 41/128 of 4 December 1986, UN Doc. A/RES/41/128.

[18] Jack Donnelly, 'In Search of the Unicorn: The Jurisprudence and Politics of the Right to Development' (1985) 15 *California Western International Law Journal* 473, 478.

[19] Noam Peleg, 'What Do We Mean When We Speak about Children's Right to Development?' in Farhad Malekiam and Kerstin Nordlöf (eds.), *The Sovereignty of Children in Law* (Cambridge Scholarly Publishing, Cambridge 2012) 134–156.

[20] United Nations General Assembly, *Vienna Declaration and Program of Action* (12 July 1993), UN Doc. A/CONF.157/23. See Obiora, *supra* n. 4, 379–380.

[21] See Articles 18, 21, 29, and 45–53.

every human person and all peoples are entitled to participate in, contribute to, and enjoy economic, social, cultural and political development, in which all human rights and fundamental freedoms can be fully realized'.[22] This definition refers to four domains of development: economic, social, cultural, and political.[23] All four are connected to societies and states, unlike the developmental domains protected by the Convention on the Rights of the Child. A textual reading suggests that the right to development can be understood as a right to enjoy the outcome of the four domains of collective development, whereas during the process of development all the rights and freedoms of individuals should be 'fully realised'. Thus, the realisation of collective development will create the necessary conditions for individuals to enjoy their human rights. The development process, as such, is external to the individual, who is, in turn, the beneficiary of this process.

Article 2(3) adds another dimension to 'development' by suggesting that development is 'the constant improvement of well-being of the entire population and of all individuals'. Here, the collective and the individual are connected, the importance of non-discrimination and inclusion is inexplicitly highlighted,[24] and the process of collective development is seen as a vehicle to improve personal well-being. In that sense, the right reaches beyond the 'notions of economic growth to the expansions of opportunities and capabilities to enjoy those opportunities'[25] by individuals. But, as Donnelly argues, 'individual development is a likely (although not a necessary) consequence of respect for economic and social rights'.[26] Which means that, yet again, and unlike the perception of development under the Convention, the individual is not the one who develops, and the individual right to development is essentially a right to enjoy the fruits of collective progress of development, which includes protection for human rights and well-being.

---

[22] Article 1(1).

[23] For more on this definition, see Hans-Otto Sano, 'Development and Human Rights: The Necessary, but Partial Integration of Human Rights and Development' (2000) 22 *Human Rights Quarterly* 734, 736. See also Allan Rosas, 'The Right to Development' in Asbjørn Eida *et al.* (eds.), *Economic, Social and Cultural Rights* (2nd edition, Kluwer International, The Hague 2001) 119–130, 123–124.

[24] Arjun Sengupta, 'The Human Right to Development' (2004) 32 *Oxford Development Studies* 179, 180.

[25] Sengupta, 'Realizing the Right to Development', *supra* n. 9, 566.

[26] Donnelly, *supra* n. 18.

The debate about whether the individual is a direct or indirect beneficiary seems less relevant to critics who argue that this right is an 'entirely pointless' idea within the framework of international human rights law and a 'hopelessly utopian'[27] concept. Further, it is suggested that the 'general' right to development does not provide any new dimension or benefit to the already existing set of recognised socioeconomic rights, and as such is nothing more than an 'umbrella concept' lacking any distinct meaning.[28] Arjun Sengupta, the former UN independent expert on the right to development, rejects this critique. He argues that the right should be seen not merely as a title that joins together civil and political rights with economic, social, and cultural rights,[29] nor as the summary of a set of rights. Instead, Sengupta asserts that all human rights are interdependent and, as such, are essential foundations for the realisation of the right to development. In other words, the realisation of the right to development depends on the protection of other rights as a precondition, but protecting other rights will not, in itself, equate to the realisation of the right to development: the sum is greater than the parts.

Moreover, Sengupta claims that the right should be perceived as an integrated whole,[30] which means the right to the 'exercise of the full range of rights; as a goal it is the self-actualization of people through the exercise of their rights'.[31] This interpretation goes beyond the immediate and inherent benefit of realising different human rights, preferring a more abstract conception of self-actualization.[32] The idea mirrors the origins of this right as a tool for emancipation, which is also embraced by the 1986 Declaration when it suggests that development 'also implies the full realization of the right of peoples to self-determination, which includes . . . their inalienable right to full sovereignty over all their natural wealth and resources' (Article 1(2)).

A somewhat different interpretation of the 1986 Declaration suggests that instead of being understood as an integrated right, the right to development can be conceptualised as a vector. According to Sengupta, a vector right means that the right to development should be understood as a composite right 'where all the rights are realised together,

---

[27] Richard Warren Perry, 'Rethinking the Right to Development: After the Critique of Development, after the Critique of Rights' (1996) 18 *Law & Society* 225, 228.

[28] Rosas, *supra* n. 23, 129.

[29] Arjun Sengupta, 'Implementing the Right to Development' in Nico J. Schrijver and Friedl Weiss (eds.), *International Law and Sustainable Development: Principles and Practice* (Martinus Nijhoff Publishers, Leiden 2004) 341–377, 343.

[30] *Ibid.*, 343.   [31] *Ibid.*   [32] *Ibid.*

recognizing their interdependence, not just their aggregation. The whole is greater than the sum of the parts ... the component rights are related in a non-linear way with positive feedback ... it is a composite of all the human rights implemented in an integrated manner as a part of a development program in the context of the growth of resources'.[33] Donnelly argues that even this interpretation fails to provide a distinct meaning for 'development', with the right to development and, more so, 'development' in itself remaining the objective of other human rights.[34] This might be too harsh a critique. 'Development' in the 'right to development' refers to the emancipation, growth, and prosperity of people. As a human right, it means that people have the right to enjoy the benefits of economic growth, which is assisted by the realisation of all their other human rights. In the next chapter, I will return to the suggestion that we understand the right to development as a composite right.

Distinguishing between the Process of Development and Its Outcome

The general right to development differentiates between two aspects of human development: the process of development and its outcome. According to the preamble of the 1986 Declaration, 'The human person is the central subject of the development *process*' (emphasis added), and the objective of this process is to improve the 'well-being of the entire population and of all individuals' (Article 2(3)). According to Sengupta, the process of development should not be seen as a means to an end: both the process and the outcome of development are not only equally important,[35] but also indivisible. Leslye Obiora further emphasises the importance of the process of development, arguing that it enables people to exercise their human rights[36] (rather than seeing the outcome of development as a precondition for realising human rights). John O'Manique suggests that the meaning and implications of protecting the process and the outcome of development can be better understood if examined from the right holder's point of view. From this perspective, the right to development can be understood as a right that protects both the process and the outcome of development, while

---

[33] Sengupta, 'The Human Right to Development', *supra* n. 24, 183.
[34] Donnelly, *supra* n. 18, 484.
[35] Sengupta, 'The Human Right to Development', *supra* n. 24, 183.
[36] Obiora, *supra* n. 4, 389.

actualising the 'human potential as defined by the individual and his or her community'.[37]

This analytical distinction between the outcome and the process of development is valuable when thinking about children. Under the 'human becomings' paradigm, most attention is placed on the end result of the development process. The expectation is to see children transform into adults. According to the 'human beings' paradigm, the process of maturation is respected too. A question that should be asked is whether the child's right to development protects the process of development (that is, the process of growing up) or the outcome of this process (that is, the end product of the process, which is the adult whom the child becomes) – or both.

Respecting People's Agency and Right to Participation

A key aspect of the right to development is the recognition of, and respect for, people's agency and right to participation. Article 1 of the 1986 Declaration acknowledges this ideal in clear terms, stating that 'every human person ... [is] entitled to participate in, contribute to, and enjoy economic, social, cultural and political development'. The Declaration further adds that the individual 'should be the active participant' in the right to development (Article 2(1)), since the 'meaningful participation' of people is essential to the realisation of the right and should be an integral part of the development process (Article 2(3)).

Respecting people's agency is the reason for, as well as the outcome of, respecting their right to self-determination.[38] Participation contributes to the elimination of exclusion and enhances community mobilisation efforts.[39] Mainstreaming the right to participation as part of the right to development conforms to the perception that empowerment and emancipation are the objectives of the right to development. The right to participate –including the right to vote as a partial, but not conclusive, element – also enhances democratic values,[40] and in turn empowers people and gives them the opportunity to shape their personal and

---

[37] John O'Manique, 'Development, Human Rights and Law' (1992) 14 *Human Rights Quarterly* 383, 384.

[38] Alston, 'The Shortcomings of a "Garfield the Cat" Approach', *supra* n. 8, 512; Sengupta, 'The Human Right to Development', *supra* n. 24, 180–181.

[39] Russel Lawrence Barsh, 'The Right to Development as a Human Right: Results of the Global Consultation' (1991) 13 *Human Rights Quarterly* 322, 329.

[40] Salomon, *supra* n. 16, 181.

collective futures. Achieving these objectives requires, inter alia, that participatory processes should be 'centred around the concept of equity and justice'.[41]

As participation gives people a voice – transforming them from passive beneficiaries of economic development or victims of political oppression into active agents of change –we can draw an important similarity between the right to development and the protection of children's right to participation in Article 12 of the Convention, and the human beings conception of childhood. As we saw in Chapter 3, the Committee on the Rights of the Child rarely links the protection of child development and the child's right to development with the right to participation.

Between an Individual and a Collective Right

As previously discussed, the right to development was envisioned as part of decolonisation and emancipation processes. Therefore, the right includes a collective element in the form of people's right to self-determination and economic development.[42] Article 1(1) states that it is the right of 'every human person and all peoples'. People 'individually and collectively' (Article 2(2)) are responsible for development, though states bear the 'duty to formulate appropriate national development policies that aim at the constant improvement of the well-being of the entire population' (Article 2(3)).

In subsequent articles, the Declaration categorises the right holders according to different goals of 'development'. For example, as a collective right, 'peoples' are the ones who enjoy the right to self-determination (Article 1(2)). Individuals, nonetheless, are the central subjects of development (Article 2(1)). This tension, Obiora argues, requires reconciling the 'antithetical and hierarchical' relationship between these two dimensions.[43] The focus should be on people, while states, as the political representations of the collective, should be seen not as right holders but rather as duty bearers.[44] Obiora further suggests that 'the assumption is that the satisfaction of the collective right and the right to development in particular is a necessary condition for the materialization of the individual right'.[45] Another possible interpretation is, according to Donnelly, to

---

[41] Sengupta, 'Realizing the Right to Development', *supra* n. 9, 566.
[42] Shelton, *supra* n. 8, 525.   [43] Obiora, *supra* n. 4, 359.   [44] Brietzke *supra* n. 10, 566.
[45] Obiora *supra* n. 4, 389.

put a greater emphasis on the individual dimension of this right, defining it as 'a right to pursue full personal development along all major dimensions of human life' and thus 'a right to full personal development can stand as a summary of traditional rights'.[46] To a large extent, this definition is aligned with the way in which the child's right to development is currently interpreted, but at the same time it undermines the categorisation of the right to development as an independent right with a distinct meaning.

Paul Brietzke suggests a different perspective on the individual–collective divide. According to his approach, the right to development should be understood as a right of individuals that can only be realised through a collective effort. Every person should be perceived as a right holder, but the right will not be realised by the actions of an individual alone. Every right holder should be located 'at the beginning and at the end of the [development] process', while 'the middle of the process, the implementing of the right to development through a broadly-defined production, can only be achieved collectively and through interdependent domestic sectors and, ultimately, the international community'.[47] The perspective is rooted in the conception of human development as a collective mobilisation process that can lead to individual development. This point is further developed by the capability approach, as will be discussed below.

Another possible way to integrate these two dimensions is to understand that the right to development 'incorporates personal rights', but nevertheless, Sengupta argues, it 'has to be implemented mainly by collective actions'.[48] But even Sengupta eventually admits that the right 'aims at the constant improvement of the well-being of the entire population on the basis of their active, free and meaningful participation and the fair distribution of benefits resulting therefrom',[49] further emphasising the importance of economic growth as 'both an objective and a means' of development.[50] This suggests that the tension between the collective and individual dimensions of the right to development leans towards favouring collective progress as a means of facilitating personal emancipation. But this approach advances the view that only economic and political progress can create the necessary material and social conditions for every individual to enjoy the full scale of human rights. To some

[46] Donnelly, *supra* n. 18, 501.   [47] Brietzke, *supra* n. 10, 593.
[48] Sengupta, 'Realizing the Right to Development', *supra* n. 9, 569.
[49] Sengupta, 'Implementing the Right to Development', *supra* n. 29, 346.   [50] *Ibid.*, 347.

extent, this conclusion undermines the view that people are at the centre of development. It also ignores personal domains of development, such as emotional or psychological development, which are affected by personal relationships (for example, between family members) and not only by material living conditions and political conditions. In that sense, human development is a collective condition that people and individuals enjoy, but it is not individuals who develop, or who are entitled to develop, their own personality and self.

What Can the General Right to Development Contribute to the Analysis of the Child's Right to Development?

The main difficulty in drawing comparisons between the general right to development and the child's right to development, and utilising the former in analysing the latter, is the somewhat contrasting objectives of these two rights. While the two rights share the yardstick of growth, the general right to development focuses on collective progress as an objective and a precondition to personal freedom, while the child's right to development looks at the multilayered process of personal change. Nonetheless, the two rights have an ultimate objective, which is essentially to enable every human being to fulfil her human potential.

The analysis of the child's right to development can benefit from this specific articulation of 'human development' and from the thematic distinction between the process of development and its outcome and the duties that these different dimensions entail. Thus far, the interpretation of the child's right to development has focused on protecting the outcome of the developmental process – creating the adult whom the child should 'become'. But if the process of development is deemed to be as important as its outcome, then it will not only reaffirm the significance of the time of childhood and respect the child as a right holder but also enable the child to see her right to participation realised in the context of her own development. In other words, it will enable the human beings model to be upheld also in the interpretation of the child's right to development.

The general right to development can also add another dimension to the interpretation of the various articles in the Convention on the Rights of the Child that refer to child development – as well as to Article 4, which speaks about international cooperation and development. The Convention focuses on individual elements of development and refers to the context of political and economic conditions as factors that affect the realisation of some socioeconomic rights of the child (for example, Articles 27 and 24). Reading these references using the lens provided by the general right to development can lead to the conclusion that children ought to enjoy the benefits of collective development as a separate objective of their individual right to development, in addition to their own personal development.

The Capability Approach and the Child's Right to Development

This section analyses the capability approach's conception of human development, the centrality of respecting people's agency in this concept, and the potential avenues for utilising the approach in analysing the child's right to development. It begins with some background on this approach before moving to discuss the concept of human development that it utilises, as well as its nexus with questions of agency and capabilities. The section concludes with some suggestions on how these conceptions can be used in the analysis of the child's right to development. There is some overlap between this section and the previous section, which discussed the general right to development. This is unavoidable due to the interrelatedness of the two, and their mutual influences, and it is necessary in order to present and discuss the capability approach in a coherent and clear way.

The capability approach (or approaches)[51] has constituted a paradigm shift in the understanding of 'development' in economics and political science, suggesting that human development should not be thought of only in terms of economic growth as a means of eliminating poverty and satisfying people's 'basic needs'.[52] Rather, development should be comprehended as a process that facilitates people's ability to live lives that are worth living.[53] Based on the seminal work of Amartya Sen and Martha Nussbaum, human development is, in a nutshell, 'freedom'.[54]

---

[51] It has also been suggested that the capability approach should be called 'the capability creation'. Des Gasper, 'What Is the Capability Approach? Its Core, Rationale, Partners and Dangers' (2007) 36 *Journal of Socio-Economics* 335, 346.

[52] Gustavo Esteva, 'Development' in Wolfgang Sachs (ed.), *The Development Dictionary* (Zed Books, London 1992) 6–25; Paul Streeten and Shahid Javed Burki, 'Basic Needs: Some Issues' (1978) 6 *World Development* 411. On women's basic needs, see Ingrid Palmer, 'Rural Women and the Basic Needs Approach to Development' (1977) 115 *International Labour Review* 97.

[53] Andrew Moore and Roger Crisp, 'Welfarism in Moral Theory' (1996) 74 *Australian Journal of Philosophy* 598; Lawrence Hamilton, 'A Theory of True Interests in the Work of Amartya Sen' (1999) 34 *Government and Opposition* 516.

[54] Amartya Sen, *Development as Freedom* (Oxford University Press, Oxford 1999).

By and large, children have been left out of the debates concerning the capability approach.[55] This book does not attempt to address all the questions raised by the relationship between this approach, children, and children's rights. Instead, I ask two questions: Can the capability approach's conception of human development be employed in analysing the child's right to development? And, if the answer is affirmative: How can this be done?

Human Development According to the Capability Approach

Against the tendency to focus on economic growth and poverty reduction as the only pillars of development,[56] or, like international children's rights law, on personal domains of development, the capability approach conceptualises human development, and its objectives, in different terms. Defining itself against the objective of advancing people's quality of life and well-being, the capability approach seeks to expand people's capability to increase their 'real opportunities' and to have a stake in shaping their own lives.[57] According to Sen, freedom to choose is 'both the primary end' and 'the principal means of development'.[58] Expanding the freedoms that people have enriches their lives[59] and 'allows them to be fuller social persons, exercising our own volitions and interacting with – and influencing – the world in which we live'.[60] The capability approach also draws attention to structural implications of disability, social exclusion, chronic poverty, democratic values and human dignity, considering the influence of these factors on an individual's freedom.[61] In that sense, similarity can be drawn with Kimberlé Crenshaw's theory of intersectionality,[62] which proposes that social categorisations – such as

---

[55] Flavio Comim et al., 'Introduction – Theoretical Foundations and the Book's Roadmap' in Mario Biggeri et al. (eds.), Children and the Capability Approach (Palgrave, Hampshire 2011) 3–21, 6.

[56] On that aspect of development, see Steven Pressman and Gale Summerfield, 'The Economic Contribution of Amartya Sen' (2000) 12 Review of Political Economy 89.

[57] Rosalind Dixon and Martha Nussbaum, 'Children's Rights and a Capability Approach: The Question of Special Priority' (2011–2012) 97 Cornell Law Review 549, 557.

[58] Sen, Development as Freedom, supra n. 54, 16.

[59] Sabina Alkire, 'Using the Capability Approach: Prospective and Evaluative Analyses' in Flavio Comim et al. (eds.), The Capability Approach (Cambridge University Press, Cambridge 2008) 26–50, 28.

[60] Sen, Development as Freedom, supra n. 54, 14.   [61] Ibid.

[62] Kimberlé Crenshaw, 'Mapping the Margins: Intersectionality, Identity Politics, and Violence against Women of Color' (1991) Stanford Law Review 1241.

race, ethnicity, religion, class, gender and sexual orientation – are inherently interconnected, mutually constituted and converging, thereby creating interdependent systems of disadvantage and discrimination. For Crenshaw, intersectionality is a theoretical prism that sheds new light on the operation of law. For the capability approach, intersections of identity and social context are a prognosis that should be used in creating the means necessary for a specific individual to be free.

'Unfreedom', according to the capability approach, is a deprivation of capabilities, such as being famine struck or undernourished; having little access to social services, such as health care, functional education, and clean water; or having no economic security. 'Unfreedom' can also be manifested in broader terms as an inequality 'between women and men [and] denial of political liberty and basic civil rights'.[63] Sen argues that social exclusion and heterogeneity are two key factors in generating inequality and unfreedom. Social, political, economic, and cultural power structures constitute the core causes of unfreedoms, since they prevent the marginalised from benefiting from economic prosperity. A related issue is household inequality and the effects of poverty. Sen claims that increasing the family income as a means of eliminating household material poverty is false, since it is based on the perception of household equality, where welfare is distributed fairly. However, this perception ignores the realities of many women, children, and the elderly, for whom decisions are made on the basis of a patriarchal order, thereby rendering them less likely to have their needs met (and girls are usually discriminated against more than boys).[64]

The capability approach further challenges the perception that poor people are a homogeneous group. Instead, it suggests that gender, disability, age, and illness are relevant factors that should be accounted for when speaking about the levels of income and accessibility to social services necessary to maintain a standard of living that is comparable to that of people who have no special needs.[65] For example, a person with physical disability often spends a larger amount of money – and probably

---

[63] Sen, *Development as Freedom*, *supra* n. 54, 15.

[64] *Ibid.*, 70–71. On the different experiences of girls and boys and the relevance to human rights, see Nura Taefi, 'The Synthesis of Age and Gender: Intersectionality, International Human Rights Law and the Marginalisation of the Girl-Child' (2009) 17 *International Journal of Human Rights* 345. See also Leena Alanen, 'Editorial: "Intersectionality" and Other Challenges to Theorizing Childhood' (2016) 23 *Childhood* 157.

[65] It is interesting to compare these arguments to the theory of intersectionality: Crenshaw, *supra* n. 62.

a larger percentage of her income – on medications and treatments (and she might also need increased and more frequent access to health care services, thus compromising her status in the job market) in comparison to a person at the same income level but without such disability. Therefore, 'developing' and maintaining a similar standard of living require a different, and probably higher, level of resources for her. The same logic should be used when thinking about children and human development, as they too have unique needs that ought to be met so they can enjoy dignified lives.[66]

Three additional concepts used by the capability approach need to be addressed: agency, functions, and capabilities. Respecting individual agency and the idea that people should live their lives according to their own wishes and aspirations, instead of being bound by a set of choices made by others,[67] or by circumstances beyond their control, such as socioeconomic conditions (which are the subject of the collective right to development discussed earlier), is one of the key principles of the capability approach. Similar to the general right to development, the capability approach sees the individual as 'someone who acts and brings about change, and whose achievements can be judged in terms of her own values and objectives, whether or not we assess them in terms of some external criteria as well'.[68] Participation of people is therefore the best way to realise those personal preferences, and it also guarantees people's freedoms since it 'enhances the ability of people to help themselves and also to influence the world ... the concern here relates to what we may call the "agency aspect" of the individual'.[69] Denying people the ability to choose not only denies their agency but also, according to Nussbaum, 'makes life not worthy of human dignity'.[70]

Functions are 'the various things a person may value being and doing'.[71] Functions include, for example, having a job and being healthy, as well as more abstract or less tangible predilections, such as being happy. The capability approach does not prescribe one definitive set of preferences,[72] as every person should be able to define their own

---

[66] Dixon and Nussbaum, *supra* n. 57, 556–563.

[67] Amartya Sen, *Inequality Re-examined* (Harvard University Press, Cambridge 1992) 39.

[68] Sen, *Development as Freedom*, *supra* n. 54, 18–19.   [69] *Ibid.*, 18.

[70] Martha C. Nussbaum, *Creating Capabilities: The Human Development Approach* (Harvard University Press, Cambridge 2011) 31.

[71] Sen, *Development as Freedom*, *supra* n. 54, 75.

[72] Amartya Sen, 'Human Rights and Capabilities' (2005) 6 *Journal of Human Development* 151, 157–160.

functions. But a necessary precondition to being able to define any set of functions and to live accordingly is having the necessary capabilities to do so. Sen uses the availability of food as an example to illustrate this point and the relationship between functions and capabilities: if a person does not eat, it might be because she does not have access to food or, alternatively, because she has made a decision to fast or to diet.[73] While the latter is a matter of choice (function), the former is a lack of capabilities. Capabilities are, therefore, 'the range of options a person has in deciding what kind of life to lead',[74] which 'represent the various combinations of functioning (being and doing) that the person can achieve',[75] and as such they constitute one's freedom. Nussbaum defines capabilities in slightly different terms, claiming that capabilities are what enable people to execute their human functions.[76] Capabilities should, therefore, be understood as 'what people are actually able to do and to be'.[77] According to Nussbaum, all human beings ought to have the freedom to choose whether or not they exercise these capabilities and the ways in which they do so, while the role of the state is to establish the 'material and institutional environment so people are actually able to function'.[78]

Distinguishing between internal capabilities and substantial freedoms can help to flush out the meanings of 'freedom' and 'capabilities' a little more. Internal capabilities are the person's intellectual and emotional capacities, fitness and health, learning skills and so on. Substantial freedom is the ability to make a choice, which depends on personal capacities, as well as the political, social, and economic environment in which a person lives, as combined capabilities. Bearing this distinction in mind, social policy that asks to promote human capabilities should support the development of internal capabilities 'through education resources to enhance physical and emotional health, support for family care and love, a system of education and much more'.[79] But providing education does not necessarily guarantee the production of an individual's internal capabilities. For example, people can be provided with literacy education

[73] Sen, *Inequality Re-examined, supra* n. 67.

[74] Jean Drèze and Amartya Sen, *India: Economic Development and Social Opportunity* (Oxford University Press, Oxford 1995) 10.

[75] Sen, *Inequality Re-examined, supra* n. 67, 4.

[76] Martha Nussbaum, 'Women's Capabilities and Social Justice' (2000) 1 *Journal of Human Development* 219, 242.

[77] *Ibid.*, 222–223.   [78] *Ibid.*, 235.

[79] Nussbaum, *Creating Capabilities, supra* n. 70, 21.

as a means of developing their capability to express themselves. But if they are denied the right to freedom of expression, their combined capability is also denied.[80] Therefore, combined capabilities cannot be provided 'without producing internal capabilities'.[81] This is a vital distinction when it comes to children and their right to development, as will be discussed in the next section.

Another aspect of capabilities that should be considered here is 'capability security'. Jonathan Wolff and Avner de-Shalit suggest that providing people with capabilities alone does not fulfil the goal of extending freedom, not least because people need some level of certainty about their future in order to enjoy the ability to choose. They therefore suggest talking about capability security as an issue concerning the length of time for which each capability will be protected, and the extent to which it will be protected. Wolff and de-Shalit further suggest that having a guarantee for a certain capability – for example, the right to education – in a constitutional document provides sufficient protection and security, in comparison to having the same capability guaranteed in law, in administrative acts, or in customs – or not guaranteed at all.

In light of this approach, Nussbaum is right to ask what new roles, if any, capability security ascribes to states and to courts.[82] After all, even this kind of constitutional instrument does not provide the necessary protection if a person lacks access to courts, or does not have confidence in the judiciary.[83] For children, as will be discussed later, capability security is important because they lack the political influence required to make capabilities accessible and available.

The Capability Approach and the Child's Right to Development

In this section, I argue that children are entitled to develop also in the capability approach's sense of the word. Further, using the capability approach's conception of human development when analysing the right to development of children can remedy two shortcomings in the current understanding of this right: first, a lack of recognition of children's

---

[80] *Ibid.*, 23.   [81] *Ibid.*   [82] *Ibid.*, 43.
[83] Jonathan Wolff and Avner de-Shalit, *Disadvantage* (Oxford University Press, Oxford 2007). See also Sano, *supra* n. 23, 749–750. To some extent, this argument is similar to the connection that some, like David Kennedy, make between the rule of law, access to justice, and development. David Kennedy, 'Laws and Development' in John Hatchard and Amanda Perry-Kessaris (eds.), *Law and Development: Facing Complexity in the 21st Century* (Cavendish, London 2003) 17–26.

agency and ignorance of their right to participation; and second, an insufficient concretisation of the right. Utilising the capability approach's conception of development in this context can also enable us to redefine the meaning of 'child development'. But first there is a need to address the preliminary questions concerning the adaptability of the capability approach to international human rights law, and the nexus between the capability approach and children.

Children have rarely featured in capability approach scholarship, and only recently do we see a change in their treatment. One of the main reasons for this silence is Sen's adoption of the human becomings model of childhood, denoting that children will have to enjoy their freedoms in the future, when they become competent adults.[84] The 'opportunities children have today and will have tomorrow, in line with what they can be reasonably expected to want', Sen writes, 'is a matter of public policy and social programmes'.[85] Competency, therefore, is the key difficulty that Sen sees in linking children and the capability approach. Madoka Saito expresses a similar concern when asking 'how can we apply the capability approach to children, since children are not mature enough to make decision by themselves?'[86] Likewise, Jérôme Ballet and colleagues assert that the 'capability approach obviously implies the individual's capacity for self-determination, which may not apply to children'.[87] David Archard holds a similar view, suggesting that a child can be denied the right to self-determination so that she will be able to exercise this right in adulthood.[88]

Questioning children's competence and capacity to choose is not unique to this context. These sorts of questions are at the heart of the debates concerning children's rights, and are being asked with respect to almost every aspect of the child's life – including, for example, consent to medical treatment,[89] sex-reassignment

---

[84] Madoka Saito, 'Amartya Sen's Capability Approach to Education: A Critical Exploration' (2003) 37 *Journal of Philosophy of Education*, 25.

[85] Amartya Sen, 'Children and Human Rights' (2007) 1 *Indian Journal of Human Development* 235, 241.

[86] Saito, *supra* n. 84, 25.

[87] Jérôme Ballet *et al.*, 'Children's Agency and the Capability Approach: A Conceptual Framework' in Mario Biggeri *et al.* (eds.), *Children and the Capability Approach* (Palgrave, Hampshire 2011) 22–45, 24.

[88] David Archard, 'Children, Adults, Best Interests and Rights' (2013) 13 *Medical Law International* 55, 70.

[89] A leading UK case is *Gillick v. West Norfolk and Wisbech Area Health Authority* [1986] AC 112. See Michael Freeman, 'Rethinking Gillick' (2005) 13 *International Journal of Children's Rights* 201; Eva De Clercq *et al.*, 'Is Decision-Making Capacity an "Essentially

operations,[90] crime and punishment,[91] the age of criminal responsibility,[92] and the right to vote.[93] Predominantly, these are debates about children's entitlement, and not about any 'empirical' capacity to choose. I therefore argue that the capability approach should be deemed as relevant to children for all the reasons that it seems relevant to all people, including the elderly and people with physical or mental disabilities. Claiming that the capability approach is not relevant to children based on the suggestion that children lack the capacity to choose undermines the core principle of the capability approach itself. One cannot advocate for respecting the human dignity and agency of all people –especially those who formerly were at the margins of their societies and were perceived as lacking (certain) capacities – and at the same time deny the applicability of this universal principle to children by arguing that they lack the capacity to choose and cannot be agents in their own rights. The unsubstantiated repeated proposition that children lack the required capacity to be free is a self-fulfilling prophecy, as it creates a situation where children are also denied the opportunity to challenge this presumption, thus perpetuating denial of their agency.[94] This vicious circle excludes children from society and deprives them of the ability to develop, in line with the capability approach's own conception of development. Even Nussbaum's definitions of internal capabilities and combined capabilities deny children the opportunity to 'develop' in the capability approach's sense of the word. Therefore, change will happen if children's internal capabilities are developed, primarily by education, and if they begin to be seen as active agents in this process too.

Contested" Concept in Pediatrics?' (2017) 20 *Medicine, Health Care and Philosophy* 425–433.

90 *Re Kelvin* [2017] FamCAFC 258.

91 *Roper v. Simmons*, 543 U.S. 551 (2005); *Miller v. Alabama*, 567 U.S. 460 (2012).

92 Different countries subscribe different ages of criminal responsibility, ranging from 7 to 18 years. Angela Melchiorre and Ed Atkins, *At What Age Are School-Children Employed, Married and Taken to Court?* (Right to Education Project, London 2011) 30–32.

93 Marc Jans, 'Children as Citizens' (2004) 11 *Childhood* 27; John Wall, 'Can Democracy Represent Children? Towards a Politics of Difference' (2012) 19 *Childhood* 86; Jeremy Roche, 'Children: Rights, Participation and Citizenship' (1999) 6 *Childhood* 475; Aoife Nolan, *Children's Socio-Economic Rights, Democracy and the Courts* (Hart, Oxford 2011) 43–92.

94 On this point, see Katherine Hunt Federle, 'Rights Flow Downhill' (1994) 2 *International Journal of Children's Rights* 343. But see Katherine Hunt Federle, 'Do Rights Still Flow Downhill?' (2017) 25 *International Journal of Children's Rights* 273.

In recent years, more attention has been given to children in discussing the capability approach. Departing from the image of children as mini adults, Comim and his colleagues investigate children's well-being and development in various domains, such as education and health, arguing that the Millennium Development Goals require paying attention to children's roles and positionalities in society.[95] Nigel Thomas and Daniel Stoecklin suggest that using the capability approach as a theoretical lens that is complementary to the recognition theory can improve our understanding of children's positionality in society and can also improve the ways in which empirical research about children is conducted.[96] The capability approach has also been used to measure what children can achieve in terms of their developmental trajectory by accounting for their available resources together with their caregivers' capabilities.[97]

In discussing the relationship between the capability approach and human rights law, Sen distinguishes between human rights norms and human rights law, claiming that the importance of the former does not necessarily require the existence of the latter. Nonetheless, Sen recognises that human rights law is a good rhetorical tool for creating and enforcing obligations on states to provide the capabilities necessary for human development.[98] Referring to the structure of international human rights law, Séverine Deneulin claims that utilising the capability approach's conception of development can enable us to 'look at the institutional framework that allows that right to be fulfilled'.[99] In other words, it is suggested not that human rights analysis should uphold the capability approach, but rather that it should utilise it in order to justify certain political obligations. Ballet et al. take a different approach to this question by suggesting that human rights and the capability approach can complement each other. While human rights can justify defending 'a list of

---

[95] Comim et al., supra n. 55.

[96] Nigel Thomas and Daniel Stoecklin, 'Recognition and Capability: A New Way to Understand How Children Can Achieve Their Rights?' in Claudio Baraldi and Tom Cockburn (eds.), Theorising Childhood: Citizenship, Rights and Participation (Palgrave Macmillan, Basingstoke 2018) 73–94, 75–80.

[97] Hinke Haisma et al., 'A Capability Approach to Child Growth: A Theoretical Approach' (2018) 14 Maternal & Child Nutrition 1.

[98] Amartya Sen, 'Capabilities and Well-Being' in Martha Nussbaum and Amartya Sen (eds.), Quality of Life (Oxford University Press, Oxford 1993) 30–53.

[99] Séverine Deneulin, 'Ideas Related to Human Development' in Séverine Deneulin and Lila Shahani (eds.), An Introduction to the Human Development and Capabilities Approach (Earthscan, London 2009) 49–70, 60.

relevant capabilities for children',[100] the capability approach 'can become a framework for normative evaluation and policy implementation'.[101] Ballet *et al.* develop this argument further, suggesting a concrete mode of operation: 'In the case of children, on the one hand human rights can be used as the main argument for defending a list of relevant capabilities for children ... and on the other the [capability approach] can become a framework for normative evaluation and policy implementation'.[102] In line with this argument, I suggest that when it comes to children, the capability approach can inform the interpretation and implementation of the Convention in general, and the right to development in particular. I will return to this idea in detail later, when discussing the potential contribution of the capability approach to concretising the child's right to development.

Polly Vizard claims that, despite Sen's reservations, international human rights law can be utilised to create 'a minimal list of central and basic capabilities with universal coverage'.[103] Likewise, Deneulin suggests that both the human rights approach and the capability approach are based on 'the maxim that individuals should not be treated as a means but as an end ... The human rights approach enhances human development with its stronger focus on obligations and duties, while the latter remains an evaluative framework for assessing states of affairs'.[104]

A different, and slightly more substantive, issue in employing the capability approach in a human rights framework is the question of equality and discrimination. While the recognition of diversity among people and the impacts that disadvantages have on people's development are central to the capability approach, Deneulin claims that 'the human rights approach does not necessarily take such differences into account'[105] and, therefore, will not fulfil the goals of the capability approach. The problem with this liberal analysis is that it ignores the notion of substantive equality and affirmative action. Human rights law does not ignore differences between people; on the contrary, it respects these differences and accounts for them. The 2007 Convention on the Rights of Persons with Disabilities is a good example of this approach,[106]

---

[100] Ballet *et al.*, *supra* n. 87, 39–40. [101] *Ibid.* [102] *Ibid.*, 39.

[103] Polly Vizard, 'Specifying and Justifying a Basic Capability Set: Should the International Human Rights Framework Be Given a More Direct Role?' (2007) 35 *Oxford Development Studies* 225, 235.

[104] Deneulin, *supra* n. 99, 60. [105] *Ibid.*, 61.

[106] See Dixon and Nussbaum's discussion about people with disabilities and US constitutional law: Dixon and Nussbaum, *supra* n. 57, 585–586.

as it includes, alongside liberal nondiscrimination clauses, some substantial equality requirements. Similarly, the differences between children and adults can and should be recognised under an equality and non-discrimination analysis.

In a similar vein, Nussbaum, in her own writing and when thinking about children in collaboration with Rosalind Dixon, probably sees more advantages in connecting the capability approach and human rights law, including children's rights law.[107] Nussbaum and Dixon argue that through the lens of the capability approach, children are recognised as human rights holders and prioritising their socioeconomic rights is justified.[108] Due to children's entitlement to see their human dignity protected, 'a range of rights for children with sensitivity both to children's welfare needs and to children's agency'[109] should be upheld. In their discussions about children's competence and agency, Dixon and Nussbaum compare children's rights to the rights of people with intellectual disabilities, arguing that recognition of children's rights is based on a similar 'moral claim of all human beings to be afforded full human dignity, regardless of their capacity for rational or reasoned participation in public or civil life'.[110] Therefore, and by taking the perspective of the capability approach, they claim that either children's 'vulnerability'[111] or, alternatively, a 'cost-effective analysis'[112] justifies affirmative action policies towards children, which can provide children with the necessary capabilities to be free.

While it might serve to illustrate why children's needs should be prioritised, the comparison between the agency of children and of people with mental disability is problematic for at least three reasons. First, it measures and compares children's capacities against adult-tailored standards of competency, perpetuating the notion that a competent adult is the standard that children must meet in order to be entitled to develop. Second, this comparison implies that childhood is some sort of disability. Third, while there may be some similarities between children's current cognitive functions and the functions of adults with mental disabilities, comparing these two groups raises the question of how children with mental disabilities should be seen and how they should be treated during

---

[107] Martha Nussbaum, 'Human Capabilities, Female Human Beings' in Martha Nussbaum and Jonathan Glover (eds.), *Women, Culture and Development: A Study of Human Capabilities* (Oxford University Press, Oxford 1995) 61–104; Martha Nussbaum, 'Capabilities as Fundamental Entitlements: Sen and Global Justice' (2003) 9 *Feminist Economics* 33.

[108] Dixon and Nussbaum, *supra* n. 57.   [109] *Ibid.*, 553.   [110] *Ibid.*

[111] *Ibid.*, 573–578.   [112] *Ibid.*, 578–584.

their childhood. In the case of children's right to development, surely, when discussed in the context of the Convention on the Rights of the Child, the positive and normative cases for special consideration have already been made. Therefore, the value of using the capability approach is in the space it opens for reimagining what child development means, and how human rights law can promote it in concrete terms.

Cultivating the Recognition of Children's Agency and Participation

An important contribution of the capability approach to the analysis of the child's right to development is in fostering the recognition of, and respect for, children's agency –for children both as individuals and as a distinct social group. This recognition will position children at the heart of the development process and will ensure the realisation of their right to participate and to enjoy both the process and the outcomes of development. In that respect, the argument shares similarities to the conclusions of the analysis of the general right to development.

As I argued in Chapter 1, the lack of recognition of children as agents enabled them to be considered as their father's property, as passive members of the family who are subjugated to the control of others, and as passive beneficiaries of welfare policies. Furthermore, despite claims that a paradigm shift in childhood studies had occurred, insufficient respect for children's agency underpinned the drafting of the right to development in the Convention on the Rights of the Child and dictated, to a large extent, the interpretation of this right by the UN Committee on the Rights of the Child.

The moral justifications and practical implications of recognising children's agency have been discussed in this book already. But, in the context of the capability approach and the right to development, attention should be given to the question of children's right to participate in shaping their own development, both present and future. If children are given the opportunity to articulate their views concerning their own freedom, it will break the dichotomous distinction between the human becomings and human beings conceptions.

Recognising the agency of children and enabling them to define and develop their individuality, Tobia Fattore and colleagues argue, also contribute to their well-being.[113] Comim claims that in the context of

---

[113] Tobia Fattore *et al.*, *Children's Understandings of Well-Being* (Springer, Dordrecht 2016) 65.

the capability approach, children usually are not consulted 'in the meaning of an active actor in society',[114] though this sort of treatment ignores the fact that 'children would probably define the meaning of being an active actor or citizen differently'.[115] While Comim flags this latter point as a potential argument against realising children's participation, I see the argument as an excellent example of why children *should* participate – not least because children's unique point of view is the reason for giving them a voice, and not a reason for continuing to silence them.

Adopting the view that children, even toddlers, can and should express their preferences enables us to overcome the main barrier for using the capability approach in analysing the right to development of children. Saito, reiterating the enjoyment theory from the 1970s, seems to be alarmed by this suggestion, warning us:

> Giving temporary freedom to a child does not always mean that the child will have freedom in future, and similarly, restricting the temporary freedom of a child may well expend the freedom that the child will have in the future. We, therefore, have to consider the freedom for a child in a lifelong perspective.[116]

While the concern for the child's future is understood, it need not come at the expense of undermining the value of the child's life in the present, or at the expense of the protection and implementation of the right to participation. The assumption that sacrificing children's freedom during their childhood, or during the early stages of their life, will lead to a greater freedom in the future, once the child becomes an adult, is empirically unfounded and morally wrong. Ensuring freedoms in the future should not – and cannot –justify denying all freedoms in the present; rather, the contrary is true. Arguably, ensuring freedoms in the present will enable children to fulfil their potential and pursue lives worth living in the future. For this reason, children's voices and opinions should be not silenced or dismissed, but rather amplified.[117]

Utilising the Capability Approach to Concretise 'Child Development'

The second usage of the capability approach to the analysis of the child's right to development is concretising the term 'child development'.

---

[114] Comim *et al., supra* n. 55, 7.   [115] *Ibid.*   [116] Saito, *supra* n. 84, 26.
[117] The moral justifications for recognising and protecting the right to participation of children have been discussed elsewhere, including in the introduction to this book.

Whereas Sen does not define a set of capabilities needed in order to be free, Nussbaum suggests a list of 10 capabilities that she qualifies as concrete, universal, inseparable, and essential to the realisation of human development. These capabilities are life; bodily health; bodily integrity; senses, imagination, and thought; emotions; practical reason; affiliation; other species; play; and control over one's environment.[118] This list is intentionally slightly ambiguous, Nussbaum adds, so that every society can elaborate and interpret the list differently, based on its own traditions and histories.[119] According to Vizard, these basic capabilities can be seen as grounds for a 'human rights based capability framework',[120] as they resemble the basic universal rights that are protected by the Universal Declaration of Human Rights and the 1966 Covenants.[121]

Despite its limitations, Nussbaum's list of capabilities is relevant in discussing children's capabilities and their right to development for three reasons. First, it corresponds with their needs and cannot be undermined on the basis of a prerequisite for capacities. Second, and similarly to Vizard's argument, many of the capabilities are defined by the Convention as children's human rights (the Convention protects the child's rights to life, health, bodily integrity, affiliations and play in Articles 6, 24, 19, 7, 8, 9, 11, and 31, respectively), which means that there is a wide recognition of the need to protect and promote them. Third, this recognition is manifested in terms of positive legal obligations, which goes beyond rhetorical weight. Therefore, and again by taking the perspective of the capability approach, these rights can be understood as substantial preconditions to the realisation of the child's right to development. Although, at first glance, the list of rights might resemble the jurisprudence of the Committee on the Rights of the Child, in the context of the capability approach these rights serve a different purpose. Here, these capabilities – and the corresponding rights that protect them – facilitate the child's freedom, while the Committee's approach is that these rights are needed to enable the child to become an adult, and thus free in the future.

---

[118] Martha Nussbaum, 'Women's Capabilities and Social Justice' (2000) 1 *Journal of Human Development* 219, 230–233; Nussbaum, *Creating Capabilities, supra* n. 70, 33–34.

[119] Nussbaum, *Creating Capabilities, supra* n. 70, 40. See Robeyns's claim that such a list should be rejected, as it narrows down Sen's approach: Ingrid Robeyns, 'An Unworkable Idea or a Promising Alternative? Sen's Capability Approach Re-examined', Center for Economic Studies Discussion Paper 00.30 (University of Leuven, Mimeo 1993).

[120] Vizard, *supra* n. 103, 234–235.   [121] *Ibid.*

Mario Biggeri and Santosh Mehrotra suggest a different, even more relevant, list of capabilities that are needed for children. Their list contains 14 capabilities: life and physical health; love and care; mental well-being; bodily integrity and safety; social relations; participation; education; freedom from economic and non-economic exploitation; shelter and environment; leisure activities; respect; religion and identity; time autonomy; and mobility.[122] Similar to Nussbaum's list, nine of the capabilities in this list can be renamed using the terms in the Convention (Articles 6, 24, 12, 28, 29, 32, 27, 31, 14, 30, 7, and 8, respectively). The remaining capabilities – such as love and care, social relations, and respect – are not considered human rights under the Convention, or in any other international human rights treaty (though it was suggested that children do have the right to be loved, and the right to 'time autonomy').[123] Ballet and colleagues claim that using the capability approach as a 'framework for normative evaluation and policy implementation'[124] with regard to children provides normative and positive grounds for promoting these capabilities. Looking at this list from the perspective of the right to development and by employing the capability approach's terminology, it can be argued that realising these rights means providing the necessary capabilities for the child to be free.

Measuring Human Capabilities: The Human Development Report

Measuring capabilities is a rather challenging task. It requires having conceptual clarity with regard to what human development stands for and what it is composed of. With this in mind, the relevant factors and variables that compose human development can be identified and quantified. The two lists of capabilities mentioned in the previous section are good starting points to this process. But these lists, or any other lists, require further development so that they can be operational when it comes to child development. Exploring a range of options in concretising the meaning of human and child development can, in turn, advance the interpretation of the right to development. This section asks that we start this process.

---

[122] Mario Biggeri and Santosh Mehrotra, 'Child Poverty as Capability Deprivation: How to Choose Domains of Child Well-being and Poverty' in Mario Biggeri *et al.* (eds.), *Children and the Capability Approach* (Palgrave, Hampshire 2011) 46–75, 51.
[123] See Chapter 1.   [124] Ballet *et al., supra* n. 87, 39.

Measuring capabilities should be based on a sound conception of human development. The project is broken down into measurable indicators, which in turn can inform decision-makers and policymakers about their successes and failures in promoting human development. Yet again, when it comes to children, there is the question of how adequate and relevant any set of indicators is to their lives and to their development, and consequently how relevant the decisions are that are being made in light of these indicators. As this section argues, great progress has been made in the last 20 years or so in defining and measuring child development. Nonetheless – and maybe because of the insufficient attention that children receive in this space – there is a need to have a closer look at the explicit and implicit conceptions of childhood and child development that underpin these endeavours, if we want to learn about the ways in which we can understand the right to development of children.

One of the most comprehensive attempts to define and measure human development is the United Nations Development Program's Human Development Report (HDR), which has been published annually since 1990. The HDR adopts the classic viewpoint on development and explores 'the relationship between economic growth and human development'.[125] It includes the Human Development Index (HDI), which is a comparison tool that measures key capabilities by relative levels in every country.

The HDR also corresponds with Sen's version of the capability approach, taking the view that 'income is not the total sum of human life'[126] and, therefore, conceptualising 'the real objective of development' as 'enlarging people's options'.[127] According to Mahbub ul Haq, the creator of the HDR, 'the objective of development is to create an enabling environment for people to enjoy long, healthy and creative lives'.[128] Ul Haq explains this approach in similar terms to those employed by Nussbaum and Sen, saying that development is more than economic well-being, and includes 'knowledge, health, a clean physical environment, political freedom and simple pleasures of life'.[129] He further adds:

---

[125] Mahbub ul Haq, *Reflections on Human Development* (Oxford University Press, Oxford 1995) 26.
[126] United Nations Development Program, *Human Development Report 1990* (Oxford University Press, New York 1990) 9.
[127] *Ibid.*, 25.   [128] Ul Haq, *supra* n. 125, 14.   [129] *Ibid.*, 14–15.

> It is fair to say that the human development paradigm is the most holistic development model that exists today. It embraces every developmental issue, including economic growth, social investment, people's empowerment, provision of basic needs and social safety nets, political and cultural freedom and all other aspects of people's lives. It is neither narrowly technocratic not overly philosophical. It is a practical reflection of life itself.[130]

The question is whether ul-Haq indeed succeeded in providing a coherent and substantive interpretation of what he defines as a 'holistic' concept of development. The first HDR states that the index 'emphasizes the development of human choices ... it is reflected in measuring development not as the expansion of commodities and wealth, but as the widening of human choices',[131] but also that it only captures 'a few of people's choices and leaves out many that people may value highly'.[132]

Consistent with the capability approach, the HDR defines three elements of human development: first, people are to be placed at the centre of attention, as both a means and an end of development; second, 'development' is a process of forming human capabilities and enabling people to acquire them; and third, the economy is not the only segment that drives development forward.[133] The essential components of development are therefore defined as equity, sustainability, productivity, and empowerment.[134] Subsequently, the HDI measures human development in three categories: longevity (life expectancy at birth), knowledge (adult literacy and years of schooling), and income (defined as 'up to the cut-off point as having full value ... The premise is that people do not need an infinite amount of income for a decent life').[135]

In comparison to the broad and complex perception of human development, the HDI measures only a fraction of a person's life experiences. The HDI was also criticised for being 'conceptually weak and empirically unsound, involving ... measurement errors and biases'.[136] Another weakness of the index, according to Anands and Sen, is the 'problematic' and ambiguous quantification of human development that it

---

[130] *Ibid.*, 23.
[131] United Nations Development Program, *Human Development Report 1990*, *supra* n. 126, 1.
[132] *Ibid.*, 16.   [133] *Ibid.*   [134] Ul Haq, *supra* n. 125, 16–20.
[135] United Nations Development Program, *Human Development Report 1990*, *supra* n. 126, 49.
[136] Thirukodikaval Nilakanta Srinivasan, 'Human Development: A New Paradigm or Reinvention of the Wheel?' (1994) 84 *AEA Papers and Proceedings* 238, 241.

upholds.[137] These measurement errors, as Mark McGillivray and Howard White call them, undermine its ambition to provide a comparative tool to evaluate development.[138] Proponents of liberal-market approaches claim that both the HDR and the index misunderstand the importance of growth and its impact,[139] and that they fail to measure human development because of the selection of functionings that they measure.[140] Claims have also been made concerning the index's lack of cultural and social sensitivity.[141] On the basis of Arturo Escobar's approach to human development,[142] the HDR was criticised for its undeclared ideological baggage and inherent biases, and for essentially being a new form of 'economics imperialism'.[143] Ambuj Sagar and Adil Najam went so far as to claim that the HDI has lost touch with the world it is attempting to portray.[144]

Arguably, the HDR is also age-biased. Although the HDI includes some variables that relate to children –for example, primary school enrolment rates and infant mortality rates – children and child development are not explicitly referred to as distinct categories in either the HDR or the HDI. Moreover, systemic developmental issues, such as poverty, do not address children's unique position in the economic order, or their experience of poverty. That the HDR overlooks children is further evidenced by another example: each of the HDRs published in the last 20 years was dedicated to a specific issue, such as power and poverty (2006), human security (1994), and participation (1993); to a specific region (the rise of the South (2013); or to a specific social group, such as gender (1995); but none of the reports were dedicated to children. Even the 2016 report, *Human Development for Everyone*, paid very little attention to children. When it did, children were primarily mentioned as subjects of family welfare policies and as passive beneficiaries of their

---

[137] Sodhir Anands and Amartya Sen, 'The Income Component of the Human Development Index' (2000) 1 *Journal of Human Development* 83, 99.

[138] Mark McGillivray and Howard White, 'Measuring Development? The UNDP's Human Development Index' (1993) 5 *Journal of International Development* 183.

[139] Martin Ravallion, 'Good and Bad Growth: The Human Development Reports' (1997) *World Development* 631, 637.

[140] Saito, *supra* n. 84, 22.   [141] *Ibid.*, 23.   [142] Escobar, *supra* n. 6.

[143] Amanda Perry-Kessaris, 'Prepare Your Indicators: Economics Imperialism on the Shores of Law and Development' (2011) 7 *International Journal of Law in Context* 401.

[144] Ambuj D. Sagar and Adil Najam, 'The Human Development Index: A Critical Review' (1998) 25 *Ecological Economy* 249.

parents' care.[145] In that sense, the empowering element of the capability approach is still ignored when it comes to children, and they are treated in accordance with what is often seen as a matter of the past: the welfare paradigm.

One HDR that is worth paying attention to in this context is the *Human Rights and Human Development* report from 2000.[146] This report upholds the human rights approach to development,[147] stating that 'the divide between the human development agenda and the human rights agenda is narrowing'.[148] The report is based on arguments similar to those of Vizard[149] and Sengupta,[150] suggesting that human rights law provides a framework of accountability for promoting human development. In response to those like Biggeri and colleagues, who cast doubts regarding the contribution and usability of human rights in promoting human development, the report suggests that 'human development is essential for realizing human rights, and human rights are essential for full human development'.[151]

Nonetheless, and similar to those that preceded it, this report includes the same few indicators concerning children, but neither child development nor children's rights, including their right to development, receives any significant attention. Children are left at the margins of the report and are mentioned only twice. The first instance is in a table titled 'Realizing the right to primary education in India'[152] and the second is in a section titled 'The rights of the child – turning words into actions'.[153]

---

[145] United Nations Development Program, *Human Development Report 2016* (New York 2016) 11–14.

[146] United Nations Development Program, *Human Development Report: Human Rights and Human Development* (Oxford University Press, Oxford and New York 2000).

[147] Andre Cornwall and Celestine Nyamu-Musembi, 'Putting the "Rights-Based Approach" to Development into Practice' (2004) 25 *Third World Quarterly* 1415, 1420; Sengupta, 'The Human Right to Development', *supra* n. 24, 181; Urban Jonsson, 'A Human Rights-Based Approach to Programming' in Paul Gready and Jonathan Ensor (eds.), *Reinventing Development?* (Zed Books, London 2005) 47–62, 47; Robert Archer, 'The Strengths of Different Traditions: What Can Be Gained and What Might Be Lost by Combining Rights and Development?' (2006) 4 *International Journal of Human Rights* 81; Mary Robinson, 'What Rights Can Add to Good Development Practices?' in Philip Alston and Mary Robinson (eds.), *Human Rights and Development* (Oxford University Press, Oxford 2005) 25–41.

[148] United Nations Development Program, *Human Development Report: Human Rights and Human Development, supra* n. 146, 2.

[149] Vizard, *supra* n. 103.

[150] Sengupta, 'The Human Right to Development', *supra* n. 24.   [151] *Ibid.*, 2.

[152] *Ibid.*,104.   [153] *Ibid.*,116.

These two references offer little substance concerning the rights of children, or the relationship between human development and human rights and child development and children's rights. More troubling is the fact that, despite the emphasis in the HDR and the HDI on empowerment and participation, children are not viewed as rights bearers or as active members of society.

To conclude, the HDR is an example of an attempt to concretise a theoretical conception of human development – and to some extent make use of it – and to establish a relationship with human rights law. Although, by and large, variables concerning child development are not part of the HDR or the HDI, the HDR does have a limited potential for telling us which rights of children need to be protected in order to support their development. For example, the HDR informs us about the connection between school enrolment as an indicator for realising the right to education and the right to nondiscrimination, and offers empirical evidence about the reciprocal relationship between these rights. But because the HDR is concerned with children's futures, giving much less weight to their present, its contribution to the analysis of the right to development is rather limited. The HDR is a good example of how the exclusion of children from theory leads to their exclusion from practice. A better place to concretise child development and the child's right to development would be in an index that focuses on children.

Concretising Child Development: The Child Indicators Movement

The child indicators movement offers a different conceptualisation of child development and child well-being. The core of this body of scholarship is the production of a body of indexes that concretise and measure both child development and child well-being in different places and in different time scales. The 'child indicators movement' is a title used to describe a range of projects that date back to the 1920s,[154] consisting of a large number of indices that gather information from local, regional, national, or international levels concerning various segments of the child's life – including education, health, contact with peer-groups and family environment.[155] The existence of these indexes demonstrates that

---

[154] Asher Ben-Arieh, 'The Child Indicators Movement: Past, Present, and Future' (2008) 1 *Child Indicators Research* 3, 3; Laura H. Lippman, 'Indicators and Indices of Child Well-Being: A Brief American History' (2007) 83 *Social Indicators Research* 39.

[155] Lippman, *supra* n. 154, 46–47; William P. O'Hare, 'Development of the Child Indicator Movement in the United States' (2012) 6 *Child Development Perspective* 79.

child development is not an abstract concept that refers to a vague future into which the child should grow; rather, it can become a concrete and measurable term. In turn, the concrete components of child development, any risk factors that undermine them, and any elements that promote them can then be articulated in human rights terms. In other words, while it is possible to study an object whose nature is not fully conceptualised, it can be assumed that a rich body of work is based on some conceptual basis about what constitutes child development or child well-being.

The early child indicators indices perceived children as human becomings and, consequently, child development and children's well-being were measured on the basis of negative factors, such as mortality rate, in an attempt to map and predict children's life expectancies and future prospects as adults. The emergence of the human beings paradigm and the normative influence of the Convention on the Rights of the Child changed the ways in which childhood is conceived and, consequently, how child development and well-being are measured.[156] These changes led to the introduction of new variables and the subsequent creation of more complex indices, which looked at, for example, school attendance and drop-out rates[157] (similarly to the HDI), children's 'health, socio-emotional status and functioning, moral and ethical attitudes and behavior, intellectual status and functioning, and other capacities such as music, art, mechanical, and athletic'.[158] This was in contrast to measures of 'education', for example, that only considered illiteracy rates among adults. Most recent indices also account for children's own perspectives on their life.[159] The importance of this last component cannot be overstated. As argued in previous sections, asking children about their views respects their agency and rights, adding important and often overlooked factors: children's experiences and their perspectives on their own lives.

Since the mid-2000s, alongside measuring children's development and well-being, some projects have also begun to qualify, quantify, and measure children's quality of life (thus suggesting that these three concepts – development, well-being, and quality of life – have distinct meanings). According to Asher Ben-Arieh, children's quality of life

---

[156] Ben-Arieh, 'The Child Indicators Movement', *supra* n. 154.   [157] *Ibid.*
[158] Lippman, *supra* n. 154, 43.
[159] Ben-Arieh, 'The Child Indicators Movement', *supra* n. 154. See Lippman, *supra* n. 154, 46. See also Kristin Anderson Moore and Laura H. Lippman, *What Do Children Need to Flourish?* (Springer, New York 2005).

relates to the 'future success of the generation' in a child-centred approach. Consequently, children's civic skills,[160] for example, ought to be measured. Nevertheless, Anne-Marie Etienne and colleagues assert that this innovative approach maintains the view of children as 'subject[s] who are constantly changing and developing',[161] thus suggesting a continued focus on children's future, primarily as adults, and undermining the claims of a paradigm shift in the way that this movement conceptualises childhood and child development. It seems that both the alleged new paradigm and its critics conceptualise childhood in a polarised way, demanding that researchers choose between one approach or the other – between the human becomings and the human beings approaches to childhood. It is, therefore, important to ask not only whether children's present lives and experiences are measured, but also why. If children's present life is measured for the sake of quantifying their future,[162] then it cannot be claimed that the human beings approach has been taken seriously.

Some new indices from recent years have sought to remedy this problem,[163] and to account for children's views,[164] by taking 'a child focused approach [that] acknowledges that children are diverse in their capacities for resilience'.[165] These participatory methods allow children to have active roles in research concerning them and, subsequently, in the policies formulated on the basis of these surveys that affect their lives. An example of an attempt to break this dichotomy can be found in recent studies in paediatrics that aim to conceptualise children's

---

[160] Ben-Arieh, 'The Child Indicators Movement', *supra* n. 154, 12.

[161] Anne-Marie Etienne *et al.*, 'The Gap Concept as a Quality of Life Measure: Validation Study of the Child Quality of Life Systemic Inventory' (2011) 100 *Social Indicators Research* 241, 242.

[162] See, for example, Jan L. Wallander and Hans M. Koot, 'Quality of Life in Children: A Critical Examination of Concepts, Approaches, Issues, and Future Directions' (2016) 45 *Clinical Psychology Review* 131.

[163] Ferran Casas, 'Children's Rights and Children's Quality of Life: Conceptual and Practical Issues' (1997) *Social Indicators Research* 283, 287–288.

[164] Asher Ben-Arieh, 'Where Are the Children? Children's Role in Measuring and Monitoring Their Well-Being' (2005) 74 *Social Indicators Research* 573, 574–579. According to Ben-Arieh, children not only can take part in research as sources of information, they also can participate in the study design and in the collection, analysis and utilisation of the data: 580–586. Gina Crivello *et al.*, 'How Can Children Tell Us about Their Well-being? Exploring the Potential of Participatory Research Approaches within *Young Lives*' (2009) 90 *Social Indicators Research* 51.

[165] Crivello *et al.*, *supra* n. 164, 54.

subjective well-being.[166] The point of departure for these studies – some of which are based on interviews with children themselves, including 8-year-olds – is that the ways in which the subjective well-being of patients is conceptualised is not adequate when talking about patients who are children. Therefore, there is a need to theoretically rethink this concept and to empirically ground it with children's own input.

Ulrike Ravens-Sieberer and her colleagues, for example, interviewed 37 children aged 8–15 years. With these interviews, they demonstrated that children were able to comprehend and respond to questions regarding evaluations of their life, and that they understood the concepts of optimism and a meaningful life.[167] This study gives children a voice and enables them to shape the ways in which their own well-being is conceptualised and subsequently measured. It then improves decision-making processes and, for our purposes, suggests that child development is a dynamic concept, that children can contribute to its definition, and that this is important not only for children's future but also for their present. In between these approaches, we can see studies that measure variables relating to the educational performance of primary school children, and their parents' educational background and professional status, as a way to develop policies targeting parents as a means of improving their children's well-being in the present and their perform-ance in the future.[168]

UNICEF's *The State of the World's Children* is probably the most comprehensive and continuous index. First published in 1980,[169] a decade before the HDR, *The State of the World's Children* reports mirror a somewhat narrow conception of child development and measure what UNICEF believes produces child poverty, as well as the implications of it on children's future, and their life and survival (similarly to the position of UNICEF during the drafting of the Convention).[170] The first report

---

[166] *C.f.* Smita Bhatia *et al.*, 'The Minneapolis-Manchester Quality of Life Instrument: Reliability and Validity of the Adolescent Form' (2002) 20 *Journal of Clinical Oncology* 4692; John Ivens, 'The Development of a Happiness Measure for Schoolchildren' (2007) 23 *Educational Psychology in Practice* 23, 221.

[167] Ulrike Ravens-Sieberer *et al.*, 'Subjective Well-Being Measures for Children Were Developed within the PROMIS Project: Presentation of First Results' (2014) 67 *Journal of Clinical Epidemiology* 207.

[168] Liliana Fernandes *et al.*, 'Assessing Child Well-Being through a New Multidimensional Child-Based Weighting Scheme Index: An Empirical Estimation for Portugal' (2013) 45 *Journal of Socio-Economics* 155.

[169] James P. Grant, *The State of the World's Children 1980–1981* (UNICEF, New York 1981).

[170] See Chapter 2.

included, for example, data on maternal ill-health and malnutrition, rates of breastfeeding, family planning, children's disability, the prevention of diseases caused by malnutrition, personal hygiene, lack of access to clean water, health education, safe sanitation and immunisation, and food security.[171] In time, and increasingly since the 2010s, *The State of the World's Children* has expanded the range of indicators it measures to include many more variables that speak to children's lives in the present, without linking them to any future trajectory – for example, flagging the disparity among children with respect to access to improved sanitation – while continuing to measure classical variables such as infant and under-five mortality rates, having a birth certificate, school enrolment, and the gender gap in this space.[172] These changes reflect a minor shift, but not a significant change, in the perceptions of children, childhood, and child development and well-being. Most indices that *The State of the World's Children* uses are negative ones, expressing concern for issues that relate to children's (mostly physical) survival, thus demonstrating the continuous domination of the human becomings paradigm and the conceptual barriers that preclude children from being seen as human 'beings'. Although the situation is changing, many indicators still measure children against their image as passive recipients of welfare, thus ignoring their agency, perspectives, and rights. In that sense, the dominant image of the child is as a person in need of protection, while provision and participation are at the margin.

Some recent indices had more success than UNICEF did in embracing the image of children as active agents and consequently broadening the meaning of child development. These indices provide more comprehensive conceptions of child development, child well-being, and children's quality of life. One of the first efforts is that of Ken Land,[173] which conceptualises children's quality of life to include 'objective and subjective axes of human existence'[174] that are divided into seven domains: material well-being, social relationship, health, safety/behavioural concerns, productive activity (educational attainments), place in community (participation in schooling or work institutions), and emotional/spiritual

---

[171] Grant, *supra* n. 169.

[172] UNICEF, *The State of the World's Children 2015: Reimagine the Future* (UNICEF, Geneva 2015).

[173] Kenneth C. Land *et al.*, 'Child and Youth Well-Being in the United States, 1975–1998: Some Findings from a New Index' (2001) 56 *Social Indicators Research* 241. See also Lippman, *supra* n. 154, 47.

[174] Land *et al.*, *supra* n. 173, 244.

well-being. Twenty-eight indicators measure these domains, including poverty rate, secure parental employment rate, median annual income, rate of children with health insurance, infant mortality rate, low-birthweight rate, mortality rate (ages 1–19), rate of children with very good or excellent health, rate of children with activity limitations (as reported by parents), rate of overweight children and adolescents (ages 6–19), teenage birth rate (ages 10–17), rate of violent crime victimisation (ages 12–19), rate of crime offenders (ages 12–17), rate of cigarette smoking, rate of alcohol drinking, rate of illicit drug use, reading test scores (ages 9, 13, and 17), mathematics test scores (ages 9, 13, and 17), rate of persons who have received a high school diploma (ages 18–24), rate of youth not working and not in school (ages 16–19), rate of pre-kindergarten enrolment (ages 3–4), rate of persons who have received a bachelor's degree (ages 25–29), rate of voting in presidential elections (ages 18–20), rate of children in families headed by a single parent, rate of children who have moved within the last year (ages1–18), suicide rate (ages 10–19), rate of weekly religious attendance, and percentage of children who report religion as being very important.[175]

This detailed directory for child development, well-being, and quality of life encompasses variants related to many aspects of children's lives and to different spaces of activities and social interactions.[176] It encompasses and respects children's lives in the present, and not only as future adults, while it accounts for and measures factors that can influence their future. In that sense, it is broader and more comprehensive than the HDI, and it appears to succeed where that index has failed in providing a holistic concept of child development and accommodating both the human beings and the human becomings conceptions of childhood. Although this index was created before the UN Committee on the Rights of the Child became operational, and even before the final text of the Convention was adopted, it is broader and more complex than the Committee's catalogue on child development.[177]

Most of the indicators in Land's index can be articulated in human rights terms and with correlation to the Convention. For example,

---

[175] *Ibid.*, 249–250.
[176] *C.f.* Index of Social Health, first published in the United States in 1987. This index addressed 'the ways in which social problems interact to create a social climate, instead of focusing on individual problems themselves'. The list of indicators is much longer than Land's list. It includes 'infant mortality, child abuse, children in poverty; and for youth, teen suicide, drug abuse, and high school drop-outs'. Lippman, *supra* n. 154, 46.
[177] See Chapter 3.

although most variables that relate to health and education can be seen as covered by the rights to health and education (Articles 24 and 28–29, respectively), it is more difficult to relate the rate of children who have moved within the last year to human rights issues. Moving houses is not a human rights violation, per se, but it can have, for example, an impact on children's stable access to education and on their ability to have a meaningful relationship with both parents – which are rights of the child under the Convention (Articles 18, 9, and again 28–29, respectively) and are known, according to the Committee, to influence children's right to development.

This index is not free from conceptual limitations. It is grounded primarily in a Unites States–centric model of family life and conservative middle-class values and lifestyles (for example, when measuring children's obesity, alcohol and drug consumption, and weekly religious attendance). As such, using its indicators in other contexts may generate a distorted picture concerning the state of children's development, well-being and quality of life. Nonetheless, from the perspective of protecting children's rights in general, and their right to development in particular, this index can prove useful in the effort to concretise child development in human rights terms – not least because it shows that the concept of child development can be concretised, and that its components resonate with children's rights law.

Based on Land's project, Kristin Moore and her colleagues developed a model of their own that tries to overcome some of the methodological and conceptual shortcomings of Land's work, as well as those of other indices that were similarly focused on the United States.[178] Their aim was:

> [To] truly measure well-being, as opposed to documenting the prevalence of risks, and to do so comprehensively by using a conceptual framework based on developmental theory, which specifies multiple levels of functioning at the individual level (physical, cognitive/educational, social, and psychological) and multiple contexts of influence (sociodemographic, family and community) that might promote or constrain development.[179]

Accordingly, the index is based upon 'developmental theory that typically considers four key domains of development: physical, intellectual/

---

[178] Kristin A. Moore et al., 'A Microdata Child Well-Being Index: Conceptualization, Creation and Findings' (2008) 1 Child Indicators Research 17.
[179] Ibid., 42.

educational, psychological, and social' and that 'embeds individuals in a system of ecological influences'.[180] In addition, the index includes four domains for measuring children's well-being: physical, psychological, social, and educational/intellectual. These are measured in three contexts: family, neighbourhood and sociodemographic. The index includes 69 variants[181] – two and a half times more than Land's index. It is a meaningful step forward in concretising what child development can mean and, like Land's index, it can be formulated, to some extent, in terms of the Convention's rights. Nonetheless, it seems that despite its clear objective to overcome cultural and class biases, this index suffers from deficiencies that are somewhat similar to those of Land's index. It too perceives children as passive actors and as recipients of welfare policies, and it does not employ any participatory methods or children's views about their own well-being and quality of life. The index is also culturally biased, reflecting Western middle-class conservative values and a liberal market ideology.

Having said that, this line of critique is also the reason why this index is comparable to the Convention, particularly to the Convention's conception of children's development. In their criticism of this index and others like it, Ashwani Saith and Rekha Wazir argue that while these indices can be valid in developed countries (and thus accurately reflect the state of children's lives in those countries), in less-developed countries they will produce a distorted picture of children's lives.[182] Saith and Wazir further suggest, in similarity to Sagar and Najam's critique on the HDI, that there is a need to develop local indexes that can accommodate a holistic view of children's well-being within the context of less developed countries.[183] But there is a growing body of evidence suggesting that reaching such a national consensus is not an easy task, and it often involves contested values that need to be mediated or reconciled.[184]

---

[180] *Ibid.*, 25.   [181] *Ibid.*, 45–48.

[182] Ashwani Saith and Rekha Wazir, 'Towards Conceptualizing Child Well-Being in India: The Need for a Paradigm Shift' (2010) 3 *Children Indication Research* 385.

[183] *Ibid.*

[184] Sinéad Hanafin *et al.*, 'Achieving Consensus in Developing a National Set of Child Well-Being Indicators' (2007) 80 *Social Indicators Research* 79. See also John Pinkerton, 'Children's Participation in the Policy Process: Some Thoughts on Policy Evaluation Based on the Irish National Children's Strategy' (2004) 18 *Children & Society* 119. But see a more positive experiences in Australia and the EU: Ann V. Sanson *et al.*, 'The Development and Validation of Australian Indices of Child Development – Part I: Conceptualization and Development' (2010) 3 *Children Indication Research* 275, 290; Jonathan Bradshaw and Dominic Richardson, 'An Index of Child Well-Being in Europe'

Many other indices are available. If the high volume of indices teaches us something, it is that there is no unified taxonomy for measuring child development and well-being[185] and the various options in understanding child development and well-being. This diversity – which, according to Ramesh Raghavan and Anna Alexandrova, reflects the lack of a unified theory[186] – led Asher Ben-Arieh and Ivar Frønes to suggest using the capability approach to define children's well-being. In their words:

> The concept of capabilities is especially suited related to children's well-being because children's movements through life produce new contexts, assigning new values to resources and commodities … The fact that capabilities influence well-being … illustrates the significance of the approach. Yet we are not suggesting a set of indicators on capabilities; rather we call for the positioning of well-being within the framework of the capability approach, underlining the differences – and dynamic relationship – between capabilities and outcomes.[187]

Here, Ben-Arieh and Frønes concentrate on the child's present and future well-being.[188] They ask people to conceptualise children's lives according to 'the developmental relationship between today and tomorrow' since 'the conditions of the present influence further development'.[189] At first glance, this approach may seem appealing – primarily because it rejects polarised views about childhood. Nonetheless, on a second look, it seems that this perspective is not significantly different from previous ones. On the one hand, the approach employs the same rhetoric concerning childhood, children and well-being that, according to Ben-Arieh himself, was used in the past.[190] On the other hand, the approach does point to the need to be context-sensitive in

---

(2009) 2 *Children Indicator Research* 319; Liliana Fernandes *et al.*, 'Assessing Child Well-Being through a New Multidimensional Child-Based Weighting Scheme Index: An Empirical Estimation for Portugal' (2013) 45 *Journal of Socio-Economics* 155; William P. O'Hare, 'A New State-Level Index of Child Well-Being for Young Children in the U.S.' (2016) 11 *Applied Research in Quality of Life* 493; Jorge Castellá Sarriera *et al.*, 'Material Resources and Children's Subjective Well-Being in Eight Countries' (2015) 8 *Child Indicators Research* 199; Gwyther Rees and Tamar Dinisman, 'Comparing Children's Experiences and Evaluations of Their Lives in 11 Different Countries' (2015) 8 *Child Indicators Research* 5.

[185] Asher Ben-Arieh and Ivar Frønes, 'Taxonomy for Child Well-Being Indicators: A Framework for the Analysis of the Well-Being of Children' (2011) 18 *Childhood* 460.

[186] Ramesh Raghavan and Anna Alexandrova, 'Toward a Theory of Child Well-Being' (2015) 121 *Social Indicator Research* 887.

[187] Ben-Arieh and Frønes, *supra* n. 185, 464.   [188] *Ibid.*, 474.   [189] *Ibid.*, 463.

[190] Ben-Arieh, 'The Child Indicators Movement: Past, Present, and Future', *supra* n. 154.

relation to the child's social and economic environments, as well as to the individual child. It also recognises diversity among children, even if only according to their age – thus reflecting a Western conception of childhood and developmental psychology models of childhood[191] – while ignoring other factors, such as gender or disability. Therefore, this not-so-new taxonomy can contribute to the realisation that children are not a homogeneous group and, subsequently, their 'development' is not homogeneous. This can lead to the development of a more nuanced and unified approach to the interpretation of the right to development.

Conclusion

This chapter has presented two conceptions of 'human development' – one according to the general right to development and the other according to the capability approach – and has discussed various ways to define child development, mainly in accordance with the child indicators movement. It has suggested that utilising key components of these various instruments – mainly the distinctions between the process of development and the outcome of it, the significance of respecting people's agency and people's voices, and the conceptualisation of development as freedom – in a framework that analyses the child's right to development will enable us to broaden the meaning of the right beyond its current limited interpretation and to develop a concrete understanding of it. The capability approach has also proposed the sort of capabilities that are necessary to support 'human development' and, in turn, how these capabilities can be articulated in human rights terms. A comprehensive – let alone conclusive – list of capabilities that can be more relevant to child development is not yet available, but the fundamental core principles exist.

The various indices measuring child development, well-being, and quality of life have demonstrated that 'child development' is not a vague concept, and that its meanings exceed the meanings used by mainstream developmental psychology, which are often utilised by law and by lawyers. The indices demonstrate that child development can be understood in broad terms, which can later be translated into measurable variables and articulated in human rights terms. In other words, the indexes show that the promotion of particular human rights of

---

[191] Allison James et al., *Theorizing Childhood* (Polity Press, Cambridge 1998) 60–61.

children – such as the right to education, the right to health, and the right to nondiscrimination – can lead to the advancement of child development as well. The question that remains unanswered is this: What is the added value of the child's right to development over respecting other enumerated rights? Or, phrased differently, is the child's right to development only a summation of other rights? The next chapter addresses these questions.

5

A New Framework for Analysing the Child's Right to Development

States Parties shall ensure to the maximum extent possible the survival and development of the child.

Article 6(2), UN Convention on the Rights of the Child

This chapter offers a new framework for analysing the child's right to development. The framework is based on a number of key elements. First, it is situated within the broad protection of 'child development' in the UN Convention on the Rights of the Child. Second, it promotes the protection of child development as a human right of children, rather than as a matter of welfare or charity.[1] Third, it utilises a hybrid conception of childhood that departs from the dichotomy of the 'human beings' and 'human becomings' models, and provides greater respect for children's agency. Fourth, it draws a clearer distinction between the meaning of the right to development as a guiding principle of the Convention and its distinct meaning as an independent human right of the child. Using this framework in conjunction with a cross-disciplinary understanding of child development can lead, I argue, to the creation of a more comprehensive and concrete interpretation of the child's right to development.

The first part of this chapter contextualises the discussion about the child's right to development within the framework of the UN Convention on the Rights of the Child and summarises some of the shortcomings in the current approach to this right that were discussed in previous chapters. The second part offers a road map for remedying these

---

[1] *C.f.* Adrian James, 'Competition or Integration? The Next Step in Childhood Studies?' (2010) 17 *Childhood* 485; Priscilla Alderson, 'Young Children's Human Rights: A Sociological Analysis' (2012) 20 *International Journal of Children's Rights* 177; Michael Freeman, 'Towards a Sociology of Children's Rights' in Michael Freeman (ed.), *Law and Childhood Studies* (Oxford University Press, Oxford 2012) 29–38; John Eekelaar, 'Family Law and Legal Theory' in Elizabeth Brake and Lucinda Ferguson (eds.), *Philosophical Foundations of Children and Family Law* (Oxford University Press, Oxford 2018) 41–58, 52–54.

shortcomings. It suggests adopting a hybrid conception of childhood that synthesises the human beings and human becomings approaches, utilising the capability approach as an additional dimension of child development and redefining the aim of the right to development accordingly. In consonance with these key themes, the part presents a new framework for the analysis of the child's right to development. It discusses the practicality of this framework and addresses some questions that require more attention.

Contextualising the Discussion: Child Rights and Child Development

The broad protection of child development in the Convention is a definitive expression of the impetus of international children's rights law to protect the child's transformation into an adult. This objective mirrors the prevailing sociological conception of childhood in the Anglo-American world, known as the human becomings approach.[2] The human beings approach – which sees children as people in their own right – emerged as a response to the human becomings approach and in parallel to the drafting of the Convention, but it had little, if any, influence on the Convention's treatment of child development.[3] Although the Convention embraces, to different degrees, both conceptions of childhood, when it comes to the right to development the Convention and its current interpretation are entrenched in the image of children as adults in the making[4] and have the sense that there is 'something very strange about thinking of children as bearers of rights'.[5]

The history of international children's rights law, including the drafting of the Convention (as discussed in Chapters 1 and 2), shows that the comprehensive protection of child development and the creation of children's unique right to development were intended to meet concerns for children's future. But what cannot be found in the historical account is a discussion about the meaning of 'child development' (and subsequent questions about the meaning of, for example, 'moral development', 'emotional development', or 'healthy development'), or about the implications of articulating the commitment to protecting child

---

[2] See Chapter 1.   [3] See Chapter 2.   [4] See Chapter 3.
[5] Harry Brighouse, 'What Rights (If Any) Do Children Have?' in David Archard and Colin Macleod (eds.), *The Moral and Political Status of Children* (Oxford University Press, Oxford 2002) 31–52, 31.

development in human rights terms and linking it to the protection for the child's right to life (Article 6(1)) and right to survival (Article 6(2)).

In Chapter 2, I suggested that in light of the drafting process of the Convention, Article 6 should be seen as the representation of a continuum, where the right to life is located at one end and the right to development at the opposite end, with the right to survival situated between the two. The two sides of the continuum represent the levels of states' obligations to the realisation of these rights (the negative–positive divide), as well as their impact on children's lives (short- and long-term).

One conclusion from the analysis of the drafting process is that the right to development was considered to be a positive right that protects what is required by the child in order to achieve a healthy process of growth. This interpretation has some inherent limitations, including its focus on the child's future and its insufficient respect for children's agency. It also assumes knowledge about the meaning of a 'healthy process of growth' and what is needed to achieve it in different contexts and for different children. Another deficiency is the insufficient differentiation between the meaning of the right to development as an independent right and the right to development as an umbrella right.

The UN Committee on the Rights of the Child interprets the child's right to development in a slightly different way, which has itself changed in recent years. The Committee understands the right to development as a right that assists the child to become an adult. At the same time, the Committee focuses on child development, but nonetheless too often ignores the right to development as a distinct human right. Further, while the Committee defines the right to development as one of the Convention's guiding principles, it says very little about the implications of this definition. So far, the Committee has not met its own guidelines for interpretation[6] and has not provided a coherent and concrete interpretation of the right to development.[7]

Despite the paradigm shift towards seeing children as human beings, the primary concern of children's rights law remains, to a large extent, children's future development. As the Supreme Court of the United States noted in a much-celebrated juvenile rights case, the 'juvenile should not be deprived of the opportunity to achieve maturity of

---

[6] UNCRC, 'General Comment No. 5 (2003): General Measures of Implementation of the Convention on the Rights of the Child' (27 November 2003) UN Doc. CRC/GC/2003/5.

[7] See Chapter 3.

judgment and self-recognition of human worth and potential'.[8] The main reason for the inability to depart from the human becomings model is, as Burman argues, that 'we cannot "unthink" development'.[9]

A New Framework for Interpretation: The Present and Future in Children's Lives

I propose framing the interpretation of the child's right to development according to the following two principles. The first is to abandon the use of binary conceptions of childhood in favour of a hybrid conception, by which the child's present and future are recognised as intertwined and equally important. Key components of the hybrid conception of childhood are respect for children's agency and respect for children as social agents. The second principle is to synthesise the capability approach's emancipatory idea of human development with a broad, interdisciplinary, and contextual understanding of child development.

A Hybrid Conception of Childhood

The two dominant conceptions of childhood – the human becomings and human beings approaches – limit, each in different ways, the scope of the interpretation of the child's legal right to development. Both approaches confine the image of the rights holder to an imaginary, homogeneous, and universal narrative of childhood:[10] the child is considered either as a person in the making or as an agent in her own right. Utilising the human becomings conception results, as the Committee's work demonstrates, in interpreting the child's right to development as a means to an end: the right to development is the right of the child to become an adult. The human beings approach has yet to sufficiently

---

[8] *Graham v. Florida*, 560 U.S. 48 at 79 (2010).

[9] Erica Burman, 'Desiring Development? Psychoanalytic Contributions to Antidevelopmental Psychology' (2011) 26(1) *International Journal of Qualitative Studies in Education* 1, 13–15.

[10] Eva Brems, 'Children's Rights and Universality' in Jan C. M. Willems (ed.), *Developmental and Autonomy Rights of Children: Empowering Children, Caregivers and Communities* (Intersentia, New York 2002) 21–45, 26–27; Alan Prout and Allison James, 'A New Paradigm for the Sociology of Childhood? Provenance, Promise and Problems' in Allison James and Alan Prout (eds.), *Constructing and Reconstructing Childhood: Contemporary Issues in the Sociological Study of Childhood* (3rd edition, Routledge, Abingdon, Oxon 2015) 7–32.

inform the analysis of the child's right to development, although using it as an alternative underpinning narrative can divert the focus from the child's future to the child's life at the present – and consequently can enhance respect for children's views about their own personal development while recognising the importance of the process of maturation, rather than focusing only on its outcome.

However, I see at least four difficulties in utilising the human beings conception as a sole narrative.

- First, applying this confined concept would inevitably lead to a polarised – and therefore rigid – interpretation of the right to development, as has been the case with the human becomings approach, as neither of these two conceptions sufficiently comprehends the complexity of children's lives.
- Second, relying solely on the human beings approach can undermine the normative grounds on which the constructions of 'childhood' and 'the child' in international children's rights law are based, entailing too sharp a departure from the travaux préparatoires (Article 31 of the Vienna Convention on the Law of Treaties).
- Third, employing a polarised conception cannot result in any holistic and contextualised interpretation of the right to development that considers the child's background, identity, and character, as well as the intersections of these factors.
- Fourth, it might be culturally biased against communities that see childhood in different terms.

Embracing the two conceptions (being and becoming) together as intertwined in the child's life might be seen as a way to remedy the limitations of adopting only one of them.[11] However, utilising both of these conceptions simultaneously with no synergy reproduces binary images of childhood and 'accepts the child/adult dualism: the being child will become an adult'.[12] A similar embracing of this dualism can be found in 'the new law of the child' that Anne Dailey and Laura Rosenbury have advocated, as recently as 2018, in the context of American constitutional law.[13] They suggest we stop thinking about children in

---

[11] Emma Uprichard, 'Children as "Being and Becomings": Children, Childhood and Temporality' (2008) 22 *Children & Society* 303.

[12] Michael Freeman, 'The Human Rights of Children' (2010) 63 *Current Legal Problems* 1, 15.

[13] Anne C. Dailey and Laura A. Rosenbury, 'The New Law of the Child' (2018) 127 *Yale Law Journal* 1448.

terms of dependency and start thinking about them in terms of autonomy. This shift might be 'radical', as they call it, in the context of the domestic system in which they operate, but not in the context of international children's rights law or many non-US domestic jurisdictions.[14]

Dailey and Rosenbury are right to suggest that the 'authorities framework', as they term the existing regime, 'focuses on the developmental arc from dependency to autonomy to the exclusion of other meaningful aspects of children's lives'[15] and thus 'overlooks the fact that children enjoy active lives in the here and now'.[16] Therefore, they distinguish between 'children's present interests' and their 'developmental interests',[17] suggesting that the two 'are inextricably linked'.[18] They ask that we put a greater emphasis on children's interests in 'the here and now', while not undermining children's interests in becoming adults.[19] In other words, they just discovered the human beings approach to childhood, and seek to utilise it in parallel to the human becomings conception. I will return to this suggestion later.

Within the context of the child's right to development, this dualism runs the risk of preserving adult supremacy over children, silencing children's voices, and ignoring children's expectations of their own processes of maturation and development.[20] Aoife Daly suggests that in cases involving a best-interests analysis, where courts are expected to consider all issues relevant to the concrete child's welfare, including the child's own preferences (in accordance with Article 12), children's voices are nonetheless supressed and their autonomy carries no or very little weight, which she deems to be insufficient. One of the reasons for this, according to Daly, is the weak protection for children's autonomy under Article 12.[21] Eventually, it seems that the being/becoming dualism results in a fragmented interpretation and implementation of the Convention that focuses on caring for the child's future while paying lip service to her life in the present. Take, for example, the *Yoder* case in the United States,[22] where the Supreme Court ruled that parents' right to freedom

---

[14] See, for example, Dawn Watkins, 'Where Do I Stand? Assessing Children's Capabilities under English Law' (2016) 28 *Child and Family Law Quarterly* 25.

[15] Dailey and Rosenbury, *supra* n. 13, 1467.   [16] *Ibid.*, 1448.   [17] *Ibid.*, 1480.

[18] *Ibid.*, 1481.   [19] *Ibid.*

[20] According to James *et al.*, the dichotomies between childhood and adulthood are structure and agency, identity and difference, continuity and change, and local and global: Allison James *et al.*, *Theorizing Childhood* (Polity Press, London 1998) 199–218.

[21] Aoife Daly, *Children, Autonomy and the Courts: Beyond the Right to Be Heard* (Brill, Leiden and Boston 2017).

[22] *Wisconsin v. Yoder*, 406 U.S. 205 (1972).

of religion outweighed the state's interest in educating its children, and therefore Amish children could not be placed under compulsory education past the eighth grade. The dissenting opinion, written by Justice William O. Douglas, points the finger towards the fact that the court was analysing the situation from a parents' rights point of view, while the matter concerns their children's rights too. Justice Douglas adds:

> I think the children should be entitled to be heard. While the parents, absent dissent, normally speak for the entire family, the education of the child is a matter on which the child will often have decided views. He may want to be a pianist or an astronaut or an oceanographer. To do so he will have to break from the Amish tradition.
>
> *It is the future of the students, not the future of the parents, that is imperiled by today's decision.* If a parent keeps his child out of school beyond the grade school, then the child will be forever barred from entry into the new and amazing world of diversity that we have today. The child may decide that that is the preferred course, or he may rebel. It is the student's judgment, not his parents', that is essential if we are to give full meaning to what we have said about the Bill of Rights and of the right of students to be masters of their own destiny[23] (emphasis added).

This is a very powerful statement about the relationship between children and their parents, and about the weight that children's wishes should be given in matters concerning their own future. More specifically, Justice Douglas is concerned with the ability – and the rights – of a child to define her own future and to make decisions during childhood that will expand the range of options for her in her adulthood. In other words, the Court accepts the suggestion that children should exercise some degree of autonomy in the present (human beings) so that they can have a say about their own future (human becomings), but it does not depart from this binary divide.

I therefore suggest thinking about childhood in hybrid terms. This approach does not embrace only the extremes,[24] nor is it a summary of the two conceptions of childhood. A hybrid conception of childhood sees the child as a person who is engaged in a process of growth in her own right and on her own terms, anticipating her future life. Growing up is something that children do, but it is not the only thing that they do, nor can it be the only thing that defines them: children participate in giving meaning to the complexity of their own childhood, which is not limited to the question of their future. This multidimensional view of children's

---

[23] *Ibid.*, at 245.   [24] *C.f.* Judith Butler, *Gender Trouble* (Routledge, New York 1999).

lives takes the child's maturation process and the child's future as being mutually constitutive and equally important, together with other dimensions of the child's life – for example, personal relationships, or areas of interest and curiosity. It offers a new way to think about the right to development, and it can also constitute a change in the way we think about other rights of the child.

Taking the right to education and the *Yoder* case as an example, the hybrid approach suggests that an Amish child's right to education requires that she can participate in choosing the format and content of her own education, thus respecting not only her right to education but also her development with its twofold and intertwined dimensions: present and the future. Such a choice might not be supported by the community, or by her siblings or parents, but nonetheless it is the parents who should make that choice available to her, as part of their duty to enable their child to exercise her rights. By having these choices, the child will be able to expend her own capabilities and exercise her rights to education, development and participation. Focusing only on the right to education and embracing either of the two rigid conceptions of childhood will result in a much narrower outlook, denying the child the opportunity to participate in her own process of development or in planning for her future. Recent occasions where children took legal actions against schools, local authorities, or ministries of education, claiming that inferior education or out-of-date school curriculum hinders their future, can be framed in terms of the right to development too, rather than in terms of the right to education.

The hybrid conception is rooted in the work of Korczak, who explains: 'When I approach a child, I have two feelings: affection for what he is today and respect for what he can become.'[25] Therefore, he writes:

> Children are not the people of tomorrow, but are people of today. They have a right to be taken seriously, and to be treated with tenderness and respect. They should be allowed to grow into whoever they were meant to be – the unknown person inside each of them is our hope for the future.[26]

In this context, the term 'child's future' requires more attention. From a child's perspective, the future is a reference not necessarily to the age of

---

[25] Janusz Korczak, *Loving Every Child* (Algonquin Books, Chapel Hill, North Carolina, 2007) 17.

[26] Quoted in Janusz Korczak, *The Child's Right to Respect: Lectures on Today's Challenges for Children* (Council of Europe, Brussels 2009; originally published 1927) 7.

18 and beyond, as the Convention deems,[27] but rather to what the child sees as her own 'future'. Time and temporality are dynamic and relational ideas, and children have a sense of time that is different from that of adults. For children, the 'future' usually includes more fluid time frames that encompass the events and changes that happen during the course of childhood.[28] The future can be the next day or the coming months, not only life in the abstract future as an adult. Therefore, discussions about a child's future in the context of her development should consider the child's age and her own perception of time.

The *Yoder* case demonstrates how adults' understanding of what the 'future' means is manifested. Caring for the future, when dealing with children's development and education, is also about events that occur during childhood. Moving from kindergarten to primary school, learning a preferred second language in school, and enrolling at a particular high school are all examples of events that will happen in the future and that require decisions in the present. All of these events, which are often examined under the legal categories of 'school choice' and 'parental rights', should also be considered as issues concerning children's rights – especially the right to development – and considered by taking a child-centred approach. Another example that can illuminate this point is a court's decision about parenting arrangements following a separation. Courts are often asked to decide how to divide legal responsibility for children between their estranged parents, and to determine the physical living arrangements. Here, a broad perspective of child development should be considered, including the concept of time. Postseparation living arrangements have different effects in the short, medium and long term depending on the age of the child. For example, a three-year-old child will be subject to these arrangements for a longer period

---

[27] Article 1. Childhood ends at the age of 18, unless domestic law sets a younger age. The Convention does not mandate setting a later age. Childhood may very well *not* end at the age of 18. As a social concept, it can end before or after that age. As James Chisholm shows, the Navajo model of childhood, for example, includes eight stages of development that are based not on age but rather on social competence. Childhood therefore does not end at a specific age, but rather after the person has progressed throughout the stages, which usually takes until the age of 30. James Chisholm, 'Learning "Respect for Everything": Navajo Images of Development' in Philip Hwang *et al.* (eds.), *Images of Childhood* (Lawrence Eribaum, Mahwah, New Jersey 1996) 167–184.

[28] See, for example, Katharine A. Tillman *et al.*, 'Today Is Tomorrow's Yesterday: Children's Acquisition of Deictic Time Words' (2017) 92 *Cognitive Psychology* 87; Sylvie Droit-Volet, 'Time Perception in Children: A Neurodevelopmental Approach' (2013) 51 *Neuropsychologia* 220.

of time – that is, 15 years – than will a 14-year-old child, who will be formally subject to the court order for four years. In both cases, the court should consider the impact that any arrangement might have on the child's present life and on the course of her childhood (that is, her future). Some domestic legislation, such as the Australian Family Law Act 1975 (Cth), requires the court to take these issues under consideration when performing a best-interests analysis (section 60CC). However, as suggested earlier, best-interests proceedings are often counter-autonomous and therefore do not respect the child's right to development.

At this point, it is worth looking at the model of Dailey and Rosenbury in more detail. Their framework for child law centres around 'relationships, responsibilities and rights', with one of its aims being to free the field from its 'developmental concerns'.[29] They distinguish between children's 'present interests' and their 'developmental interests',[30] suggesting – similarly to the hybrid conception – that the two 'are inextricably linked'. Like James and Prout, they ask that we put a greater emphasis on children's interests in 'the here and now', but without undermining children's interests in becoming adults.[31] This move, self-described by the authors as a radical one, is not, I argue, radical enough. Instead, welding together the two contesting images of the child – acknowledging that the child is simultaneously a human being and a human becoming – will enable the law to move beyond the dependency–autonomy dualism. It is in this context that respecting the right to development will provide children with a legal framework to enjoy what Dailey and Rosenbury claim to be children's interests. It is interesting to note that they base some of their arguments on developmental research, suggesting that the 'new law for the child' is a better vehicle to ensure children's ability to develop a complex web of meaningful relationships, and therefore promote their social and mental development.[32] The problem with this argument is not the potential intrinsic weight that it carries – that is, the idea that their model can improve the protection of child development – but rather the qualification of ensuring child development as a matter of children's interests. Dailey and Rosenbury identify children's interests and needs and translate those into a claim for rights, which are nonetheless 'rooted' in children's interests.[33] Under the Convention, children's rights already exist, and the question is how to interpret them, and in light of which conceptions of childhood and rights.

---

[29] Dailey and Rosenbury, *supra* n. 13, 1506.   [30] *Ibid.*, 1480.   [31] *Ibid.*, 1481.
[32] *Ibid.*, 1485.   [33] *Ibid.*, 1527.

The hybrid conception is not free from ideological biases. It is based on a moral claim with regard to children and human rights, and it assumes that the period of childhood is as significant as the time of adulthood. The African Charter on the Rights and Welfare of the Child[34] – similarly to the Convention, and like many domestic legal systems – focuses on the distinctiveness of childhood. It thus adopts a culturally biased division of the human lifespan into childhood and adulthood, as well as the intradivision of childhood into different stages (such as infancy and adolescence).[35] These stages should be taken into account when employing the hybrid conception and the suggested framework in different cultural contexts, but without compromising its core components. Contextualising the implications of the concept – including with respect to the right to development – is not a justification to retreat from the idea that children are human rights holders who have the rights to life, to survive, and to grow up to their fullest potential.

Children's Agency and Participation in the Context of Their Right to Development

The hybrid conception of childhood mainstreams respect for children's agency and their right to participation as substantial and procedural elements of the right to development. The theoretical significance and practical implications of respecting children's agency and voice have been discussed in detail in previous chapters. Here, I would like to focus on the importance of respecting children's agency and voice in the specific context of the right to development.

Respecting children's agency can shift the focus of the discussion from questions of competence and welfare to questions of empowerment and human rights.[36] It will open a space in which to articulate the child's right to development as a distinct and concrete human right, essentially transforming Durkheim's 'law of growth'[37] into an issue of human rights law. As an agent in her own right, the child will be entitled to grow up and not be seen merely as someone in need of growing and in need for

---

[34] African Charter on the Rights and Welfare of the Child (OAU Doc. CAB/LEG/ 24.9/49 (1990)), entered into force Nov. 29, 1999.

[35] See Erica Burman, 'Local, Global or Globalized? Child Development and International Child Rights Legislation' (1996) 3 *Childhood* 46.

[36] C.f. Dailey and Rosenbury's suggestion that we move from the 'authorities framework' to the 'tripartite model' of relationships, responsibilities and rights.

[37] Émile Durkheim, 'Childhood' in W. S. F. Pickering (ed.), *Durkheim: Essays on Morals and Education* (trans. H. L. Sutcliffe, Routledge, London 1979; first published 1911) 149.

support and protection in this process. Recognising children's agency will also enable a broadening of the meaning of the term 'child development' in the context of the right to development, so that it moves beyond the often-used psychosocial developmental framework to include knowledge from other disciplines, as well as children's own experiences and views.

Ignoring children's views in the context of their development perpetuates the image of children as passive subjects whose sole purpose in life is to grow up. When it comes to the challenging task of developing the meaning and interpretation of the right to development, children should have the opportunity to engage in a meaningful participatory process in which they can offer their own opinions.[38] Children should also be part of the process of implementing the right to development, including in the design of tools and practices (for example, devising policies and programs, and drafting new legislation).[39] Following this suggestion can mitigate the possibility that the right to development will be interpreted in paternalistic terms, which would undermine the potential for children's empowerment and self-determination. This does not mandate 'full liberation' or 'abandoning' children to their rights,[40] not least because the right to participation under the Convention (Article 12) does not give children – whether we like it or not – the right to make decisions by themselves. In this context, I speak not about decision-making power, but rather about understanding childhood as a time when children should be empowered and should have opportunities to develop their autonomy. The latter is one of the objectives of the right to participation, and it is a main justification for respecting children as rights holders.[41] Therefore, and in line with the logics of the general right to development and the capability approach in promoting human development,[42] it should also be an essential element of the interpretation and implementation of the child's right to development. The contributions of using the capability approach are discussed further in the next section. At this point, I would like to emphasise that the manifestation of the right to

---

[38] *C.f.* UNCRC, 'General Comment No. 20 (2016) on the Implementation of the Rights of the Child during Adolescence' (6 December 2016) UN Doc. CRC/C/GC/20. See also Laura Lundy, 'In Defence of Tokenism? Implementing Children's Right to Participate in Collective Decision-Making' (2018) 25 *Childhood* 340.

[39] UNCRC, 'General Comment No. 20', *supra* n. 37.

[40] Bruce C. Hafen and Jonathan O. Hafen, 'Abandoning Children to Their Autonomy: The United Nations Convention on the Rights of the Child' (1996) 37 *Harvard International Law Journal* 449.

[41] Freeman, *supra* n. 12.   [42] See Chapter 4.

development as an emancipatory right and giving children a voice in this process require a social and cultural transformation,[43] which includes the creation of a 'political space in which children are empowered to express their own distinctive and submerged point of view'.[44] The hybrid conception of childhood can help in creating this space, as it empowers children to be active, if they wish, in their own lives and in the lives of their communities, including their families and schools.

A holistic interpretation of the Convention requires that the interpretation of the right to participation in the context of the right to development should also take into account other rights of the Convention – including the right of children to have their best interests taken as a primary consideration[45] – and the evolving-capacities principle.

Law and Child Development

The hybrid conception of childhood relates to the meaning of 'child development' in the context of interpreting the child's right to development. So far, little attention has been given to the interpretation of this term, even though it is a challenging, and challenged, one. Unpacking its potential meanings is a necessary first step in discussing how to protect and promote child development. In order to provide children with the widest possible developmental processes and outcomes, I suggest employing a broad and multidisciplinary understanding of child development, which includes the meanings of this term in pedagogy, sociology, psychiatry, psychology, anthropology, medicine, and political science, instead of the often, albeit inexplicitly, used meaning – which is perhaps outdated and biased – that is taken from developmental psychology.[46] This can ensure that the child's rights and developmental needs will take into account a range of factors that can hinder or promote

---

[43] Ragnhild Lund, 'At the Interface of Development Studies and Child Research: Rethinking the Participating Child' (2007) 5 *Children's Geographies* 131.

[44] John Wall, 'Can Democracy Represent Children? Towards a Politics of Difference' (2012) 19 *Childhood* 86, 92. See also Nigel Thomas, 'Towards a Theory of Children's Participation' (2007) 15 *International Journal of Children's Rights* 199, 210.

[45] UNCRC, 'General Comment No. 14 (2013) on the Right of the Child to Have His or Her Best Interests Taken as a Primary Consideration (Art. 3, para. 1)' (29 May 2013) UN Doc. CRC.C/GC/14.

[46] *C.f.* Huntington's suggestion with respect to the relationship between the law and early childhood development: Clare Huntington, 'Early Childhood Development and the Law' (2017) 90 *Southern California Law Review* 755.

different elements and dimensions of child development, such as physical or mental development, as well as the qualifications ('normal' or 'healthy') and outcomes ('full' or 'optimum') of the development process.

There are two reasons for the ambiguity surrounding the current interpretation of 'child development' in the context of the right to development. The first is that the term is not part of the legal vocabulary in the sense that the law, as a discipline, does not explain or engage with its intrinsic meaning. The second concerns the communication between lawyers and other professionals who employ this term as part of their discipline-specific discourse and knowledge. When a psychologist talks about child development, for example, she may have in mind the theories of Piaget or Freud, and she will basically be occupied with events that can hinder or support good or normal 'development', while for a paediatrician, the term 'child development' is associated with physical development: it represents a matrix of age, weight, and height. Thus, the psychologist and the medical doctor may use the same vocabulary, but the meaning of 'child development' varies according to the particular discipline. Lawyers and judges will probably have very little ability to contribute to the conversation about the meanings of 'child development',[47] essentially because this term is not part of their professional lexicon.

The problem with the ways in which players in the legal profession engage with child development can be explained by comparison with the treatment of the right to freedom of speech. When a lawyer interprets that right, the meaning of 'speech' seems quite clear. 'Speech' and the corresponding right to 'freedom of speech' were, and still are, the subjects of extensive scholarly debates and have been adjudicated in the courts for many years. The meaning of 'speech' in the context of the right to freedom of speech has evolved over the years – from political speech, and the corresponding right to stand at Speakers' Corner in Hyde Park and protest against the king, to commercial speech and the right of corporations to advertise their products freely. The question of what is 'speech' has evolved too, primarily with changes in technology, and the term has been transformed to encompass spoken, written and printed speech, as well as online communications – including those on social media. A tweet, therefore, is also speech these days, which might be protected under the right to freedom of speech, which includes, so it seems, the right to tweet. The point is that the law was able to adapt to

---

[47] *Ibid.*

these changes in the forms, fora, and content of 'speech', and to reinter-
pret the right to freedom of speech accordingly. But changes in the
meaning of 'child development' happen outside the legal arena, and legal
actors not only are unaware to these changes, but they also, by and large,
are not part of the discussion about them.

Most research about the relationship between the law and child development science focuses on the question of how courts utilise the social
and life sciences in children's cases. These studies have highlighted, for
example, the limited ability of judges to handle expert witnesses' testi-
mony regarding child development, lawyers' manipulations of this evidence, and the judges' own explicit or inexplicit – or even unconscious –
biases and reliance on their personal experiences as adults and parents.[48]
It has also been suggested that complicated procedures in which neither
the parties nor the judges have the time, resources, or skills to encompass
the complexity of child development can engender misunderstanding or
manipulation of the evidence, thus resulting in misinformed or ill-
informed decisions.[49] It has therefore been recommended that some
training should be provided whereby judges and lawyers who deal with
child-related cases will learn about research methodologies in the life and
social sciences, so that they have the tools to evaluate the validity of the
scientific evidence presented to them. These suggestions seem to ignore
the constitutive role of the law in this process.[50] The decisions of courts
are made within legal frameworks, and judges are not expected to rubber-
stamp whatever a random expert witness might suggest.

For example, section 61DA of Australia's Family Law Act 1975 (Cth)
outlines a legislative pathway for ensuring that the interests of child
development are served in a postseparation situation. It states that when
parents separate, the child's development will be best served if both

---

[48] Martha Fineman and Anne Opie, 'The Uses of Social Science Data in Legal Policymaking:
Custody Determination at Divorce' (1987) *Wisconsin Law Review* 107; Judith Cashmore
and Patrick Parkinson, 'The Use and Abuse of Social Science Research Evidence in
Children's Cases' (2014) 20 *Psychology, Public Policy and Law* 239; Dana Prescott,
'Forensic Experts and Family Courts: Science or Privilege-by-License?' (2016) 28 *Journal
of the American Academy of Matrimonial Lawyers* 521; Judith Cashmore, 'Best Interests
in Care Proceedings: Law, Policy and Practice' in Elaine E. Sutherland and Lesley-Anne
Barnes Macfarlane (eds.), *Implementing Article 3 of the United Nations Convention on the
Rights of the Child* (Cambridge University Press, Cambridge 2016).

[49] Helen Stalford and Kathryn Hollingsworth, 'Judging Children's Rights: Tendencies,
Tensions, Constraints and Opportunities' in Helen Stalford *et al.* (eds.), *Rewriting
Children's Rights Judgments* (Hart, Oxford 2017) 17–53, 47.

[50] Emily Buss, 'Developmental Jurisprudence' (2016) 88 *Temple Law Review* 741.

parents equally share parental responsibility. Only where there is strong evidence suggesting that this will not be the case is the Family Court permitted to depart from this legislative position.

Therefore, the process of engagement between law and child development should include consultation with professionals from other fields. Such consultation will probably not result in a unified understanding of the term 'child development' – not least because it involves not only empirical and scientific points of view, but also normative ideas about childhood, adulthood, life cycles, parenting, relationships, risk assessment, and so on. Consultation does not – and will not – make lawyers experts in any other discipline, nor should they be. But lawyers should be able to understand what child development means in other disciplines, so that they can overcome their inherent professional limitations and articulate the care for this concept in human rights terms. For example, what are the various meanings of the eight developmental domains that the Convention mentions (physical, mental, moral, social, cultural, spiritual, personality, and talent)? Are there additional developmental aspects that should be accounted for but are not explicitly mentioned? How should 'physical' development or 'moral' development – to name just two of the eight – be defined, and according to which discipline? Only after the establishment of the normative grounds will it be possible to ask what sorts of entitlements this right creates, and what kinds of duties it imposes on the different duty bearers. Subsequently, it will be possible to concretise the components and meaning of this right and to develop empirical indicators to measure its implementation. Without having a clearer idea of what child development means, any attempt to interpret the legal right to development is destined to have limited success.

Adapting the term 'child development' into legal norms is a process that should be undertaken with caution.[51] In her investigation of the relationship between law and the science of child development in the context of juvenile justice in the United States,[52] Emily Buss claims that discussions about children's rights usually focus on children's capacities in order to determine their guilt – or, more precisely, their capacity to be

---

[51] For a general overview of the relationship between law and science, see Helen Reece (ed.), *Law and Science* (Oxford University Press, Oxford 1998). See also Barbara Beatty *et al.* (eds.), *When Science Encounters the Child: Education, Parenting and Child Welfare in 20th-Century America* (Teachers College Press, New York 2006).

[52] Emily Buss, 'What the Law Should (and Should Not) Learn from Child Development Research' (2009–2010) 38 *Hofstra Law Review* 13.

held responsible for their actions – and the correspondingly appropriate sentencing, as well as, more broadly, the interpretation of their constitutional right not to be subject to inhumane punishment. Buss suggests that the law does not currently accommodate the complexity of social science and that interpreting children's rights considering their capacities, or in light of neuroscientific evidence that speaks to their brain functions, perpetuates the supremacy of the competent-adult model in law and dictates assessing children accordingly. This, Buss argues, prevents us from achieving coherence in the law regarding children's constitutional rights, as their rights are contested against those of adults. She further suggests that focusing on children's current capacities in order to determine their legal competence and culpability diverts attention from children's future.[53] Therefore, Buss suggests that we need to change the way in which the law treats child development, essentially putting law back in the driver's seat.[54] This is a different objective from that of Dailey and Rosenbury, who ask to free the field of children and the law from its 'developmental concerns'.[55] In other words, Buss convincingly suggests, the insights that science can give us should be filtered and used via the law's overall objectives. It is the law, Buss argues, that provides children with the opportunities to exercise agency as part of their 'healthy development'.[56]

The hybrid conception of childhood can help us to overcome the problems that Buss identifies, as it changes the way in which the discussion of children's competency and rights is framed, the normative values that it suggests child development should have, and the objectives of protecting the right to development. If we look at these issues as representations of different perspectives on the relationship between children and human rights, then the child's current capacities should not be seen as a reason for denying children their right to development. At the same time, care for the child's future should not be so easily dismissed. These two dimensions – current and anticipated capacities – and the concern for both are not mutually exclusive. Rather, they are complementary to each other. At this point, the contribution of the capability approach to the interpretation of the child's right to development becomes even clearer. I suggest integrating the capability approach's view of human

[53] *Ibid.*, 20–34.   [54] *Ibid.*, 15.   [55] Dailey and Rosenbury, *supra* n. 13, 1506.
[56] Emily Buss, 'Roper v. Simmons: 543 US 551 (2005) Commentary' in Helen Stalford *et al.* (eds.), *Rewriting Children's Rights Judgments: From Academic Vision to New Practice* (Hart, Oxford 2017) 405–410, 408.

development as a process of emancipation into the interpretation of the child's right to development. While medicine or psychology can suggest what qualifies as a 'good' or 'normal' course of development, and how this can be best served, utilising the capability approach will redefine the objectives of this right. It will then mean more than a right to grow up. As a human right, the right to development should provide the child with the entitlement to be an active agent in her own development. The right to development will not merely mean the right to become an adult. Rather, it will mean the right to be a free child, while becoming a free adult.

Interpreting the Right to Development

The interpretation of the right to development in accordance with the hybrid conception of childhood, the drafting history of the Convention, the remarks of the Committee, and a broader understanding of child development can support an interpretation whereby the right to development can be seen as a right that respects, protects, and promotes the child's process of development, as well as its outcomes, with the aim of enabling the child to fulfil her human potential to the maximum. This interpretation should be applied in context, accounting for each individual child, and in accordance with her capacities, her capabilities and the intersectionality[57] of social categories that shape her experience.

Kimberlé Crenshaw's theory of intersectionality suggests that social categorisations – such as race, ethnicity, religion, class, gender, sexuality and, I would add, age – are inherently interconnected, mutually constituted, and converging, thereby creating interdependent systems of disadvantage and discrimination. In her work, Crenshaw demonstrates how the law can be blind to categories of difference, which results in subjugating marginalised and disempowered women to oppressive structures of power. Similar arguments can be made about children, whose experiences in relation to their development should be understood in light of their various overlapping and intersecting social positions and the opportunity structures that are available to them. Nancy Dowd's model of 'developmental equality' can be a complementary framework in this context, and in interpreting the right to development,[58] even though

---

[57] Kimberlé Crenshaw, 'Mapping the Margins: Intersectionality, Identity Politics, and Violence against Women of Color' (1991) *Stanford Law Review* 1241–1299.

[58] Nancy E. Dowd, 'Black Boys Matter: Developmental Equality' (2016) 45 *Hofstra Law Review* 47.

her model and the Convention are based on different legal frameworks
and vary in their objectives. Developmental equality identifies the structural components of inequality created and sustained by the state, with
the aims of exposing and dismissing barriers to equality, recognising and
celebrating positive racial identity development, and achieving equality
by maximising potential for all children.[59]

Taking an intersectional approach to the interpretation and implementation of the right to development requires acknowledging as constitutive to the experiences of children not only age, ethnicity, culture, race,
and socioeconomic background, but also other social categories of exclusion, such as gender, sexuality, class and (dis)ability,[60] about which the
Convention is, by and large, silent.[61] For example, girls; lesbian, gay,
bisexual, transgender, intersex, and queer (LGBTIQ) children; children
with disabilities; and young children have different developmental
needs.[62] Therefore, the meaning of the right to development might be
different for these children when compared to most white, European,
middle-class boys. At this point, Sengupta's suggestion that we understand the general right to development as a composite right becomes
relevant to the context of children's rights too. He suggests that 'the
whole is greater than the sum of the parts ... the component rights are
related in a non-linear way with positive feedback'.[63] If the child's right to
development is interpreted as a composite right, then it will comprehend
all eight development domains protected by the Convention, any other
developmental aspects that will be deemed to be relevant in any given
situation, and the child's rights to participation and nondiscrimination.[64]
In this sense, the right to development can be seen as the right that

---

[59] *Ibid.*, 49–50.
[60] Leslie McCall, 'The Complexity of Intersectionality' (2005) 30 *Journal of Women in
      Culture and Society* 1771, 1780–1784.
[61] Recent jurisprudence of the Committee begins to make explicit references to these groups
      of children. See, for example, UNCRC, 'General Comment No. 20', *supra* n. 37; Kirsten
      Sandberg, 'The Rights of LGBTI Children under the Convention on the Rights of the
      Child' (2015) 33 *Nordic Journal of Human Rights* 337.
[62] Woodhead is wrong to suggest that the right to development is only relevant to young
      children, not least in light of Article 2 of the Convention: Martin Woodhead, 'Early
      Childhood Development: A Question of Rights' (2005) 37 *International Journal of Early
      Childhood* 80.
[63] Arjun Sengupta, 'The Human Right to Development' (2004) 32 *Oxford Development
      Studies* 179, 183.
[64] Compare to UNCRC, 'General Comment No. 5', *supra* n. 6.

enables the child to have as many options as possible for living her life (during both her childhood and her adulthood).

Defining the child's right to development as the right to fulfil her human potential to the maximum does not suggest overlooking the process of development or its significance. In the context of the hybrid conception of childhood, this interpretation requires that facilitating the process of development will not cast a shadow over the means necessary to enable the child to achieve her developmental potential. The process of maturation and the experiences of children throughout it are inherently important to the child's ability to form her own view about the process and its outcomes, and to fulfil her potential at every step of the way. Moreover, caring for the child's potential is an objective shared by many cultures – not only those of the West – and thus carries less cultural bias and less ideological baggage than the dismissal of the child's agency (having said that, no child's rights should be violated in achieving this objective). Therefore, this concept can be more easily accepted in different contexts, and more easily implemented (or enforced, if needed).

The lives of transgender children can illuminate this point. For many of these children, the process of development and its result – questioning their own gender identity, coming to terms with their sexuality, and deciding to undergo long and often painful medical processes so that their physical appearance will match their gender identity – occur during their childhood. The process often begins during the second decade of their lives, but for some children it can occur much earlier, at the age of six or seven. The toll on children's mental health is high, and the distress that is created by the incongruence between their gender identity and the sex they were assigned at birth should be diagnosed, as per the *Diagnostic and Statistical Manual of Mental Disorders, Fifth Edition*, as Gender Dysphoria.[65] Stage 1 of the suggested medical treatment for children with Gender Dysphoria is to suppress the onset of puberty through the use of hormones (puberty-blocking treatment) and subsequently to commence further hormone treatment so as to promote the development of non-natal physical attributes (gender-affirming hormone treatment).[66] Stage 2 treatment has physiological effects that are irreversible (either breast growth or decreased sperm production) and partially irreversible (decreased testicular volume and decreased terminal hair growth). Stage

[65] Felicity Bell, 'Children with Gender Dysphoria and the Jurisdiction of the Family Court' (2015) 38 *University of New South Wales Law Journal* 426.
[66] *Ibid.*

3 treatment involves surgical interventions (chest reconstructive surgery, phalloplasty, hysterectomy, bilateral salpingectomy, creation of the neo-vagina, and vaginoplasty), which are irreversible.

In Australia, the Full Court of the Family Court decided in 2017 that a *Gillick*-competent child[67] can consent to stage 1 and stage 2 without the need for a court to approve the procedure.[68] In this decision, the court reversed its previous rulings, where it was determined that due to the risk associated with stage 2 treatment, and its irreversible nature, court approval must always be obtained.[69] One of the reasons for this change of heart was the court's conclusion that 'psychologically, the treatment will allow Kelvin [the child's nickname. – N.P] to continue to develop his self-esteem, the confidence in his body and appearance and to consequently develop the congruence necessary for a healthy future outlook'.[70]

When these stages of treatment are considered, then – both for children who are determined to be *Gillick* competent and for those who are not (though one can wonder whether a child with such strong views about her own body, soul, and identity can be deemed incompetent) – the right to development, as interpreted in this book, should come into play. The court, when asked to approve these medical procedures, should consider the right to development of the specific child, the effects and significance of the process that she would undergo, and the result that she wishes to achieve – which is completing the physical transformation of her body, so that she can continue her life as a child, and in the future as an adult, as whomever she wants to be and in accordance with her gender identity.

The Right to Development as a Guiding Principle of the Convention

Another dimension of Article 6 and the right to development is the definition of Article 6 as a guiding principle of the Convention by the UN Committee on the Rights of the Child.[71] This aspect of Article 6 is rarely discussed in the literature and the Committee so far has done very little in substantiating it. This oversight was one of the reasons that led Karl Hanson and Laura Lundy to suggest that Article 6 should not be considered as a guiding principle at all (in addition to questioning the

---

[67] See *Gillick v West Norfolk and Wisbech Area Health Authority* [1986] AC 112.
[68] *Re: Kelvin* [2017] FamCAFC 258.   [69] *Re: Jamie* [2013] FamCAFC 110.
[70] *Re: Kelvin, supra* n. 67, at [para. 47].
[71] UNCRC, 'General Comment No. 5', *supra* n. 6.

'added value' that Article 6 has over other Articles, or whether the Convention's drafters considered Article 6 to represent an overarching principle).[72] While I agree with Hanson and Lundy's analysis, I disagree with their suggestion to replace Article 6 with Article 5.[73] Article 5 and the evolving-capacities principle is, essentially, a mechanism to achieve balance between autonomy and protection, and between provision and paternalism (by the requirement of parents to provide guidelines to their children), while Article 6 stands for substantial rights in itself, as well as providing a procedural benchmark as a general principle.

As a guiding principle of the Convention, the right to development should be interpreted as a procedural requirement, or as a benchmark for scrutinising decisions that affect children both as a collective and as individuals. As a litmus test, it requires assessing any actions that can have an impact on children's development in the present, during the process of development, and in the future once the process has come to a resolution. This means that when a duty bearer takes an action or drafts a policy, it is not only the right to non-discrimination, the right to participation, and the best interests of the child that should be respected, but also the right to development. Every decision, policy and legislative provision should be measured against its impact on the right to development.[74] Understanding the right to development as a guiding principle – similar to the functioning of Article 3 – requires that decisions about children are made after assessing their impact on the ability of children to develop, on the process of their development, and on the potential outcomes of the process. The attention to, and care for, child development should exceed the confines of the five Articles of the Convention that mention child development explicitly (Articles 18(1), 23(3), 27(1), 29(1)(a) and 32(1)) and the eight specific child development domains to which reference is made. As such, the right to development should not be seen merely as a summary of other rights that support child development. This approach is different – in terms of both the process it

---

[72] Karl Hanson and Laura Lundy, 'Does Exactly What It Says on the Tin? A Critical Analysis and Alternative Conceptualisation of the So-Called "General Principles" of the Convention on the Rights of the Child' (2017) 25 *International Journal of Children's Rights* 285.

[73] *Ibid.*, 304.

[74] Compare with Marta Maurás's suggestion regarding the relationship between public policies and the implementation of the Convention: Marta Maurás, 'Public Policies and Child Rights: Entering the Third Decade of the Convention on the Rights of the Child' (2011) 633 *Annals of the American Academy of Political and Social Sciences* 52, 56.

sanctions and its comprehensive application – from the position that sees the promotion of child development as a by-product of the realisation of other human rights of the child, such as the right to education or health.

To a limited extent, the Committee utilises this approach. In its work, it examines legislation and policies against their potential or actual impact on child development (but usually without referring to the right to development). Using the example of education, understanding the right to development as a guiding principle means that every decision that affects children's access to education – for example, the national budget allocated for the Ministry of Education, or the questions of curricula and school discipline – should also be measured against its impact on the child's right to development.

Additional Considerations when Protecting the Right to Development

Realising the right to development requires States to take into account the 'maximum available resources' test set by Article 6(2),[75] as well as the division of responsibilities between different actors according to Articles 5 and 18 of the Convention. These actors include parents and other guardians, the extended family, the government (with its different layers and bodies – municipal, regional, and national) and, according to Article 4, the international community when its cooperation is required.

Another dimension that requires attention in the process of realising the right to development, in light of the capabilities approach, is making children aware of the range of options available to them – thus increasing their choices and freedoms. A child should be provided with the necessary capabilities to choose, and with the voice to articulate her choices, and those preferences should be considered in a nondiscriminatory way. Comparing this objective, using the right to education as an example once again, results in a conclusion that the right to education serves ends other than those served by the right to development, and those ends to some extent overlap but are not identical.[76] The right to education also reflects different, but partially overlapping, justifications, including, but not limited to, the support for the child's development. Teaching the child how to read and write has its own values and rationales. Inter alia, it

---

[75] See Noam Peleg and John Tobin, 'Article 6' in John Tobin (ed.), *The UN Convention on the Rights of the Child: A Commentary* (Oxford University Press, Oxford, forthcoming 2019).

[76] Article 29(1) defines the aim of education as developing the child's personality.

allows the child to acquire new skills and knowledge, which promotes the child's intellectual development. It also contributes to the child's emancipation by creating opportunities for her, and in doing so promotes the fulfilment of the child's potential. But realising the child's right to education does not satisfy all of the child's developmental needs – not even in the education context – nor is it sufficient to support the child's realisation of her fullest potential. Realising the child's fullest potential requires more than literary capabilities. Therefore, while education and the right to education are necessary components of supporting child development and realising the right to development, they are not enough to achieve comprehensive protection for the right to development.

Conclusion

There is no paradigmatic child and there is no singular and universal childhood.[77] Therefore, there is no one right way for children to develop. Children have different experiences of childhood and different processes of development, with different expectations, hopes, and fears forming each child's process and its outcomes.[78] Hence, there is a place to argue that in interpreting the child's right to development, a universal and context-free meaning for the term 'child development' should be employed. Furthermore, as an emancipatory right, the right to development should acknowledge the child's right to develop in different ways, as long as it enables the child to fulfil her potential. This suggested framework, however, does not provide a conclusive definition for the child's right to development. Such a definition should be the result of applying this framework with a specific understanding of child development.

What is required as 'support' for the child's development depends on how we define child development. The eight components of development that are mentioned in the Convention should be the starting point for this interpretation process. Other sources are the lists of capabilities necessary for development, and the rich understanding of the term employed in the context of child indicators research, which were

---

[77] Michael Freeman, 'Towards a Sociology of Children's Rights', *supra* n. 1, 33.

[78] Helga Kelle, 'The Discourse of "Development": How 9- to 12-Year-Old Children Construct "Childish" and "Further Developed" Identities within Their Peer Culture' (2001) 8 *Childhood* 95, 109. In a different context, see Richard Maclure, 'The Dynamics of Youth Participation: Insights from Research Fieldwork with Female Youth in Senegal' in Myriam Denov *et al.* (eds.), *Children's Rights and International Development: Lessons and Challenges from the Field* (Palgrave, New York 2011) 155–174.

described in Chapter 4. Although Nussbaum's list of 10 capabilities is not tailored for children, Biggeri and Mehrotra's list of 14 capabilities seems more adequate.[79] The various indices that the child indicators movement has created are potential sources for providing concrete benchmarks. These examples demonstrate the feasibility of articulating children's development in concrete terms, identifying its components, and then adapting these components to human rights terms. Further articulation of a child-specific list of capabilities is needed. Such a list should be based on a conception of child development that is different from those currently available.

[79] See Chapter 4.

~

Conclusion

The UN Convention on the Rights of the Child tells a familiar, and very convincing, story about children, childhood, child development, and human rights. Under the Convention, the child is perceived as a person in the making who should enjoy the maximum available resources in order to develop into a competent adult at the age of 18. Consequently, many of the Convention's rights explicitly, or by way of interpretation, support child development in one way or another – in addition to protecting the distinct and unique right of children to development.

The child, the Convention's preamble asserts, should 'grow up in a family environment, in an atmosphere of happiness, love and under-standing'. Accordingly, parents not only need to love and understand their child, but also bear the responsibility for 'the upbringing and development of the child' (Article 18). The child's material standard of living should be adequate for 'the child's physical, mental, spiritual, moral and social development' (Article 27). Education is expected to develop 'the child's personality, talents and mental and physical abilities' (Article 29). The Convention therefore tells us how 'development' should be supported, and the inclusion of these elements might have either a complementary or overlapping relationship with Article 6 and other provisions under the Convention.[1] Little is said about how 'development' should end. With the exception of Article 29, the Convention is silent about the person whom the child should turn into upon becoming an adult – saving the assumption that once a child becomes an adult, she also becomes a fully competent person who is stripped of the unique protection that children receive.

Chapters 1 and 2 described and analysed the socio-legal background that led to the creation of children's unique right to development in

---

[1] Julia Sloth-Nielsen and Sue Philpott, 'The Intersection between Article 6 of the UN Convention on the Rights of the Child and Early Childhood Development' (2015) 26 *Stellenbosch Law Review* 295.

international law. Chapter 1 reviewed the development of children's rights law and theory, highlighting the importance given to the protection of child development, and the ways in which this term was understood. Based on original archival research, Chapter 2 systematically analysed the drafting process of the Convention, aiming to understand the motivations for including a broad protection for child development. I argued that understanding the social conceptions that led to the creation of the Convention is vital to the effort of understanding the objectives of the child's right to development and the potential meanings it can have for children. But, as the chapter demonstrates, while the concern for child development was always an issue for the Convention's drafters, no significant attention was given to the meaning of the legal right to development.

Chapter 3 focused on the work of the UN Committee on the Rights of the Child and critically analysed the Committee's interpretation of this right during the last 25 years. The findings in this chapter reaffirm the hypothesis about the dominance of the 'human becomings' conception of childhood in the interpretation of the Convention's protection for child development, essentially considering this right as a right of the child to become an adult. Although the Committee ascribes protection for a broad but nonetheless undefined and thus vague concept of 'child development,' it ignores, almost entirely, the child's legal right to development. Chapter 4 addressed two of the main obstacles in the current interpretation of the right to development – namely, the diverse meanings of 'human development' and 'child development', and the difficulty of concretising these terms as a human right in human-rights law. The chapter suggested comparing the child's right to development with some elements of the 'general' right to development, the capability approach's conceptualisation of human development, and the child indicators movement. It demonstrated the importance of recognising the agency of the rights holder, the differentiation between the process of development and its outcomes, and the articulation of development as an emancipatory idea. The chapter further analysed a number of indices that take specific conceptions of development and delineate their measurable components.

Following this trajectory, Chapter 5 offered a new framework for the analysis of the child's right to development. The suggested framework is broad and comprehensive. It is based on a new conceptualisation of childhood – namely, a hybrid conception that respects children's agency and comprehends wide-ranging perspectives of child development. These include, but are not limited to, the Convention's eight developmental domains and the capability approach's idea of development as freedom and emancipation. These conceptions of development are a good starting point for conducting a cross-disciplinary consultation about the meaning of 'child development'. The suggested framework can lead to the creation of a concrete interpretation of the child's right to development, which includes substantial and procedural elements, in order to create a right that is greater than the sum of its parts. The aim of this right is to enable the child to fulfil her potential to the maximum. This right can and should be taken into account in every decision concerning a child, and every time that a court needs to make a decision about a child. It is relevant when deciding on the child's living arrangements after parental separation, whether to allow or deny a medical treatment, either therapeutic or nontherapeutic treatment for a Gillick-competent child or a non–Gillick competent child, or when deciding whether a school enrolment policy or disciplinary method is lawful or not. The child's right to development, in the broad and comprehensive interpretation that this book suggests, is relevant in all these cases.

To paraphrase the words of Janusz Korczak, the right to development should be understood as a right to ensure the 'optimal conditions to grow and develop', as well as the right to 'live in the present'.[2] These aims are not mutually exclusive; rather, they complement each other. They represent a concept that acknowledges the right to development of children while defining the idea of 'development' in complex terms.

The framework I suggest is articulated in relatively general terms so that it can meet the 'challenge', as Carol Smart and her colleagues put it,[3] of exploring the plurality of childhood and of child development. The suggested framework should be employed in a context-sensitive manner, with the realisation that children are not a homogeneous group. Since there is no paradigmatic 'child', there is no paradigmatic 'development'. Children vary in their experiences of their childhood, which in turn is shaped by their identities and the ways those identities intersect. Children develop in different ways, experience their childhoods differently, and grow up to become different people. The meaning of 'normal' development therefore varies in different contexts and cultures and for different children. There is a need to be aware of the differences among

---

[2] Janusz Korczak, *Loving Every Child* (Algonquin Books of Chapel Hill, North Carolina 2007; originally published in 1919) 355.
[3] Carol Smart *et al.*, *The Changing Experience of Childhood: Families and Divorce* (Polity Press, Cambridge 2001) 12.

children with respect to gender, sexual orientation, class, race, ethnicity, disability, religion, culture, and age, and their intersections. These characteristics should first apply to children themselves, and not to adults; respecting children's agency means that we should not measure or consider them in comparison to adults. All those factors mentioned above can influence children's perceptions about their life, shape the opportunities that they can generate for themselves, and determine the opportunities that society offers them. The interpretation of the legal right to development should reflect this understanding.

REFERENCES

Books

Ajodhia-Andrews, A., *Voices and Visions from Ethnoculturally Diverse Young People with Disabilities* (Sense Publishers, Boston, Rotterdam, 2016).

Archard, D., *Children: Rights and Childhood* (3rd edition, Routledge, London 2014).

Ariès, P., *Centuries of Childhood: A Social History of Family Life* (translated by Robert Baldick, Jonathan Cape, London 1962).

Barbara, B., Grant, J., and Cahan, E. D., (eds.), *When Science Encounters the Child: Education, Parenting and Child Welfare in 20th Century America* (Teachers College Press, New York 2006).

Beiter, K. D., *The Protection of the Right to Education by International Law* (Martinus Nijhoff Publisher, Leiden 2006).

Berger, K. S., *The Developing Person* (7th edition, Worth Publishers, New York 2006).

Bluebond-Langer, M., *The Private Worlds of Dying Children* (Princeton University Press, Princeton 1978).

Boserup, E., *Women's Role in Economic Development* (Earthscan, revised edition 2007. Originally published in 1970).

Bowlby, J., *A Secure Base: Clinical Applications of Attachment Theory* (Routledge, London 1988).

Bridges, K. M. B., *The Social and Emotional Development of the Pre-School Child* (Kegan Paul, Trench, Trubner & Co., London 1931).

Burman, E., *Developments: Child, Image, Nation* (Routledge, London 2008).
Deconstructing Developmental Psychology (3rd edition, Routledge, London 2017).

Butler, J., *Gender Trouble* (Routledge, New York and London 1999).

Cunningham, H., and Morpurgo, M., *The Invention of Childhood* (BBC Books 2007).

Diduck, A., *Law's Families* (LexisNexis, London 2003).

Drèze J., and Sen, A., *India: Economic Development and Social Opportunity* (Oxford University Press, Oxford 1995).

Easterly, W., *The White Man's Burden* (Oxford University Press, Oxford 2006).

Eppler, K. S., *Dependent States: The Child's Part in Nineteenth-Century American Culture* (University of Chicago Press, Chicago 2005).

Escobar, A., *Encountering Development: The Making and Unmaking of the Third World* (Princeton University Press, Princeton 1995).

Farson, R. E., *Birthrights* (Macmillan, New York 1974).

Fass, P. S., *The Damned and the Beautiful: American Youth in the 1920s* (Oxford University Press, Oxford 1977).

Fattore, T., Mason, J., and Watson, E., *Children's Understandings of Well-Being* (Springer, Dordrecht 2016).

Franklin, B. (ed.), *The Rights of Children* (Basil Blackwell, Oxford 1986).

Freeman, D., *Margaret Mead and Samoa: The Making and Unmaking of an Anthropological Myth* (Harvard University Press, Cambridge, Massachusetts, and London 1983).

Freeman, M., *The Rights and Wrongs of Children* (Frances Pinter, London 1983).
The Moral Status of Children (Martinus Nijhoff Publishers, The Hague 1997).
Article 3: The Best Interests of the Child (Martinus Nijhoff Publishers, Leiden 2007).

Gilligan, C., *In a Different Voice* (Harvard University Press, Cambridge, Massachusetts, 1982).

Goldstein, J., Solnit, A., and Goldstein, S., *The Best Interests of the Child: The Least Detrimental Alternative* (Simon & Schuster, New York 1996).

Grant, J. P., *The State of the World's Children 1980–1981* (UNICEF, New York 1981).

Griffin, J., *Well-Being: Its Meaning, Measurement, and Moral Importance* (Clarendon Press, Oxford 1986).

Heywood, C., *History of Childhood: Children and Childhood in the West from Medieval to Modern Times* (Polity Press, London 2001).

Holt, J., *Escape from Childhood* (Penguin Books, Middlesex 1974).

Hopkins, B. (ed.), *The Cambridge Encyclopedia of Child Development* (Cambridge University Press, Cambridge 2005).

Hulme, D., and Turner, M. M., *Sociology and Development: Theories, Policies and Practices* (Harvester Wheatsheaf, New York 1990).

Illich, I. D., *Celebration of Awareness : A Call for Institutional Revolution* (Calder, London 1969).

Ishay, M. R., *The History of Human Rights* (University of California Press, Berkeley 2008).

James, A., Jenks, C., and Prout, A., *Theorizing Childhood* (Polity, Cambridge 1998).

James, A., and James, A. L., *Constructing Childhood: Theory, Policy and Social Practice* (Palgrave Macmillan, Basingstoke 2004).

Kabeer, N., *Reversed Realities: Gender Hierarchies in Development Thought* (Verso, London 1994).

Key, E., *The Century of the Child* (G. P. Putnam's Sons, New York and London 1909).

King, M., and Piper, C., *How the Law Thinks about Children* (Gower, Vermont 1990).

Korczak, J., *Loving Every Child* (Algonquin Books of Chapel Hill, North Carolina 2007).

The *Child's Right to Respect* (Council of Europe, Brussels 2009. Originally published in 1927).

Kraut, R., *What Is Good and Why: The Ethics of Well-Being* (Harvard University Press 2007).

Lansdown, G., *The Evolving Capacities of the Child* (Save the Children and UNICEF, Innocenti Research Centre, Florence 2005).

Lee, N., *Childhood and Society: Growing Up in an Age of Uncertainty* (Open University Press, Buckingham 2001).

LeVine, R. A., and New, R. S., *Anthropology and Child Development : A Cross-Cultural Reader* (Blackwell Publishing, Malden, Massachusetts, and Oxford, England 2008).

Lewis, W. A., *The Theory of Economic Growth* (Routledge, London 2007. Originally published in 1950).

Lifton, B. J., *The King of Children: The Life and Death of Janusz Korczak* (Chatto & Windus, London 1988).

Mason, J., *Gender and Development*, 2nd edition (Routledge, London, 2011).

Mason, M. A., *From Father's Property to Children's Rights: The History of Child Custody in the United States* (Columbia University Press, New York 1994).

Mayall, B., *Towards a Sociology for Childhood: Thinking from Children's Lives* (Open University Press, Gosport 2002).

Maynes, M. J., *Schooling in Western Europe* (State University of New York Press, Albany 1985).

McEwan, C., *Postcolonialism and Development* (Routledge, New York 2009).

Mead, M., *Coming of Age in Samoa: A Psychological Study of Primitive Youth for Western Civilisation* (Harmondsworth, Penguin Books 1943. First published in 1928).

Mintz, S., *Huck's Raft: A History of American Childhood* (Harvard University Press, Cambridge 2004).

Montgomery, H., *An Introduction to Childhood* (Wiley Blackwell, Chichester 2009).

Moore, K. A., and Lippman, L. H., *What Do Children Need to Flourish? Conceptualizing and Measuring Indicators of Positive Development* (Springer, New York 2005).

Morsink, J., *The Universal Declaration of Human Rights: Origins, Drafting and Intent* (University of Pennsylvania Press, Philadelphia 1999).

Mulley, C., *The Women Who Saved the Children* (Oneworld, Oxford 2009).

Nolan, A., *Children's Socio-Economic Rights, Democracy and the Courts* (Hart, Oxford 2011).

Nowak, M., *U.N. Covenant on Civil and Political Rights: CCPR Commentary* (N.P. Engel, Kehl 1993).

Article 6: The Right to Life, Survival and Development (Martinus Nijhoff Publishers, Leiden 2005).

Nussbaum, M., *Creating Capabilities – The Human Development Approach* (Harvard University Press, Cambridge 2011).

Patterson, D., *Law and Truth* (Oxford University Press, Oxford 1996).

Platt, A. M., *The Child Savers: The Invention of Delinquency* (2nd edition, University of Chicago Press, Chicago 1977).

Postman, N., *The Disappearance of Childhood* (Vintage Books, New York 1984).

Prout, A. (ed.), *The Future of Childhood: Towards the Interdisciplinary Study of Children* (Routledge, London 2005).

Reece, H. (ed.), *Law and Science* (Oxford University Press, Oxford 1998).

Rogers, R. S., and Rogers, W. S., *Stories of Childhood: Shifting Agendas of Child Concern* (University of Toronto Press, Toronto 1992).

Salomon, M., *Global Responsibility for Human Rights* (Oxford University Press, Oxford 2007).

Sen, A., *Inequality Re-examined* (Harvard University Press, Cambridge, Massachusetts 1992).

Development as Freedom (Oxford University Press, Oxford 1999).

Smart, C., Neale, B., and Wade, A., *The Changing Experience of Childhood: Families and Divorce* (Polity, Cambridge 2001).

Stafford, C., *The Roads of Chinese Childhood* (Cambridge University Press, Cambridge 1995).

Stainton R. R., and Stainton, R. W., *Stories of Childhood* (University of Toronto Press, Toronto 1992).

Tomuschat, C., *Human Rights: Between Idealism and Realism* (2nd edition, Oxford University Press, Oxford 2008).

Turmel, A., *A Historical Sociology of Childhood: Developmental Thinking, Categorization and Graphic Visualisation* (Cambridge University Press, Cambridge 2008).

ul Haq, M., *Reflections on Human Development* (Oxford University Press, Oxford 1995).

UNHCHR, *Legislative History of the Convention on the Rights of the Child*, Volumes I–II (Office of the High Commissioner for Human Rights and Save the Children Sweden, New York and Geneva 2007).

Uvin, P., *Human Rights and Development* (Kumarian Press, Sterling, Virginia 2004).

Van Bueren, G., *The International Law on the Rights of the Child* (Martinus Nijhoff Publishers, The Hague 1998).

Veerman, P., *The Rights of the Child and the Changing Image of Childhood* (Martinus Nijhoff Publishers, Leiden 1992).

Wells, K., *Childhood in a Global Perspective* (Polity Press, Cambridge 2009).

Whelan, D. J., *Indivisible Human Rights* (University of Pennsylvania Press, Philadelphia 2010).

Wolff, J., and De-Shalit, A., *Disadvantage* (Oxford University Press, Oxford 2007).

Wyness, M., *Childhood and Society: An Introduction to the Sociology of Childhood* (Palgrave, Basingstoke 2006).

Chapters in Books

Adams, P., 'The Infant, the Family and Society' in Adams, P., Berg, L., Berger, N. *et al.* (eds.) *Children's Rights: Towards the Liberation of the Child* (Elek Books, London 1971) 51–90.

Aldgate, J. 'Child Well-Being, Child Development and Family Life' in McAuley, C., and Rose, W. (eds.) *Child Well-Being: Understanding Children's Lives* (Jessica Kingsley Publishers, London 2010) 21–38.

Alkire, S., 'Using the Capability Approach: Prospective and Evaluative Analyses' in Comim, F., Qizilbash, M., and Alkire S. (eds.), *The Capability Approach: Concepts, Measures and Applications* (Cambridge University Press, Cambridge 2008) 26–50.

Arajärvi, P., 'Article 26' in Alfredsson, G., and Eide, A. (eds.) *The Universal Declaration of Human Rights* (Martinus Nijhoff, The Hague 1999) 551–574.

Archard, D., 'John Locke's Children' in Turner, S. M., and Matthews, G. B. (eds.) *The Philosopher's Child: Critical Perspectives in the Western Tradition* (University of Rochester Press, Rochester 1998) 85–104.

'Philosophical Perspectives on Childhood' in Fionda, J. (ed.) *Legal Concepts of Childhood* (Hart, Oxford 2001) 43–56.

Ballet, J., Biggeri, M., and Comim, F., 'Children Agency and the Capability Approach – A Conceptual Framework' in Biggeri, M., Ballet, J., and F. Comim (eds.) *Children and the Capability Approach* (Palgrave Macmillan, Basingstoke 2011) 22–46.

Barnes, A., 'CRC's Performance of the Child as Developing' in Freeman, M. (ed.) *Law and Childhood Studies* (Oxford University Press, Oxford 2012) 392–418.

Basu, K., 'Prologue' in Biggeri, M., Ballet, J., and Comim, F. (eds.) *Children and the Capability Approach* (Palgrave Macmillan, Basingstoke 2011).

Berger, N., 'The Child, the Law and the State' in Adams, P., Berg, L., Berger, N. *et al.* (eds.), *Children's Rights: Towards the Liberation of the Child* (Elek Books, London 1971) 153–179.

Biggeri, M., and Mehrotra, S., 'Child Poverty as Capability Deprivation: How to Choose Domains of Child Well-Being and Poverty', in Biggeri, M., Ballet, J., and Comim F. (eds.), *Children and the Capability Approach* (Palgrave, Basingstoke 2011) 46–75.

Bishop, S., 'Children, Autonomy, and the Right to Self-determination' in Aiken, W., and LaFollette, H. (eds.), *Whose Child?* (Rowman and Littlefield, Totowa, New Jersey 1980) 154–177.

Brems, E., 'Children's Rights and Universality' in Willems, J. C. M. (ed.) *Developmental and Autonomy Rights of Children: Empowering Children, Caregivers and Communities* (Intersentia, Antwerp, Oxford 2002) 21–45.

Brighouse, H., 'What Rights (If Any) Do Children Have?' in Archard, D. and Macleod, C. (eds.), *The Moral and Political Status of Children* (Oxford University Press, Oxford 2002) 31–52.

Cashmore, J., 'Best Interests in Care Proceedings: Law, Policy and Practice' in Sutherland, E., and Macfarlane, L. A. B. (eds.), *Implementing Article 3 of the United Nations Convention on the Rights of the Child* (Cambridge University Press, 2016).

Chisholm, J., 'Learning "Respect for Everything": Navajo Image of Development' in Hwang, P., and Lamb, M. (eds.), *Images of Childhood* (Lawrence Eribaum, New Jersey 1996) 167–184.

deMause, L., 'The Evolution of Childhood', in deMause, L. (ed.), *The History of Childhood* (Souvenir Press, London 1976) 1–74.

Deneulin, S., 'Ideas Related to Human Development' in Deneulin, S., and Shahani, L. (eds.), *An Introduction to the Human Development and Capabilities Approach* (Earthscan, London 2009) 49–70.

Doek, J. E., 'The CRC: Dynamics and Directions of Monitoring Its implementation' in Invernizzi, A., and Williams, J. (eds.), *The Human Rights of Children* (Ashgate Falmer, London 2011) 99–116.

Durkheim, E., 'Childhood', in Pickering W. S. F. (ed.), *Durkheim: Essays on Morals and Education* (translated into English by H. L. Sutchliffe, Routledge, London 1979. First published in 1919) 150.

Eekelaar, J., 'Family Law and Legal Theory' in Brake, E., and Ferguson, L. (eds.), *Philosophical Foundations of Children and Family Law* (Oxford, Oxford University Press 2018) 41–58.

Eide, A., and Eide, W. B., 'Article 25' in Alfredsson, G. and Eide, A. (eds.), *The Universal Declaration on Human Rights* (Martinus Nijhoff, The Hague 1999) 523–550.

Ennew, J., 'Time for Children or Time for Adults?' in Qvortrup, J., Bardy, M., Sgritta, G. *et al.* (eds.), *Childhood Matters: Social Theory, Practice and Politics* (Ashgate, Farnham 1994) 125–134.

Esteva, G., 'Development' in Sachs, W. (ed.), *The Development Dictionary* (Zed Books, London 1992) 6–25.

Feinberg, J., 'The Child's Right to an Open Future' in Aiken, W., and LaFollette, H. (eds.), *Whose Child?* (Rowman and Littlefield, Totowa, New Jersey 1980) 124–153.

Franklin, A., and Franklin, B., 'Growing Pains: The Developing Children's Rights Movement in the UK' in Pilcher, J. and Wagg, S. (eds.), *Thatcher's Children?* (Falmer Press, London 1996) 94–113.

Freeman, M., 'Towards a Sociology of Children's Rights' in Freeman, M. (ed.), *Law and Childhood Studies* (Oxford University Press, Oxford 2012) 29–38.

Heintze, H-J., 'Children's Rights within Human Rights Protection' in Freeman, M., and Veerman, P. (eds.), *The Ideologies of Children's Rights* (Martinus Nijhoff Publishers, Dordrecht 1992) 71–78.

Hopkins, B., 'What Is Ontogenetic Development?' in Hopkins, B. (ed.), *The Cambridge Encyclopedia of Child Development* (Cambridge University Press, Cambridge 2005) 18–24.

Jackson, C., 'Rescue Gender from the Poverty Trap' in Jackson, C., and Person, R. (eds.), *Feminist Vision of Development: Gender Analysis and Policy* (Routledge, London 1998) 39–64.

James, A. 'Agency' in Qvortrup, J., Corsaro, W., and Honig, M. (eds.), *The Palgrave Handbook of Childhood Studies* (Palgrave, Basingstoke 2009) 34–45.

James, A., and Prout A., 'Re-presenting Childhood: Time and Transition in the Study of Childhood' in James, A., and Prout, A. *Constructing and Reconstructing Childhood: Contemporary Issues in the Sociological Study of Childhood* (2nd edition, Routledge, London 1997) 230–250.

Jaquette, J. S., and Staudt, K., 'Women, Gender and Development' in Jaquette, J. S., and Summerfield, G. (eds.), *Women and Gender Equality in Development Theory and Practice* (Duke University Press, Durham and London 2006) 17–52.

Johns, F. 'Introduction' in Johns, F., Joyce, R., and Pahuja, S. (eds.), *Events: The Force of International Law* (Routledge, Oxford 2011) 1–17. HERE

Jonsson, U., 'A Human Rights-Based Approach to Programming' in Gready, P., and Ensor, J. (eds.), *Reinventing Development?* (Zed Books, London 2005) 47–62.

Kennedy, D., 'Laws and Developments' in Hatchard, J., and Perry-Kessaris, A. (eds.), *Law and Development: Facing Complexity in the 21st Century* (Cavendish, London 2003) 17–26.

King, P. O., 'Thomas Hobbes's Children' in Turner. S. M.. and Matthews. G. B. (eds.), *The Philosopher's Child: Critical Perspectives in the WesternTradition* (University of Rochester Press, Rochester 1998) 65–84.

Korczak, J., 'How to Love a Child' in Wolins, M. (ed.), *Selected Works of Janusz Korczak* (National Science Foundation, Washington D.C. 1967) 355–356.

Kothari, U., 'From Colonial Administration to Development Studies: A Post-Colonial Critique on the History of Development Studies', in Kothari, U.

(ed.), *A Radical History of Development Studies* (Zed Books, New York 2005) 47–66.

Lansdown, G., 'The Reporting Process Under the Convention on the Rights of the Child' in Alston, P., and Crawford, J. (eds.), *The Future of UN Human Rights Treaty Monitoring* (Cambridge University Press, Cambridge 2000) 113–128.

Lervese, V., 'Introduction: Theoretical Foundations and the Book's Roadmap' in Biggeri, M., Ballet, J., and Comim, F. (eds.), *Children and the Capability Approach* (Palgrave, Hampshire 2011) 3–21.

Lopatka, A., 'The Rights of the Child Are Universal: The Perspective of the UN Convention on the Rights of the Child' in Freeman, M., and Veerman, P. (eds.), *The Ideologies of Children's Rights* (Martinus Nijhoff Publishers, Dordrecht 1992) 47–52.

Lundy, L., Welty, E., Swadener, B. B. *et al.*, 'What If Children Had Been Involved in Drafting the United Nations Convention on the Rights of the Child?' in Diduck, A., Peleg, N., and Reece, H. (eds.), *Law in Society: Reflections on Children, Family, Culture, and Philosophy; Essays in Honour of Michael Freeman* (Brill, The Hague, 2015) 223–242.

Maclure, R., 'The Dynamics of Youth Participation: Insights from Research Fieldwork with Female Youth in Senegal' in Denov, M., Maclure, R., and Campbell, K. (eds.), *Children's Rights and International Development: Lessons and Challenges from the Field* (Palgrave, New York 2011) 155–174.

Marshall, T. H., 'Citizenship and Social Class' in Marshall, T. H. (ed.), *Citizenship and Social Class and Other Essays* (Cambridge University Press, Cambridge 1951) 1–86.

Menghistu, F., 'The Satisfaction of Survival Requirements' in Ramcharan, B. G. (ed.), *The Right to Life in International Law* (Martinus Nijhoff Publishers, Dordrecht 1985) 63–83.

Neill, A. S., 'Freedom Works' in Adams, P., Berg, L., Berger, N. *et al.* (eds.), *Children's Rights: Towards the Liberation of the Child* (Elek Books, London 1971) 127–152.

Nussbaum, M., 'Human Capabilities, Female Human Beings' in Nussbaum, M. and Glover, J. (eds.), *Women, Culture and Development: A Study of Human Capabilities* (Oxford University Press, Oxford 1995) 61–104.

O'Dell, L., Brownlow, C., and Bertilsdotter-Rosqvist, H., 'Introducing Normative and Different Childhoods, Developmental Trajectory and Transgression' in O'Dell, L., Brownlow, C., and Bertilsdotter-Rosqvist, H. (eds.), *Different Childhoods: Non/normative and Transgressive Trajectories* (Routledge 2018).

Ollendorf, R., 'The Rights of Adolescents' in Adams, P., Berg, L., Berger, N. *et al.* (eds.), *Children's Rights: Towards the Liberation of the Child* (Elek Books, London 1971) 91–126.

Palmeri, A., 'Childhood's End: Toward the Liberation of Children' in Aiken, W., and LaFollette, H. (eds.), *Whose Child?* (Rowman and Littlefield, Totowa, New Jersey 1980) 105–124.

Peleg, N., 'What Do We Mean When We Speak about Children's Right to Development?' in Malekiam, F., and Nordlöf, K. (eds.), *The Sovereignty of Children in Law* (Cambridge Scholarly Publishing, Cambridge 2012) 134–156.

Peleg, N., and Tobin, J., 'Article 6 – The Right to Life, Survival and Development' in Tobin, J. (ed.), *The UN Convention on the Rights of the Child: A Commentary* (Oxford University Press, 2019) 186–236.

Price Cohen, C., 'The Relevance of Theories of Natural Law and Legal Positivism' in Freeman, M., and Veerman, P. (eds.), *The Ideologies of Children's Rights* (Martinus Nijhoff Publishers, Dordrecht 1992) 53–70.

Prout, A., and James, A., 'A New Paradigm for the Sociology of Childhood? Provenance Promise and Problems' in James, A., and Prout, A. (eds.), *Constructing and Reconstructing Childhood* (3rd edition, Routledge, Oxon 2015) 7–33.

Robertson, P., 'Home as a Nest: Middle Class Childhood in Nineteenth-Century Europe' in deMause L. (ed.), *The History of Childhood* (Souvenir Press, London 1976) 407–431.

Robinson, M., 'What Rights Can Add to Good Development Practice' in Alston, P., and Robinson, M. (eds.), *Human Rights and Development: Towards Mutual Reinforcement* (Oxford University Press, Oxford 2005) 25–41.

Rosas, A., 'The Right to Development' in Eida, A., Krause, C., and Rosas, A. (eds.), *Economic, Social and Cultural Rights* (2nd edition, Kluwer International, The Hague 2001) 119–130.

Sen, A., 'Capabilities and Well-Being' in Nussbaum, M., and Sen, A. (eds.), *Quality of Life* (Oxford University Press, Oxford 1993) 30–53.

Sengupta, A., 'Implementing the Right to Development' in Schrijver, N., and Weiss, F. (eds.), *International Law and Sustainable Development: Principles and Practice* (Martinus Nijhoff Publishers, Leiden 2004) 341–377.

Simon, J., 'Jean-Jacques Rousseau's Children', in Turner, S. M., and Matthews, G. B. (eds.), *The Philosopher's Child: Critical Perspectives in the Western Tradition* (University of Rochester Press, New York 1998) 105–120.

Stalford, H., and Hollingsworth, K., 'Judging Children's Rights: Tendencies, Tensions, Constraints' in Stalford, H., Hollingsworth, K., and Gilmore, S. (eds.), *Rewriting Children's Rights Judgments* (Hart 2017) 17–52.

Thomas, N., and Stoecklin, D., 'Recognition and Capability: A New Way to Understand How Children Can Achieve Their Rights?' in Baraldi, C., and Cockburn, T. (eds.), *Theorising Childhood: Citizenship, Rights and Participation* (Palgrave Macmillan, Basingstoke 2018) 73–94.

Woodhead, M., 'Child Development and the Development of Childhood' in Qvortrup, J., Corsaro, W., and Honig, M. (eds.), *The Palgrave Handbook of Childhood Studies* (Palgrave, Basingstoke 2009, 2011) 46–61.

Journal Articles

Ajodhia-Andrews, A., and Berman, R., 'Exploring School Life From the Lens of a Child Who Does Not Use Speech to Communicate' (2009) 15 *Qualitative Inquiry* 931.

Anonymous note, 'The Development of Young Children' (1931) 218 (5638) *The Lancet* 668.

Alanen, L., 'Editorial: "Intersectionality" and Other Challenges to Theorizing Childhood' (2016) 23 *Childhood* 157.

Alderson, P., 'Young Children's Human Rights: A Sociological Analysis' (2012) 20 *International Journal of Children's Rights* 177.

Alderson, P., Hawthorne, J., and Killen M., 'The Participation Rights of Premature Babies' (2005) 13 *International Journal of Children's Rights* 31.

Alston, A., 'A Third Generation of Solidarity Rights: Progressive Development or Obfuscation on International Human Rights Law?' (1982) 29 *Netherlands International Law Review* 307.

Alston, P., 'The Shortcomings of a "Garfield the Cat" Approach to the Right to Development' (1985) 15 *California Western International Law Journal* 510.
'Making Space for New Human Rights: The Case of the Right to Development' (1988) 1 *Harvard Human Rights Yearbook* 3

Anands, S., and Sen, A., 'The Income Component of the Human Development Index' (2000) 1 *Journal of Human Development* 83.

Archard, D., 'Children, Adults, Best Interests and Rights' (2013) 13 *Medical Law International* 55.

Archer, R., 'The Strengths of Different Traditions: What Can Be Gained and What Might Be Lost by Combining Rights and Development?' (2006) 4 *The International Journal of Human Rights* 81.

Barsh, R. L., 'The Right to Development as a Human Right: Results of the Global Consultation' (1991) 13 *Human Rights Quarterly* 322.

Beck, R., 'White House Conferences on Children: An Historical Perspective' (1973) 43 *Harvard Educational Review* 653.

Bell, F., 'Children with Gender Dysphoria and the Jurisdiction of the Family Court" (2015) 38 *University of New South Wales Law Journal* 426.

Ben-Arieh, A., 'Where Are the Children? Children's Role in Measuring and Monitoring Their Well-Being' (2005) 74 *Social Indicators Research* 573.
'The Child Indicators Movement: Past, Present, and Future' (2008) 1 *Child Indicators Research* 3.

Ben-Arieh, A., and Frønes, I., 'Taxonomy for Child Well-Being Indicators: A Framework for the Analysis of the Well-Being of Children' (2011) 18 *Childhood* 460.

Bhatia, S., Jenney, M. E., Bogue, M. K. *et al.*, 'The Minneapolis-Manchester Quality of Life Instrument: Reliability and Validity of the Adolescent Form' (2002) 20 *Journal of Clinical Oncology* 4692.

Bishop, K., 'Challenging Research: Completing Participatory Social Research with Children and Adolescents in a Hospital Setting' (2014) 7 *Health Environments Research & Design Journal* 76.

Bradshaw, J., and Richardson, D., 'An Index of Child Well-Being in Europe' (2009) 2 *Children Indication Research* 319.

Brietzke, P. H., 'Consorting with the Chameleon, or Realizing the Right to Development' (1985) 15 *California Western International Law Journal* 560.

Burman, E., 'Local, Global or Globalized' (1996) 3 *Childhood* 46.

'Desiring Development? Psychoanalytic Contribution to Antidevelopmental Psychology' (2011) 26 *International Journal of Qualitative Studies in Education* 1.

'Deconstructing Neoliberal Childhood: Towards a Feminist Antipsychological Approach' (2012) 19 *Childhood* 423.

Buss, E., 'What the Law Should (and Should Not) Learn from Child Development Research' (2009–2010) 38 *Hofstra Law Review* 13.

'Developmental Jurisprudence' (2016) 88 *Temple Law Review* 741.

'Roper v Simmons: Commentary' in Stalford, H., Hollingsworth, K., and Gilmore, S. (eds.), *Rewriting Children's Rights Judgments* (Hart 2017) 405–410.

Butler, U. M., 'Freedom, Revolt and 'Citizenship' (2009) 16 *Childhood* 11;

Camfield, L., Streuli, N., and Woodhead, M., 'What's the Use of "Well-Being" in Contexts of Child Poverty? Approaches to Research, Monitoring and Children's Participation' (2009) 17 *International Journal of Children's Rights* 65.

Casas, F., 'Children's Rights and Children's Quality of Life: Conceptual and Practical Issues' (1997) *Social Indicators Research* 283.

Cashmore, J., and Parkinson, P., 'The Use and Abuse of Social Science Research Evidence in Children's Cases' (2014) 20 *Psychology, Public Policy and Law* 239.

Chinkin, C., 'The Challenges of Soft Law: Development and Change in International law' (1989) 28 *International and Comparative Law Quarterly* 850.

Chow, P. Y. S., 'Has Intersectionality Reached Its Limits? Intersectionality in the UN Human Rights Treaty Body Practice and the Issue of Ambivalence' (2016) 16 *Human Rights Law Review* 453.

Cornwall, A., and Nyamu-Musembi, C., 'Putting the "Rights-Based Approach" to Development into Practice' (2004) 25 *Third World Quarterly* 1415.

Crenshaw, K., 'Mapping the Margins: Intersectionality, Identity Politics, and Violence against Women of Color' (1991) 43 *Stanford Law Review* 1241.

Crivello, G., Camfield, L., and Woodhead, M., 'How Can Children Tell Us about Their Wellbeing? Exploring the Potential of Participatory Research Approaches within Young Lives' (2009) 90 *Social Indicators Research* 51.

Dailey, A. C., and Rosenbury, L. A., 'The New Law of the Child' (2018) 127 *The Yale Law Journal* 1448.

Daiute, C., 'The Rights of Children, The Rights of Nations: Developmental Theory and the Politics of Children's Rights' (2008) 64 *Journal of Social Issues* 701.

De Clercq, E., Ruhe, K., Rost, M., et al., 'Is Decision-Making Capacity an "Essentially Contested" Concept in Pediatrics?' (2017) 20 *Medicine, Health Care and Philosophy* 425–433.

Dekker, J. J. J., 'The Century of the Child Revisited' (2000) 8 *International Journal of Children's Rights* 133.

Dixon, R., and Nussbaum, M., 'Children's Rights and a Capability Approach: The Question of Special Priority' (2011–2012) 97 *Cornell Law Review* 549.

Donnelly, J., 'In Search of the Unicorn: The Jurisprudence and Politics of the Right to Development' (1985) 15 *California Western International Law Journal* 473.

Douglas, H., and Walsh, T., 'Continuing the Stolen Generations: Child Protection Interventions and Indigenous People' (2013) 21 *International Journal of Children's Rights* 59.

Dowd, N. E., 'Black Boys Matter: Developmental Equality' (2016) 45 *Hofstra Law Review* 47.

Droit-Volet, S., 'Time Perception in Children: A Neurodevelopmental Approach' (2013) 51 *Neuropsychologia* 220.

Dworkin, R., 'Law as Interpretation' (1982) 9 *Critical Inquiry* 179.

Eichsteller, G., 'Janusz Korczak: His Legacy and Its Relevance for Children's Rights Today' (2009) 17 *International Journal of Children's Rights* 377.

Etienne, A.-M., Dupuis, G., Spitz E. et al., 'The Gap Concept as a Quality of Life Measure: Validation Study of the Child Quality of Life Systemic Inventory' (2011) 100 *Social Indicators Research* 241.

Fass, P. A, 'A Historical Context for the United Nations Convention on the Rights of the Child' (2011) 633 *Annals of the American Academy of Political and Social Science* 17.

Federle, K. H., 'Rights Flow Downhill' (1994) 2 *International Journal of Children's Rights* 343.

'Looking Ahead: An Empowerment Perspective on the Rights of the Child' (1995) 689 *Temple Law Review* 1585.

'Do Rights Still Flow Downhill?' (2017) 25 *International Journal of Children's Rights* 273.

Fernandes, L., Mendes, A., and Teixeira, A., 'Assessing Child Well-Being through a New Multidimensional Child-Based Weighting Scheme Index: An Empirical Estimation for Portugal' (2013) 45 *Journal of Socio-Economics* 155.

Fineman, M., and Opie, A., 'The Use of Social Science Data in Legal Policymaking: Custody Determination at Divorce' (1987) *Wisconsin Law Review* 107.

Fish, S., 'Working on the Chain Gang: Interpretation in the Law and in Literary Criticism' (1982) 9 *Critical Inquiry* 201.

Freeman, M., 'Children's Rights and Some Unanswered Questions and Some Unquestioned Answers' (1979–1980) 5 *Poly Law Review* 9, 15.

'The Morality of Cultural Pluralism' (1995) 3 *International Journal of Children's Rights* 1.

'Rethinking Gillick' (2005) 13 *International Journal of Children's Rights* 201.

'Why It Remains Important to Take Children's Rights Seriously' (2007) 15 *International Journal of Children's Rights* 5.

'The Human Rights of Children' (2010) 63 *Current Legal Problems* 1.

Gasper, D., 'What Is the Capability Approach? Its Core, Rationale, Partners and Dangers' (2007) 36 *Journal of Socio-Economics* 335.

Geiser, R. L., 'The Rights of Children' (1976–1977) 28 *Hastings Law Journal* 1027.

Goswami, H., 'Social Relationships and Children's Subjective Well-Being' (2011) 107 *Social Indicator Research* 575.

Hafen, B. C., 'Children's Liberation and the New Egalitarianism: Some Reservations about Abandoning Youth to Their "Rights"' [1976] *BYU Law Review* 605.

Hafen, B. C., and Hafen, J. O., 'Abandoning Children to Their Autonomy: The United Nations Convention on the Rights of the Child' (1996) 37 *Harvard International Law Journal* 449.

Haisma, H., Yousefzadeh, S., Boele Van Hensbroek, P., 'Toward a Capability Approach to Child Growth: A Theoretical Framework' (2018) 14 *Maternal & Child Nutrition* 1.

Hamilton, L., 'A Theory of True Interests in the Work of Amartya Sen' (1999) 34 *Government and Opposition* 516.

Hanafin, S., Brooks, A.-M., Carroll, E., *et al.*, 'Achieving Consensus in Developing a National Set of Child Well-Being Indicators' (2007) 80 *Social Indicators Research* 79.

Hanson, K., and Lundy, L., 'Does Exactly What It Says on the Tin? A Critical Analysis and Alternative Conceptualisation of the So-Called "General Principles" of the Convention on the Rights of the Child' (2017) 25 *The International Journal of Children's Rights* 285.

Harris-Short, S., 'International Human Rights Law: Imperialist, Inept and Ineffective? Cultural Relativism and the UN Convention on the Rights of the Child' (2003) 25 *Human Rights Quarterly* 130.

Heesterman, W., 'An Assessment of the Impact of Youth Submissions to the United Nations Committee on the Rights of the Child' (2005) 13 *International Journal of Children's Rights* 351–378.

Heywood, C., 'Centuries of Childhood: An Anniversary – and an Epitaph?' (2010) 3 *Journal of History of Childhood and Youth* 343, 357–358.

Himes, J. R., 'Children's Rights: Moralists, Lawyers and the Right to Development' (1993) 1 *International Journal of Children's Rights* 81.

Hodgson, D., 'The Child's Right to Life, Survival and Development' (1994) 2 *International Journal of Children's Rights* 369.

Holland, S., Renold, E., Ross, N. *et al.*, 'Power, Agency and Participatory Agendas: A Critical Exploration of Young's People's Engagement in Participative Qualitative Research' (2010) 17 *Childhood* 360–375.

Huntington, C., 'Early Childhood Development and the Law' (2017) 90 *Southern California Law Review* 755.

Ito, T., 'New Education for Underprivileged Children: The Condition of Children's Rights in Japanese Law' (2012) 48 *Paedagogica Historica* 153.

Ivens J., 'The Development of a Happiness Measure for Schoolchildren' (2007) 23 *Educational Psychology in Practice* 203.

James, A., 'The Standardized Child: Issues of Openness, Objectivity and Agency in Promoting Childhood Health' (2004) 13 *Anthropological Journal on European Culture* 93.

'Competition or Integration? The Next Step in Childhood Studies?' (2010) 17 *Childhood* 485.

Jans, M., 'Children as Citizens' (2004) 11 *Childhood* 27.

Jones, L., Bellis, M. A., Wood, S. *et al.*, 'Prevalence and Risk of Violence Against Children with Disabilities: A Systematic Review and Meta-analysis of Observational Studies' (2012) 380 *Lancet* 899–907.

Kahn-Freund, O., 'On Uses and Misuses of Comparative Law' (1974) 37 *Modern Law Review* 1.

Karkness, S., 'The Cultural Context of Child Development' (1980) 8 *New Directions of Child Development* 7.

Kelle H., 'The Discourse of "Development": How 9- to 12-Year-Old Children Construct "Childish" and "Further Developed" Identities within Their Peer Culture' (2001) 8 *Childhood* 95.

Kelle, H., "Age Appropriate Development' as Measure and Norm' (2010) 17 *Childhood* 9.

Kosher, H., and Ben-Arieh, A., 'What Children Think about Their Rights and Their Well-Being: A Cross-National Comparison' (2017) 87 *American Journal of Orthopsychiatry* 256.

Land, K. C., Lamb, V. L., and Mustillo, S. K., 'Child and Youth Well-Being in the United States, 1975–1998: Some Findings from a New Index' (2001) 56 *Social Indicators Research* 241.

Lindenmeyer, K., and Sandin, B., 'National Citizenship and Early Policies Shaping 'The Century of the Child' in Sweden and the United States' (2008) 1 *Journal of History of Childhood and Youth* 50.

Lippman, L. H., 'Indicators and Indices of Child Well-Being: A Brief American History' (2007) 83 *Social Indicators Research* 39.

Lund, R., 'At the Interface of Development Studies and Child Research: Rethinking Participating Child' (2007) 5 *Children's Geographies* 131.

Lundy, L., '"Voice" Is Not Enough: Conceptualising Article 12 of the UN Convention on the Rights of the Child' (2007) 33 *British Educational Research Journal* 927.

   'In Defence of Tokenism? Implementing Children's Right to Participate in Collective Decision-Making' (2018) 25 *Childhood* 340.

Margolin, C. R., 'Salvation versus Liberation: The Movement for Children's Rights in a Historical Context' (1977–1978) 25 *Social Problems* 441.

Marks, S., 'The Human Right to Development: Between Rhetoric and Reality' (2004) 17 *Harvard Human Rights Journal* 137.

Marshall, D., 'The Construction of Children as an Object of International Relations: the Declaration of Children's Rights and the Child Welfare Committee of League of Nations, 1990–1924' (1999) 7 *International Journal of Children's Rights* 103.

Maurás, M., 'Public Policies and Child Rights: Entering the Third Decade of the Convention on the Rights of the Child' (2011) 633 *Annals of the American Academy of Political and Social Sciences* 52.

McCall, L., 'The Complexity of Intersectionality' (2005) 30 *Journal of Women in Culture and Society* 1771.

McGillivray, M., and White, H., 'Measuring Development? The UNDP's Human Development Index' (1993) 5 *Journal of International Development* 183.

Minow, M., 'What Ever Happened to Children's Rights?' (1995) 80 *Minnesota Law Review* 267.

Modell, J., 'How May Children's Development Be Seen Historically?' (2000) 7 *Childhood* 81.

Moore, A., and Crisp, R., 'Welfarism in Moral Theory' (1996) 74 *Australian Journal of Philosophy* 598.

Moore, A., Theokas, C., Lippman, L. *et al.*, 'A Microdata Child Well-Being Index: Conceptualization, Creation and Findings' (2008) 1 *Child Indicators Research* 17.

Nelson, P. J., and Dorsey, E., 'At the Nexus of Human Rights and Development: New Methods and Strategies of Global NGOs' (2003) 31 *World Development* 2013.

Nolan, A., 'The Child as 'Democratic Citizen': Challenging the 'Participation Gap'' (2010) 4 *Public Law* 767.

Nussbaum, M., 'Capabilities as Fundamental Entitlements: Sen and Global Justice' (2003) 9 *Feminist Economics* 33.

'Women's Capabilities and Social Justice' (2000) 1 *Journal of Human Development* 219.

Obiora, L. A., 'Beyond the Rhetoric of a Right to Development' (1996) 18 *Law & Policy* 355.

O'Hare, W. P., 'Development of the Child Indicator Movement in the United States' (2012) 6 *Child Development Perspective* 79.

'A New State-Level Index of Child Well-Being for Young Children in the U.S.' (2016) 11 *Applied Research in Quality of Life* 493.

O'Manique, J., 'Development, Human Rights and Law' (1992) 14 *Human Rights Quarterly* 383.

'Human Rights and Development' (1992) 14 *Human Rights Quarterly* 78.

O'Neill, O., 'Children's Rights and Children's Lives' (1988) 98 *Ethics* 445.

Palmer, I., 'Rural Women and the Basic Needs Approach to Development' (1977) 115 *International Labour Review* 97.

Pavlovic, Z., and Leban, T. R., 'Children's Rights International Study Project (CRISP) – A Shift from the Focus on Children's Rights to a Quality of Life Assessment Instrument' (2009) 2 *Child Indicators Research* 265.

Peleg, N., 'Marginalisation by the Court: The Case of Roma Children and the European Court of Human Rights' (2018) 18 *Human Rights Law Review* 111.

Perry, R. W., 'Rethinking the Right to Development: After the Critique of Development, After the Critique of Rights' (1996) 18 *Law & Society* 225.

Perry-Kessaris, A., 'Prepare Your Indicators: Economic Imperialism on the Shores of Law and Development' (2011) 7 *International Journal of Law in Context* 401.

Pinkerton, J., 'Children's Participation in the Policy Process: Some Thoughts on Policy Evaluation Based on the Irish National Children's Strategy' (2004) 18 *Children & Society* 119.

Prescott, D., 'Forensic Experts and Family Courts: Science or Privilege-by-License?' (2016) 28 *Journal of the American Academy of Matrimonial Lawyers* 521.

Pressman, S., and Summerfield, G., 'The Economic Contribution of Amartya Sen' (2000) 12 *Review of Political Economy* 89.

Quennerstedt, A., 'Children's Rights Research Moving into the Future: Challenges on the Way Forward' (2013) 21 *International Journal of Children's Rights* 233.

Raffaelli, M., 'How Do Brazilian Street Youth Experience "the Street"?' (2001) 8 *Childhood* 396.

Raghavan, R., and Alexandrova, A., 'Toward a Theory of Child Well-Being' (2015) 121 *Social Indicator Research* 887.

Ravallion, M., 'Good and Bad Growth: The Human Development Reports' (1997) *World Development* 631.

Ravens-Sieberer, U. Devine, J., Bevans, K., *et al.*, 'Subjective Well-Being Measures for Children Were Developed within the PROMIS Project: Presentation of First Results' (2014) 67 *Journal of Clinical Epidemiology* 207.

Rees, G., and Dinisman, T., 'Comparing Children's Experiences and Evaluations of Their Lives in 11 Different Countries' (2015) 8 *Child Indicators Research* 5.

Reynart, D., Bie, M., and Vandevelde, S., 'A Review of Children's Rights Literature since the Adoption of the United Nations Convention on the Rights of the Child' (2009) 16 *Childhood* 518.

Roche, J., 'Children: Rights, Participation and Citizenship' (1999) 6 *Childhood* 475.

Rochelle, V., 'White House Conferences on Children: an Historical Perspective' (1973) 43 *Harvard Educational Review* 653.

Rodham, H., 'Children Under the Law' (1973) 43 *Harvard Educational Review* 487.

Ruck, M. D., Abramovitch, R., and Keating, D. P., 'Children's and Adolescents' Understanding of Rights: Balancing Nurturance and Self-Determination' (1988) 69 *Child Development* 404.

Ruck, M. D., Keating, D. P., Abramovitch R., *et al.*, 'Adolescents' and Children's Knowledge about Rights: Some Evidence for How Young People View Rights in Their Own Lives' (1998) 21 *Journal of Adolescence* 275.

Ryan, K. W., 'The New Wave of Childhood Studies: Breaking the Grip of Bio-social Dualism?' (2011) 19 *Childhood* 439.

Sagar, A. D., and Najam, A., 'The Human Development Index: A Critical Review' (1998) 25 *Ecological Economy* 249.

Saith, A., and Wazir, R., 'Towards Conceptualizing Child Well-being in India: The Need for a Paradigm Shift' (2010) 3 *Children Indication Research* 385.

Saito, M., 'Amartya Sen's Capability Approach to Education: A Critical Exploration' (2003) 37 *Journal of Philosophy of Education* 17.

Sandberg, K., 'The Rights of LGBTI Children under the Convention on the Rights of the Child' (2015) 33 *Nordic Journal of Human Rights* 337.

Sano, H.-O., 'Development and Human Rights: The Necessary, but Partial Integration of Human Rights and Development' (2000) 22 *Human Rights Quarterly* 734.

Sanson, A. V., Mission, S., Hawkins, M. T., *et al.*, 'The Development and Validation of Australian Indices of Child Development – Part I: Conceptualisation and Development' (2010) 3 *Children Indication Research* 275.

Sarriera, J. C., Casas, F., Bedin, L. *et al.*, 'Material Resources and Children's Subjective Well-Being in Eight Countries' (2015) 8 *Child Indicators Research* 199.

Sen, A., 'Human Rights and Capabilities' (2005) 6 *Journal of Human Development* 151.
  'Children and Human Rights' (2007) 1 *Indian Journal of Human Development* 235, 241.

Sengupta, A., 'The Human Right to Development' (2004) 32 *Oxford Development Studies* 179.
  'Realizing the Right to Development' (2000) 31 *Development and Change* 553.

Shanahan, S., 'Lost and Found: The Sociological Ambivalence towards Childhood' (2007) 33 *Annual Review of Sociology* 407.

Shelton, D., 'A Response to Donnelly and Alston' (1985) 15 *California Western International Law Journal* 524.

Skolnick, A., 'The Limits of Childhood: Conceptions of Child Development and Social Context' (1975) 39 *Law & Contemporary Problems* 38.

Sloth-Nielsen, J., and Philpott, S., 'The Intersection between Article 6 of the UN Convention on the Rights of the Child and Early Childhood Development' (2015) 26 *Stellenbosch Law Review* 295.

Srinivasan, T. N., 'Human Development: A New Paradigm or Reinvention of the Wheel?' (1994) 84 *AEA Papers and Proceedings* 238.

Stearns, P. N., 'Defining Happy Childhoods: Assessing a Recent Change' (2010) 3 *Journal of the History of Childhood and Youth* 165.

Stewart, J., '"The Dangerous Age of Childhood": Child Guidance and the "Normal" Child in Great Britain, 1920–1950' (2011) 47 *Paedagogica Historica* 785.

Streeten, P., and Burki, S. J., 'Basic Needs: Some Issues' (1978) 6 *World Development* 411.

Taefi, N., 'The Synthesis of Age and Gender: Intersectionality, International Human Rights Law and the Marginalisation of the Girl-Child' (2009) 17 *International Journal of Human Rights* 345.

Tillman, K. A., Marghetis, T., Barner, D. *et al.*, 'Today Is Tomorrow's Yesterday: Children's Acquisition of Deictic Time Words' (2017) 92 *Cognitive Psychology* 87.

Thomas, N., 'Towards a Theory of Children's Participation' (2007) 15 *International Journal of Children's Rights* 199.

Thorne, B., 'Crafting the Interdisciplinary Field of Childhood Studies' (2007) 24 *Childhood* 147.

Tobin, J., 'Justifying Children's Rights' (2013) 21 *International Journal of Children's Rights* 395.

Turner, B., 'Personhood and Citizenship' (1986) 3 *Theory Culture Society* 1.

Uprichard, E., 'Children as "Being and Becomings": Children, Childhood and Temporality' (2008) 22 *Children & Society* 303.

Vandenhole, W., 'Economic, Social and Cultural Rights in the CRC: Is There a Legal Obligation to Cooperate Internationally for Development?' (2009) 17 *International Journal of Children's Rights* 23.

Van Drenth, A., and Myers, K., 'Normalising Childhood: Politics and Interventions Concerning Special Children in the United States and Europe (1900–1960)' (2011) 47 *Paedagogica Historica* 719.

Vann, R. T., 'The Youth of *Centuries of Childhood*' (1982) 21 *History and Theory* 279.

Vizard, P., 'Specifying and Justifying a Basic Capability Set: Should the International Human Rights Framework be Given a More Direct Role?' (2007) 35 *Oxford Development Studies* 225.

Wald, M. S., 'Children's Rights: A Framework for Analysis' (1979) 12 *University California Davis Law Review* 255.

Wall, J., 'Can Democracy Represent Children? Towards a Politics of Difference' (2012) 19 *Childhood* 86.

Wallander, J. L., and Koot, H. M., 'Quality of Life in Children: A Critical Examination of Concepts, Approaches, Issues, and Future Directions' (2016) 45 *Clinical Psychology Review* 131.

Watkins, D., 'Where Do I Stand? Assessing Children's Capabilities Under English Law' (2016) 28 *Child and Family Law Quarterly* 25.

Wilson, A., 'The Infancy of the History of Childhood: An Appraisal of Philippe Ariès' (1980) 19 *History and Theory* 132.

Woodhead, M., 'Reconstructing Developmental Psychology: Some First Steps' (1999) 13 *Children & Society* 3.

'Early Childhood Development: A Question of Rights' (2005) 37 *International Journal of Early Childhood* 80.

Reports

Australian Human Rights Commission, *Bringing Them Home: The 'Stolen Children' Report* (1997)

Grant, J. P., *The State of the World's Children 1980–1981* (UNICEF, New York 1981).

Lundy, L., Orr, K., Marshall, C., *et al.*, *Towards Better Investment in the Rights of the Child: The Views of Children* (2015, Geneva: Child Rights Connect).

Melchiorre, A., and Atkins, E., *At What Age Are School-Children Employed, Married and Taken to Court?* (Right to Education Project, London 2011) 30–32.

Orr, K., Emerson, L., Lundy, L., *et al.*, *Enabling the Exercise of Civil and Political Rights: The Views of Children* (2016 London: Save the Children and Queen's University Belfast).

Robeyns, I., 'An Unworkable Idea or a Promising Alternative? Sen's Capability Approach Re-examined' (1993) Centre of Economic Discussion on Paper 00.30. University of Leuven, Mimeo.

UNDP, *Human Development Report* 1990 (Oxford University Press, New York 1990).

Human Development Report: Human Rights and Human Development (Oxford University Press, Oxford and New York 2000).

Human Development Report 2016: Human Development for Everyone (United Nations Development Programme, New York 2016) 11–14.

UNICEF, *The State of the World's Children 2011* (UNICEF, New York 2011).

The State of the World's Children 2015: Reimagine the Future (UNICEF, Geneva 2015).

Legislation

Australia

Family Law Act 1975 (Cth)

Cases

Australia

Re: Jamie [2013] FamCAFC 110.
Re Kelvin [2017] FamCAFC 258.

United Kingdom

Gillick v. West Norfolk and Wisbech Area Health Authority [1986] AC 112.
ZH (Tanzania) (FC) v. Secretary of State for the Home Department [2011]
    UKSC 4.

United States of America

In Re Gault, 387 U.S. 1 (1967).
Wisconsin v. Yoder, 406 U.S. 205 (1972).
Roper v. Simmons 543 U.S 551 (2005).
Graham v. Florida 560 U.S 48 (2010).
Miller v. Alabama 567 U.S 460 (2012).

International Conventions and Declarations

The Covenant of the League of Nations, 1924.
The Declaration on the Rights of the Child, League of Nations O.J. Spec. Supp. 21,
    at 43 (1924).
Charter of the United Nations (1945).
UN General Assembly, *Universal Declaration of Human Rights*, 10 December
    1948, 217 A (III).
  Declaration on the Rights of the Child (Adopted by UN General Assembly
    Resolution 1386 (XIV) of 10 December 1959).
The Declaration on the Right to Development, adopted by General Assembly
    Resolution 41/128 of 4 December 1986.
The International Covenant on Civil and Political Rights (ICCPR), Adopted
    and opened to signature, ratification and accession by General Assembly
    Resolution 2200A (XXI) of 16 December 1996. Entered into force on
    23 March 1976.

The International Covenant on Economic, Social and Cultural Rights (ICESCR), Adopted and opened to signature, ratification and accession by General Assembly Resolution 2200A (XXI) of 16 December 1966. Enter into force on 3 January 1976.

Vienna Convention on the Laws of Treaties (Done at Vienna on 23 May 1969, Entered into Force on 27 January 1980). *United Nations Treaty Series*, Vol. 1155, 331.

UN Convention on the Rights of the Child 1989 (Adopted by General Assembly Resolution 44/25 of 20 November 1989, entered into force on 2 September 1990).

African Charter on the Rights and Welfare of the Child (OAU Doc. CAB/LEG/ 24.9/49 (1990)), entered into force Nov. 29, 1999.

UNGA, *Vienna Declaration and Program of Action* (12 July 1993), UN Doc. A/ CONF.157/23.

UN Documents

General Assembly Resolution 31/169, adopted on 21 December 1976.

'International Year of the Child' adopted on 21 December 1976.

UN Commission on Human Rights Resolution 4 (XXXIII) of 21 February 1977 UN Doc. E/CN.4/RES/4(XXXIII).

Letter to the UN Commission on Human Rights from the Permanent representative of Poland to the United Nations Office at Geneva E/CN.4/1284 (18 January 1978).

UN Economic and Social Council (18 January 1978) UN Doc. E/CN.4/1284.

'Question of a Convention on the Rights of the Child' (23 February 1978), UN Doc. E/CN.4/NGO/225.

Open-Ended Working Group on the UN Convention on the Rights of the Child

UN Commission on Human Rights (UNCHR), 'Question of a Convention on the Rights of the Child' (7 February 1978) UN Doc. E/CN.4/L.1366.

UNCHR, 'Question on a Convention on the Rights of the Child' (6 February – 10 March 1978) UN Doc. E/1978/34/E/CN.4/1292.

'Summary Record of the 1438th Meeting' (15 February 1978) UN Doc. E/CN.4/ SR.1438.

'Summary Record of the 1471st Meeting' (13 March 1978) UN Doc. E/CN.4/ SR.1471.

'Question of a Convention on the Rights of the Child' (1 February 1979) UN Doc. E/CN.4/1324/Add. 1.

'Report of the Open-Ended Working Group on a Draft Convention on the Rights of the Child' (12 March 1979) UN Doc. E/CN.4/L.1468.

'Report of the Working Group on a Draft Convention on the Rights of the Child' (10 March 1980) UN Doc. E/CN.4/L.1542.

'Report of the Working Group on a Draft Convention on the Rights of the Child' (17 February 1981) UN Doc. E/CN.4/L.1975.

'Report of the Working Group on a Draft Convention on the Rights of the Child' (8 March 1982) UN Doc. E/CN.4/1982/30/Add. 1.

'Report of the Working Group on a Draft Convention on the Rights of the Child' (25 March 1983) UN Doc. E/CN.4/1983/62.

'Report of the Working Group on a Draft Convention on the Rights of the Child' (23 February 1984) UN Doc. E/CN.4/1984/71.

'Report of the Working Group on a Draft Convention on the Rights of the Child' (11 March 1985) UN Doc. E/CN.4/1985/L.1.

'Report of the Working Group on a Draft Convention on the Rights of the Child' (13 March 1986) UN Doc. E/CN.4/1986/39.

'Report of the Working Group on a Draft Convention on the Rights of the Child' (23 February 1987) UN Doc. E/CN.4/1987/25.

'Pre-Sessional Open-Ended Working Group on the Question of a Convention on the Rights of the Child, "Proposal Submitted By India"'(28 January 1988) UN Doc. E/CN.4/1988/WG1/WG.13.

'Report of the Working Group on a Draft Convention on the Rights of the Child' (6 April 1988) UN Doc. E/CN.4/1988/28.

'Report of the Working Group on a Draft Convention on the Rights of the Child' (2 March 1989) UN Doc. E/CN.4/1989/48.

'Draft Convention on the Rights of the Child, Working Paper Submitted by the Chairman, Text as Adopted at First Reading with Suggested Revisions' (24 November 1988) UN Doc. E/CN.4/1989/WG.1/WP.2.

UN Committee on the Rights of the Child (UNCRC)

General Documents

UNCRC (UN Committee on the Rights of the Child), 'General Guidelines Regarding Form and Content of Initial Reports to Be Submitted by States Parties Under Article 44(1)(a) of the Convention' (30 October 1991) UN Doc. CRC/C/5.

'General Guidelines Regarding the Forms and Content of Period Reports to be Submitted by States Parties Under Article 44(1)(b) of the Convention' (29 November 2005) UN Doc. CRC/C/58/Rev. 1.

'Treaty-Specific Guidelines Regarding the Form and Content of Periodic Reports to Be Submitted by States Parties Under Article 44, Paragraph 1 (b), of the Convention on the Rights of the Child' (25 November 2010) CRC/C/58/Rev. 2.

'Treaty-Specific Guidelines Regarding the Form and Content of Periodic Reports to be Submitted by States Parties Under Article 44, paragraph 1 (b), of the Convention on the Rights of the Child' (3 March 2015) UN Doc. CRC/C/58/Rev.3.

General Comments

UNCCPR (UN Convention on Civil and Political Rights), 'General Comment No. 36 (2018) on Article 6 of the International Covenant on Civil and Political Rights, on the Right to Life' (30 October 2018) UN Doc. CCPR/C/GC/36.

UNCRC 'General Comment Number 1 – Article 29(1): The Aims of Education' (17 April 2001) UN Doc. CRC/GC/1/2001.

'General Comment Number 3 – HIV/AIDS and the Rights of the Child' (17 March 2003) UN Doc. CRC/GC/3/2003.

'General Comment Number 4 – Adolescent Health and Development in the Context of the Convention on the Rights of the Child' (1 July 2003) UN Doc. CRC/GC/4/2003.

'General Comment Number 5 – General Measures of Implementation of the Convention on the Rights of the Child' (27 November 2003) UN Doc. CRC/GC/5/2003.

'General Comment Number 6 – Treatment of Unaccompanied and Separated Children Outside Their Country of Origin' (1 September 2005) UN Doc. CRC/GC/2005/6.

'General Comment Number 7 – Implementing Child Rights in Early Childhood' (20 September 2006) UN Doc. CRC/GC/7/Rev.1.

'General Comment Number 8 – The Rights of the Child for Protection From Corporal Punishment and other Cruel or Degrading Forms of Punishment' (2 March 2007) UN Doc. CRC/GC/8.

'General Comment Number 9 – The Rights of Children with Disabilities' (27 February 2007) UN Doc. CRC/C/GC/9.

'General Comment Number 10 – Children's Rights in Juvenile Justice' (25 April 2007) UN Doc. CRC/C/GC/10.

'General Comment Number 11 – Indigenous Children and Their Rights under the Convention' (12 February 2009) UN Doc. CRC/C/GC/11.

'General Comment Number 12 – The Right of the Child to Be Heard' (20 July 2009) UN Doc. CRC/C/GC/12.

'General Comment Number 13 – The Right of the Child to Freedom from All Forms of Violence' (18 April 2011) UN Doc. CRC/C/GC/13.

'General Comment No. 14 (2013) on the Right of the Child to Have His or Her Best Interests Taken as a Primary Consideration (art. 3, para. 1)' (29 May 2013) UN Doc. CRC/C/GC/14.

'General Comment No. 15 (2013) on the Right of the Child to the Enjoyment of the Highest Attainable Standard of Health (art. 24)' (17 April 2013) UN Doc. CRC/C/GC/15.

'General Comment 17 on the Right of the Child to Rest, Leisure, Play, Recreational Activities, Cultural Life and the Arts' (17 April 2013) UN Docs CRC/C/GC/17.

UNCRC and CEDAW, 'Joint General Recommendation No. 31 of the Committee on the Elimination of Discrimination against Women/General Comment No. 18 of the Committee on the Rights of the Child on Harmful Practices' (14 November 2014) UN Docs. CEDAW/C/GC/31-CRC/C/GC/18.

UNCRC, 'General Comment 20 on the Implementation of the Rights of the Child during Adolescence' (6 December 2016) UN Docs CRC/C/GC/20

'General Comment No. 21 (2017) on Children in Street Situations' (21 June 2017) UNCRC/C/GC/21.

UNCRC and UNCMW, 'Joint General Comment No. 3 (2017) of the Committee on the Protection of the Rights of All Migrant Workers and Members of Their Families and No. 22 (2017) of the Committee on the Rights of the Child on the General Principles Regarding the Human Rights of Children in the Context of International Migration' (16 November 2017) UN Docs. CMW/C/GC/3-CRC/C/GC/22.

'Joint General Comment No. 4 (2017) of the Committee on the Protection of the Rights of All Migrant Workers and Members of Their Families and No. 23 (2017) of the Committee on the Rights of the Child on State Obligations Regarding the Human Rights of Children in the Context of International Migration in Countries of Origin, Transit, Destination and Return' (16 November 2017) UN Docs. CMW/C/GC/4-CRC/C/GC/23.

Concluding Observations

UNCRC 'Concluding Observations: Bolivia' (18 February 1993) UN Doc. CRC/C/15/Add.1.

'Concluding Observations: Sweden' (18 February 1993) UN Doc. CRC/C/15/Add. 2.

'Concluding Observations: Viet Nam' (18 February 1993) UN Doc. CRC/C/15/Add. 3.

'Concluding Observations: Russian Federation' (18 February 1993) UN Doc. CRC/C/15/Add.4.

'Concluding Observations: Egypt' (18 February 1993) UN Doc. CRC/C/15/Add.5.

'Concluding Observations: Sudan' (18 October 1993) UN Doc. CRC/C/15/Add.10.

'Concluding Observations: France' (25 April 1994) UN Doc. CRC/C/15/Add. 20.

'Concluding Observations: Honduras' (24 October 1994) UN Doc. CRC/C/15/ Add. 24.

'Concluding Observations: Indonesia' (24 October 1994) UN Doc. CRC/C/15/ Add. 25.

'Concluding Observations: Madagascar' (24 October 1994) UN Doc. CRC/C/15/ Add. 26.

'Concluding Observations: Spain' (24 October 1994) UN Doc. CRC/C/15/ Add. 28.

'Concluding Observations: Philippines' (15 February 1995) UN Doc. CRC/C/15/ Add. 29.

'Concluding Observations: Jamaica' (15 February 1995) UN Doc. CRC/C/15/ Add. 32.

'Concluding Observations: United Kingdom' (15 February 1995) UN Doc. CRC/ C/15/Add. 34.

'Concluding Observations: Nicaragua' (20 June 1995) UN Doc. CRC/C/15/ Add. 36.

'Concluding Observations: Canada' (20 June 1995) UN Doc. CRC/C/15/ Add. 37.

'Concluding Observations: Sri Lanka' (21 June 1995) UN Doc. CRC/C/15/ Add. 40.

'Concluding Observations: Senegal' (27 November 1995) UN Doc. CRC/C/15/ Add. 44.

'Concluding Observations: Lebanon' (7 June 1996) UN Doc. CRC/C/15/ Add. 54.

'Concluding Observations: Cyprus' (7 June 1996) UN Doc. CRC/C/15/ Add. 59.

'Concluding Observations: Nigeria' (30 October 1996) UN Doc CRC/C/15/ Add. 61.

'Concluding Observations: Uruguay' (30 October 1996) UN Doc. CRC/C/15/ Add. 62.

'Concluding Observations: Bulgaria' (24 January 1997) UN Doc. CRC/C/15/ Add. 66.

'Concluding Observations: Ethiopia' (24 January 1997) UN Doc. CRC/C/15/ Add. 67.

'Concluding Observations: New Zealand' (24 January 1997) UN Doc. CRC/C/ 15/Add. 71.

'Concluding Observations: Bangladesh' (18 June 1997) UN Doc. CRC/15/C/ Add. 74.

'Concluding Observations: Laos' (10 October 1997) UN Doc. CRC/C/15/ Add. 78.

'Concluding Observations: Czech Republic' (27 October 1997) UN Doc. CRC/C/ 15/Add. 81.

'Concluding Observations: Trinidad and Tobago' (10 October 1997) UN Doc. CRC/C/15/Add. 82.

'Concluding Observations: Federated State of Micronesia' (4 February 1998) UN Doc. CRC/C/15/Add. 86.

'Concluding Observations: Hungary' (5 June 1998) UN Doc. CRC/C/15/Add. 87.

'Concluding Observations: Fiji (24 June 1998) UN. Doc. CRC/C/15/Add. 89

'Concluding Observations: Japan (24 June 1998) UN. Doc. CRC/C/15/Add. 90

'Concluding Observations: Ecuador' (26 October 1998) UN Doc. CRC/C/15/Add. 93.

'Concluding Observations: Iraq' (26 October 1998) UN Doc. CRC/C/15/Add. 94.

'Concluding Observations: Bolivia' (26 October 1998) UN Doc. CRC/C/15/Add. 95.

'Concluding Observations: Kuwait' (26 October 1998) UN Doc. CRC/C/15/Add. 96.

'Concluding Observations: Austria' (7 May 1999) UN Doc. CRC/C/15/Add. 98.

'Concluding Observations: Belize' (10 May 1999) UN Doc. CRC/C/15/Add. 99.

'Concluding Observations: Yemen' (10 May 1999) UN Doc. CRC/C/15/Add. 102.

'Concluding Observations: Barbados' (24 August 1999) UN Doc. CRC/C/15/Add. 103.

'Concluding Observations: Honduras' (24 August 1999) UN Doc. CRC/C/15/Add. 105.

'Concluding Observations: Benin' (24 August 1999) UN Doc. CRC/C/15/Add. 106.

'Concluding Observations: Nicaragua' (24 August 1999) UN Doc. CRC/C/15/Add. 108.

'Concluding Observations: Russian Federation' (10 November 1999) UN Doc. CRC/C/15/Add. 110.

'Concluding Observations: Vanuatu' (10 November 1999) UN Doc. CRC/C/15/Add. 111.

'Concluding Observations: Mali' (2 November 1999) UN Doc. CRC/C/15/Add. 113.

'Concluding Observations: India' (23 February 2000) UN Doc. CRC/C/15/Add. 115.

'Concluding Observations: Sierra Leone' (24 February 2000) UN Doc. CRC/C/15/Add. 116.

'Concluding Observations: Costa Rica' (24 February 2000) UN Doc. CRC/C/15/Add. 117.

'Concluding Observations: Macedonia' (23 February 2000) UN Doc. CRC/C/15/Add. 118.

'Concluding Observations: Peru' (22 February 2000) UN Doc. CRC/C/15/Add. 120.

'Concluding Observations: South Africa' (23 February 2000) UN Doc. CRC/C/15/Add. 122.

'Concluding Observations: Jordan' (28 June 2000) UN Doc. CRC/C/15/Add. 125.

'Concluding Observations: Djibouti' (28 June 2000) UN Doc. CRC/C/15/Add. 131.

'Concluding Observations: Burundi' (16 October 2000) UN Doc. CRC/C/15/Add. 133.

'Concluding Observations: Columbia' (16 October 2000) UN Doc. CRC/C/15/Add. 137.

'Concluding Observations: Central African Republic' (18 October 2000) UN Doc. CRC/C/15/Add. 138.

'Concluding Observations: Marshall Islands' (16 October 2000) UN Doc. CRC/C/15/Add. 139.

'Concluding Observations: Slovakia' (23 October 2000) UN Doc. CRC/C/15/Add. 140.

'Concluding Observations: Comoros' (23 October 2000) UN Doc. CRC/C/15/Add. 141.

'Concluding Observations: Latvia' (21 February 2001) UN Doc. CRC/C/15/Add. 142.

'Concluding Observations: Ethiopia' (21 February 2000) UN Doc. CRC/C/15/Add. 144.

'Concluding Observations: Lithuania' (21 February 2000) UN Doc. CRC/C/15/Add. 146.

'Concluding Observations: Dominican Republic' (21 February 2000) UN Doc. CRC/C/15/Add. 150.

'Concluding Observations: Turkey' (9 July 2001) UN Doc. CRC/C/15/Add. 152.

'Concluding Observations: Democratic Republic of Congo' (9 July 2001) UN Doc. CRC/C/15/Add. 153.

'Concluding Observations: Ivory Coast' (9 July 2001) UN Doc. CRC/C/15/Add. 155.

'Concluding Observations: United Republic of Tanzania' (9 July 2001) UN Doc. CRC/C/15/Add. 156.

'Concluding Observations: Mauritania' (6 November 2001) UN Doc. CRC/C/15/Add. 159.

'Concluding Observations: Kenya' (7 November 2001) UN Doc. CRC/C/15/Add. 160.

'Concluding Observations: Cameroon' (6 November 2001) UN Doc. CRC/C/15/Add. 164.

'Concluding Observations: Paraguay' (6 November 2001) UN Doc. CRC/C/15/Add. 166.

'Concluding Observations: Sudan' (9 October 2002) UN Doc. CRC/C/15/Add. 190.

'Concluding Observations: Ukraine' (9 October 2002) UN Doc. CRC/C/15/Add. 191.

'Concluding Observations: Moldova' (31 October 2002) UN Doc. CRC/C/15/Add. 192.

'Concluding Observations: Burkina Faso' (9 October 2002) UN Doc. CRC/C/15/Add. 193.

'Concluding Observations: Poland' (30 October 2002) UN Doc. CRC/C/15/Add. 194.

'Concluding Observations: Estonia' (17 March 2003) UN Doc. CRC/C/15/Add. 196.

'Concluding Observations: Republic of Korea' (18 March 2003) UN Doc. CRC/C/15/Add. 197.

'Concluding Observations: Romania' (18 March 2003) UN Doc. CRC/C/15/Add. 199.

'Concluding Observations: Czech Republic' (18 March 2003) UN Doc. CRC/C/15/Add. 201.

'Concluding Observations: Haiti' (18 March 2003) UN Doc. CRC/C/15/Add. 202.

'Concluding Observations: Zambia' (2 July 2003) UN Doc. CRC/C/15/Add. 206.

'Concluding Observations: Libya Arab Jamahiriya' (4 July 2003) UN Doc. CRC/C/15/Add. 209.

'Concluding Observations: Jamaica' (4 July 2003) UN Doc. CRC/C/15/Add. 210.

'Concluding Observations: Morocco' (10 July 2003) UN Doc. CRC/C/15/Add. 211.

'Concluding Observations: New Zealand' (27 October 2003) UN Doc. CRC/C/15/Add. 216.

'Concluding Observations: Pakistan' (27 July 2003) UN Doc. CRC/C/15/Add. 217.

'Concluding Observations: Madagascar' (27 October 2003) UN Doc. CRC/C/15/Add. 218.

'Concluding Observations: Singapore' (27 July 2003) UN Doc. CRC/C/15/Add. 220.

'Concluding Observations: Bangladesh' (27 July 2003) UN Doc. CRC/C/15/Add. 221.

'Concluding Observations: Georgia' (27 July 2003) UN Doc. CRC/C/15/Add. 222.

'Concluding Observations: Germany' (26 February 2004) UN Doc. CRC/C/15/Add. 226.

'Concluding Observations: India' (26 February 2004) UN Doc. CRC/C/15/Add. 228.

'Concluding Observations: Japan' (26 February 2004) UN Doc. CRC/C/15/Add. 231.

'Concluding Observations: Rwanda' (1 July 2004) UN Doc. CRC/C/15/Add. 234.

'Concluding Observations: Liberia' (1 July 2004) UN Doc. CRC/C/15/Add. 236.s

'Concluding Observations: Myanmar' (30 June 2004) UN Doc. CRC/C/15/Add. 237.

'Concluding Observations: Democratic People's Republic of Korea (1 July 2004) UN Doc. CRC/C/15/Add. 239.

'Concluding Observations: France' (30 June 2004) UN Doc. CRC/C/15/Add. 240.

'Concluding Observations: Brazil' (3 November 2004) UN Doc. CRC/C/15/Add. 241.

'Concluding Observations: Croatia' (3 November 2004) UN Doc. CRC/C/15/Add. 243.

'Concluding Observations: Equatorial Guinea' (3 November 2004) UN Doc. CRC/C/15/Add. 245.

'Concluding Observations: Angola' (3 November 2004) UN Doc. CRC/C/15/Add. 246.

'Concluding Observations: Antigua and Barbuda' (3 November 2004) UN Doc. CRC/C/15/Add. 247.

'Concluding Observations: Austria' (January 2005) UN Doc. CRC/C/15/Add. 251.

'Concluding Observations: Islamic Republic of Iran' (31 March 2005) UN Doc. CRC/C/15/Add. 254.

'Concluding Observations: Togo' (31 March 2005) UN Doc. CRC/C/15/Add. 255.

'Concluding Observations: Bolivia' (11 February 2005) UN Doc. CRC/C/15/Add. 256.

'Concluding Observations: Nigeria' (13 April 2005) UN Doc. CRC/C/15/Add. 257.

'Concluding Observations: Philippines' (21 September 2005) UN Doc. CRC/C/15/Add. 259.

'Concluding Observations: Nepal' (21 September 2005) UN Doc. CRC/C/15/Add. 261.

'Concluding Observations: Mongolia' (21 September 2005) UN Doc. CRC/C/15/Add. 264.

'Concluding Observations: Nicaragua' (21 September 2005) UN Doc. CRC/C/15/Add. 265.

'Concluding Observations: Yemen' (21 September 2005) UN Doc. CRC/C/15/ Add. 267.

'Concluding Observations: Australia' (20 October 2005) UN Doc. CRC/C/15/ Add. 268.

'Concluding Observations: Algeria' (12 October 2005) UN Doc. CRC/C/15/ Add. 269.

'Concluding Observations: Russian Federation' (23 November 2005) UN Doc. CRC/C/RUS/CO/3.

'Concluding Observations: Uganda' (23 November 2005) UN Doc. CRC/C/ UGA/CO/2.

'Concluding Observations: Finland' (20 October 2005) UN Doc. CRC/C/15/ Add. 272.

'Concluding Observations: China' (24 November 2005) UN Doc. CRC/C/CHN/ CO/2.

'Concluding Observations: Azerbaijan (17 March 2006) UN Doc. CRC/C/AZE/ CO/2.

'Concluding Observations: Thailand' (17 March 2006) UN Doc. CRC/C/THA/ CO/2.

'Concluding Observations: Republic on Congo' (20 October 2006) UN Doc. CRC/C/COG/CO/1.

'Concluding Observations: Latvia' (28 June 2006) UN Doc. CRC/C/LTC/ CO/2.

'Concluding Observations: Lebanon' (8 June 2006) UN Doc. CRC/C/LBN/CO/2.

'Concluding Observations: Lithuania' (17 March 2006) UN Doc. CRC/C/LTU/ CO/2.

'Concluding Observations: Benin' (20 October 2006) UN Doc. CRC/C/BEN/ CO/2.

'Concluding Observations: United Republic of Tanzania' (21 June 2006) UN Doc. CRC/C/TZA/CO/2.

'Concluding Observations: Mexico' (2 June 2006) UN Doc. CRC/C/MEX/CO/3.

'Concluding Observations: Jordan' (29 September 2006) UN Doc. CRC/C/JOR/ CO/3.

'Concluding Observations: Ghana' (17 March 2006) UN Doc. CRC/C/GHA/ CO/2.

'Concluding Observations: Ireland' (29 September 2006) UN Doc. CRC/C/IRL/ CO/2.

'Concluding Observations: Swaziland' (16 October 2006) UN Doc. CRC/C/ SWZ/CO/1.

'Concluding Observations: Uzbekistan' (2 June 2006) UN Doc. CRC/C/UZB/ CO/2.

'Concluding Observations: Colombia' (8 June 2006) UN Doc. CRC/C/COL/CO/3.

'Concluding Observations: Uruguay' (5 July 2007) UN Doc. CRC/C/URY/CO/2.

'Concluding Observations: Kazakhstan' (19 June 2007) UN Doc. CRC/C/KAZ/CO/3.

'Concluding Observations: Venezuela' (5 October 2007) UN Doc. CRC/C/VEN/CO/2.

'Concluding Observations: Kenya' (19 June 2007) UN Doc. CRC/C/KEN/CO/2.

'Concluding Observations: Malaysia' (25 June 2007) UN Doc. CRC/C/MYS/CO/1.

'Concluding Observations: Marshall Islands' (19 November 2007) UN Doc. CRC/C/MHL/CO/2.

'Concluding Observations: Maldives' (13 July 2007) UN Doc. CRC/C/MDV/CO/3.

'Concluding Observations: Bulgaria' (23 June 2008) UN Doc. CRC/C/BGR/CO/2.

'Concluding Observations: Georgia' (23 June 2008) UN Doc. CRC/C/GEO/CO/3.

'Concluding Observations: Republic of Serbia' (20 June 2008) UN Doc. CRC/C/SRB/CO/1.

'Concluding Observations: Sierra Leone' (20 June 2008) UN Doc. CRC/C/SLE/CO/2.

'Concluding Observations: Djibouti' (7 October 2008) UN Doc. CRC/C/DJI/CO/2.

'Concluding Observations: United Kingdom' (20 October 2008) UN Doc. CRC/C/GBR/CO/4.

'Concluding Observations: Dominican Republic' (11 February 2008) UN Doc. CRC/C/DOM/CO/2.

'Concluding Observations: Timor-Leste' (14 February 2008) UN Doc. CRC/C/TLS/CO/1.

'Concluding Observations: Democratic People's Republic of Korea' (27 March 2009) UN Doc. CRC/C/PRK/CO/4.

'Concluding Observations: Democratic Republic of the Congo' (10 February 2009) UN Doc. CRC/C/COD/CO/2.

'Concluding Observations: Republic of Chad' (12 February 2009) UN Doc. CRC/C/TCD/CO/2.

'Concluding Observations: Bangladesh' (26 June 2009) UN Doc. CRC/C/BGD/CO/4.

'Concluding Observations: Romania' (30 June 2009) UN Doc. CRC/C/ROM/CO/4.

'Concluding Observations: The Plurinational State of Bolivia' (16 October 2009) UN Doc. CRC/C/BOL/CO/4.

'Concluding Observations: Pakistan' (15 October 2009) UN Doc. CRC/C/PAK/CO/3-4.

'Concluding Observations: The Philippines' (22 October 2009) UN Doc. CRC/C/PHL/CO/3-4.

'Concluding Observations: Qatar' (14 October 2009) UN Doc. CRC/C/QAT/CO/2.

'Concluding Observations: Burkina Faso' (9 February 2010) UN Doc. CRC/C/BFA/CO/3-4.

'Concluding Observations: Ecuador' (29 January 2010) UN Doc. CRC/C/ECU/CO/4.

'Concluding Observations: Mongolia' (29 January 2010) UN Doc. CRC/C/MNG/CO/3-4.

'Concluding Observations: Norway' (3 March 2010) UN Doc. CRC/C/NOR/CO/4.

'Concluding Observations: Paraguay' (10 February 2010) UN Doc. CRC/C/PRY/CO/3.

'Concluding Observations: Tajikistan' (5 February 2010) UN Doc. CRC/C/TJK/CO/2.

'Concluding Observations: Argentina' (11 June 2010) UN Doc. CRC/C/ARG/CO/3-4.

'Concluding Observations: Belgium' (18 June 2010) UN Doc. CRC/C/BEL/CO/3-4.

'Concluding Observations: The Former Yugoslav Republic of Macedonia' (11 June 2010) UN Doc. CRC/C/CO/2.

'Concluding Observations: Nigeria' (11 June 2010) UN Doc. CRC/C/NGA/CO/3-4.

'Concluding Observations: Angola' (11 October 2010) UN Doc. CRC/C/CO/2-4.

'Concluding Observations: Burundi' (1 October 2010) UN Doc. CRC/C/BDI/CO/2.

'Concluding Observations: Guatemala' (1 October 2010) UN Doc. CRC/C/GTM/CO/3-4.

'Concluding Observations: Spain' (29 September 2010) UN Doc. CRC/C/ESP/CO/3-4.

'Concluding Observations: Sudan' (1 October 2010) UN Doc. CRC/C/SDN/CO/3-4.

'Concluding Observation: Holy See' (25 February 2014) UN Doc. CRC/C/VAT/CO/2.

'Concluding Observations: Fiji' (13 October 2014) UN Doc. CRC/C/FJI/CO/2-4.

'Concluding Observations: Ethiopia' (3 June 2015) UN Doc. CRC/C/ETH/CO/4-5.

'Concluding Observations: Brunei Darussalam' (24 February 2016) CRC/C/BRN/CO/2-3.

'Concluding Observations: Peru' (2 March 2016) CRC/C/PER/CO/4-5.

'Concluding Observations: Zimbabwe' (7 March 2016) UN Doc. CRC/C/ZWE/CO/2.

'Concluding Observations: Senegal' (7 March 2016) UN Doc. CRC/C/SEN/CO/3-5.

'Concluding Observations: Central African Republic' (8 March 2016) UN Doc. CRC/C/CAF/CO/2.

'Concluding Observations: Kenya' (21 March 2016) CRC/C/KEN/CO/3-5.

'Concluding Observations: Gabon' (8 July 2016) UN Doc. CRC/C/GAB/CO/2.

'Concluding Observations: Pakistan' (11 July 2016) UN Doc. CRC/C/PAK/CO/5.

'Concluding Observations: Slovakia' (20 July 2016) UN Doc. CRC/C/SVK/CO/3-5.

'Concluding Observations: New Zealand' (21 October 2016) UN Doc. CRC/C/NZL/CO/5.

'Concluding Observations: Bulgaria' (21 November 2016) UN Doc. CRC/C/BGR/CO/3-5.

'Concluding Observations: Democratic Republic of Congo' (28 February 2017) UN Doc. CRC/C/COD/CO/3-5.

'Concluding Observations: Georgia' (9 March 2017) UN Doc. CRC/C/GEO/CO/4.

'Concluding Observations: Republic of Moldova' (20 October 2017) UN Doc. CRC/C/MDA/CO/4-5.

'Concluding Observations: Democratic People's Republic of Korea' (23 October 2017) UN Doc. CRC/C/PRK/CO/5.

'Concluding Observations: Denmark' (26 October 2017) UN Doc. CRC/C/DNK/CO/5.